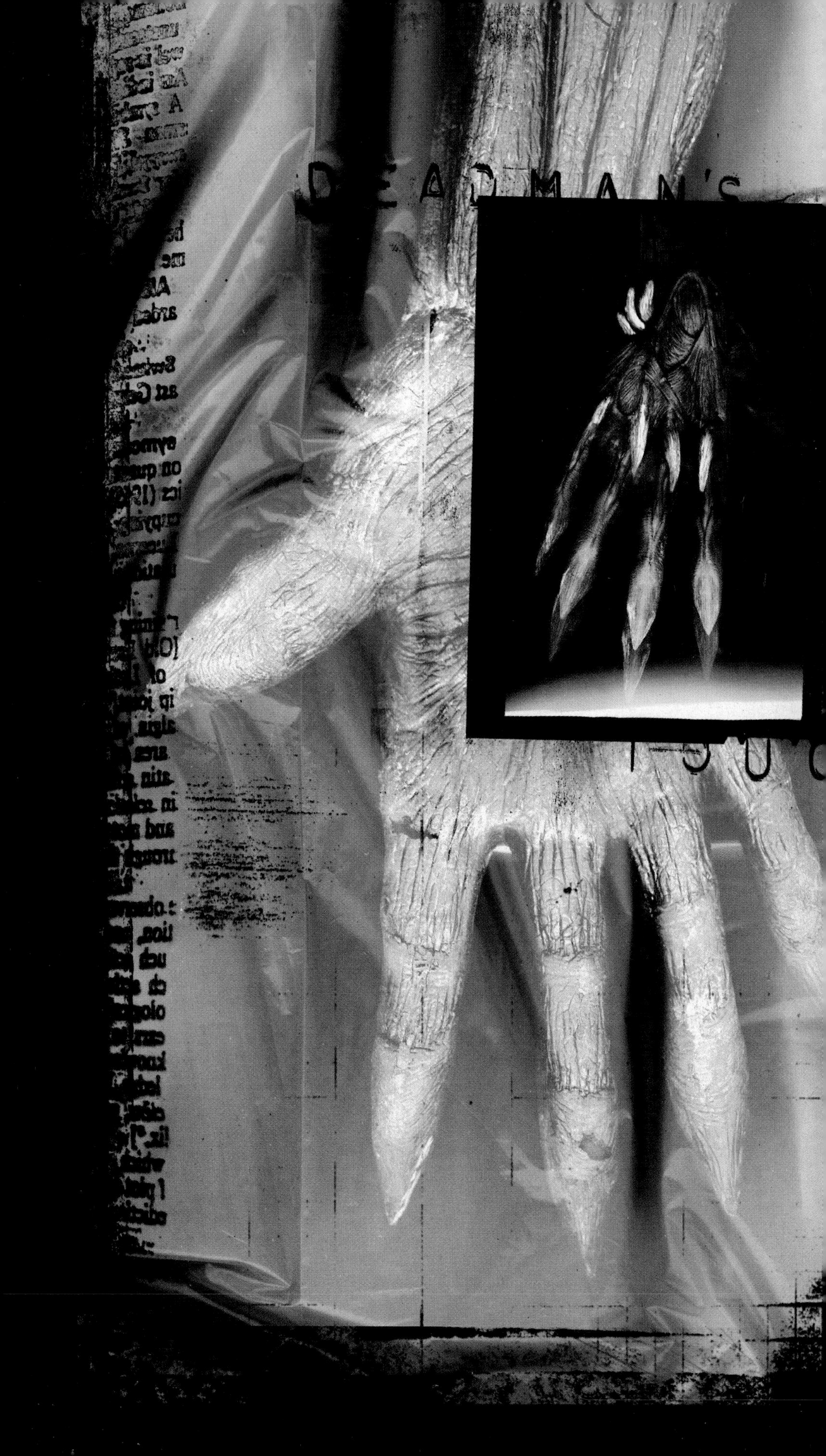
DEADMAN'S

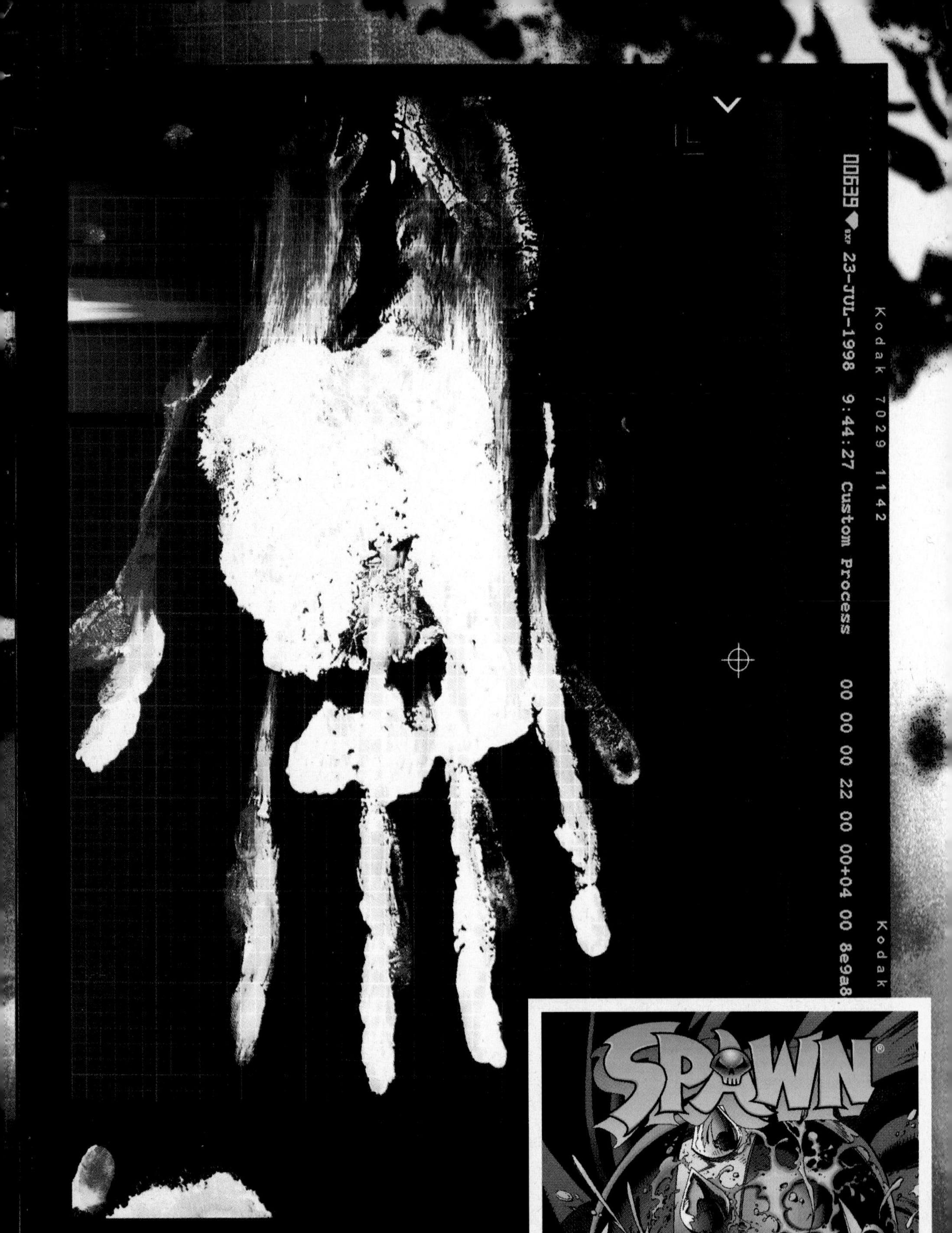
Kodak 7029 1142
00639 23-JUL-1998 9:44:27 Custom Process 00 00 00 22 00 00+04 00 8e9a8
Kodak

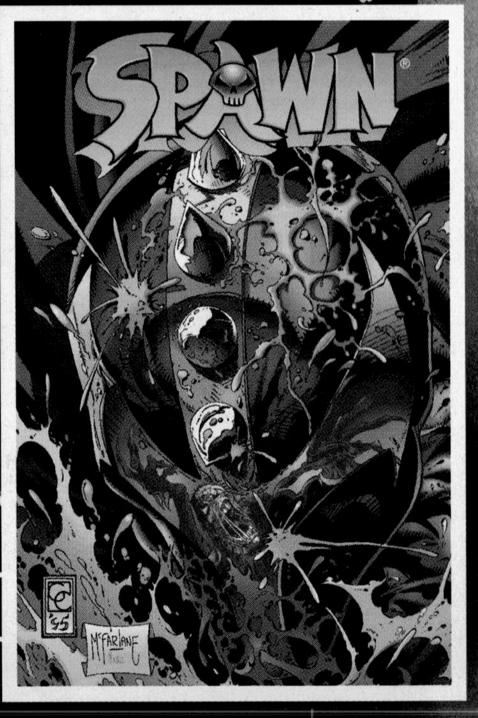
SPAWN
McFARLANE

THE HOMECOMING 3

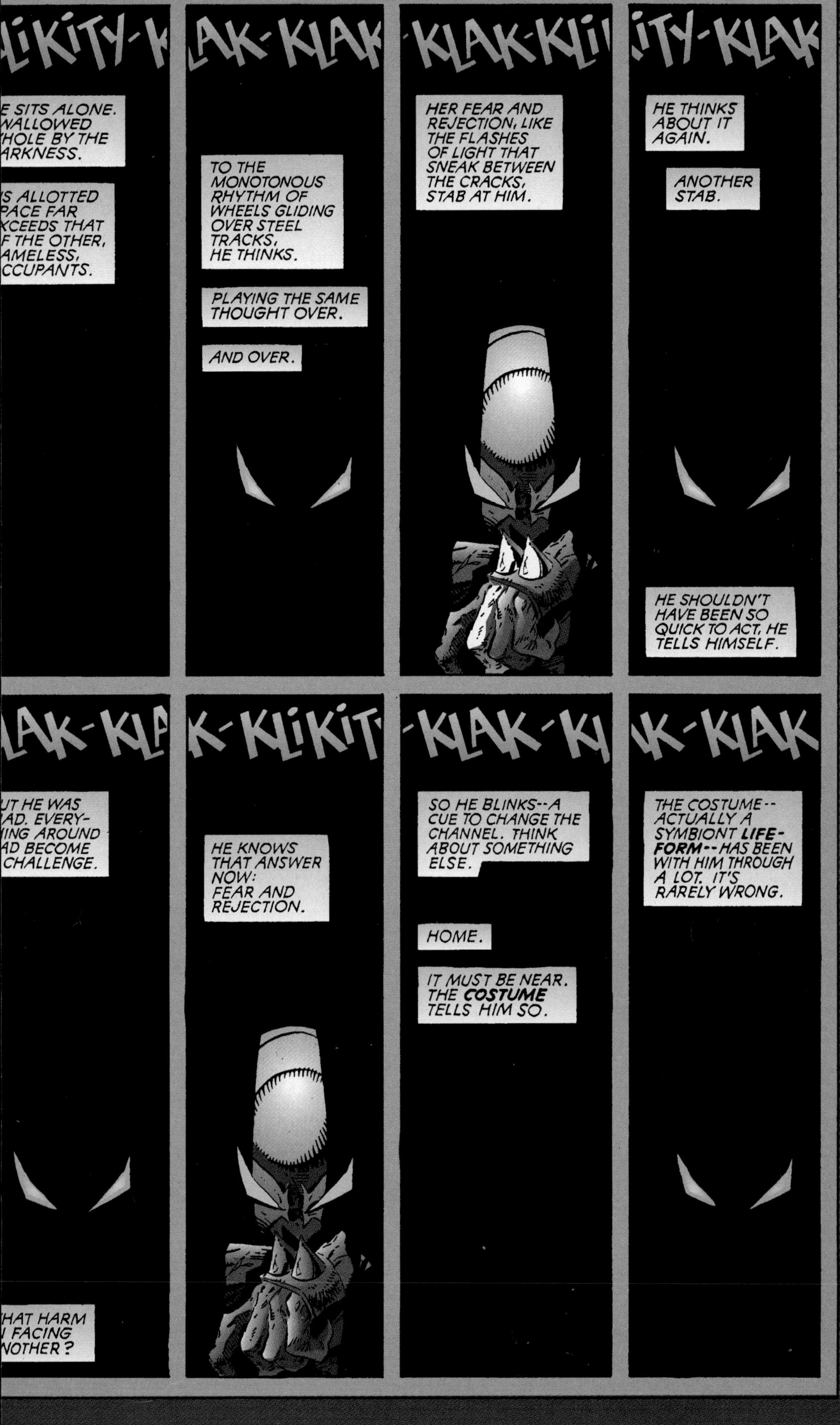
LIKITY-K
E SITS ALONE. WALLOWED HOLE BY THE ARKNESS.
S ALLOTTED PACE FAR XCEEDS THAT F THE OTHER, AMELESS, CCUPANTS.
LAK-KLAK
TO THE MONOTONOUS RHYTHM OF WHEELS GLIDING OVER STEEL TRACKS, HE THINKS.
PLAYING THE SAME THOUGHT OVER.
AND OVER.
-KLAK-KLI
HER FEAR AND REJECTION, LIKE THE FLASHES OF LIGHT THAT SNEAK BETWEEN THE CRACKS, STAB AT HIM.
ITY-KLAK
HE THINKS ABOUT IT AGAIN.
ANOTHER STAB.
HE SHOULDN'T HAVE BEEN SO QUICK TO ACT, HE TELLS HIMSELF.
LAK-KLA
UT HE WAS AD. EVERY- HING AROUND AD BECOME CHALLENGE.
HAT HARM FACING NOTHER?
K-KLIKIT
HE KNOWS THAT ANSWER NOW: FEAR AND REJECTION.
-KLAK-K
SO HE BLINKS--A CUE TO CHANGE THE CHANNEL. THINK ABOUT SOMETHING ELSE.
HOME.
IT MUST BE NEAR. THE COSTUME TELLS HIM SO.
K-KLAK
THE COSTUME-- ACTUALLY A SYMBIONT LIFE-FORM--HAS BEEN WITH HIM THROUGH A LOT. IT'S RARELY WRONG.

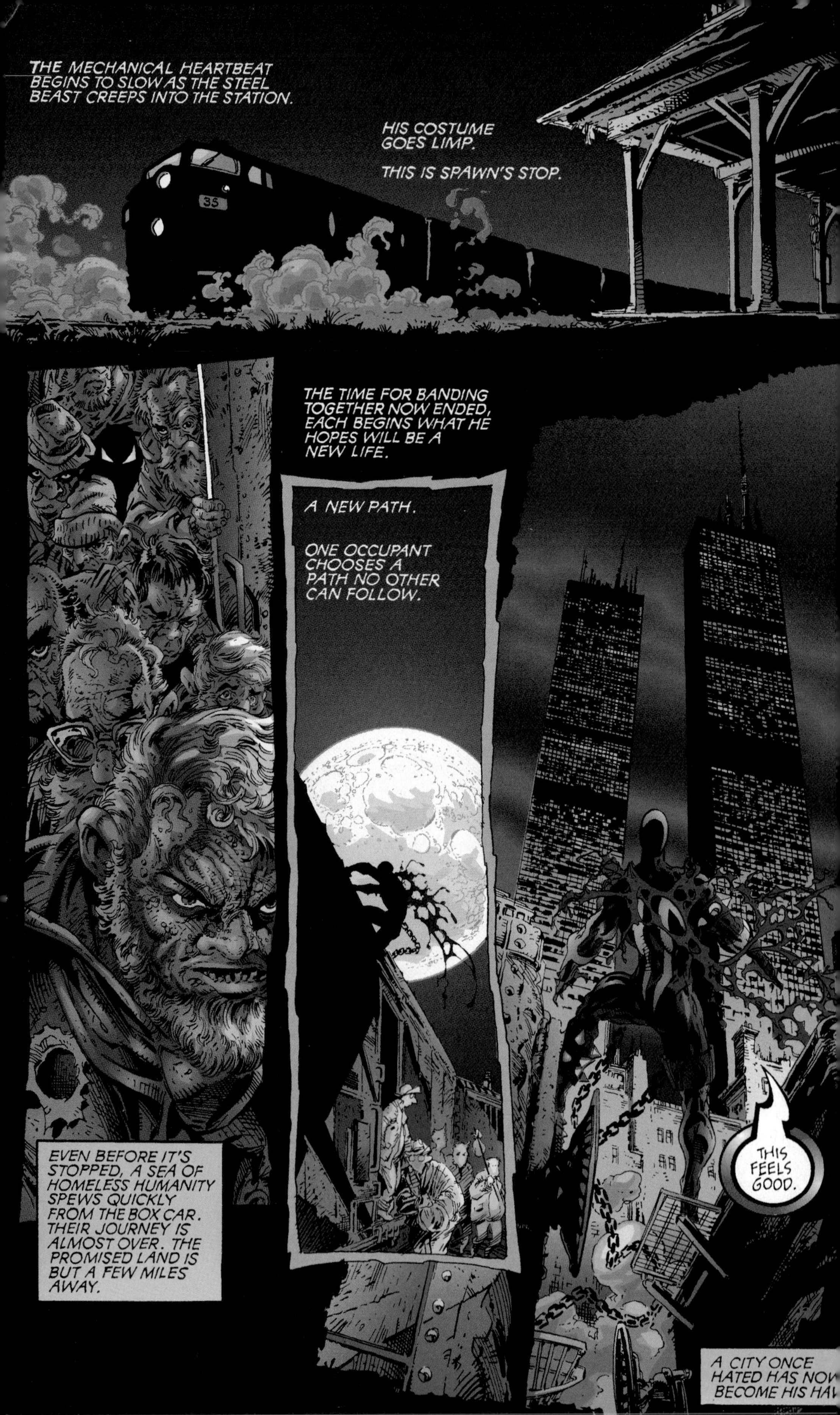
THE MECHANICAL HEARTBEAT BEGINS TO SLOW AS THE STEEL BEAST CREEPS INTO THE STATION.
HIS COSTUME GOES LIMP.
THIS IS SPAWN'S STOP.
35
EVEN BEFORE IT'S STOPPED, A SEA OF HOMELESS HUMANITY SPEWS QUICKLY FROM THE BOX CAR. THEIR JOURNEY IS ALMOST OVER. THE PROMISED LAND IS BUT A FEW MILES AWAY.
THE TIME FOR BANDING TOGETHER NOW ENDED, EACH BEGINS WHAT HE HOPES WILL BE A NEW LIFE.
A NEW PATH.
ONE OCCUPANT CHOOSES A PATH NO OTHER CAN FOLLOW.
THIS FEELS GOOD.
A CITY ONCE HATED HAS NOW BECOME HIS HA

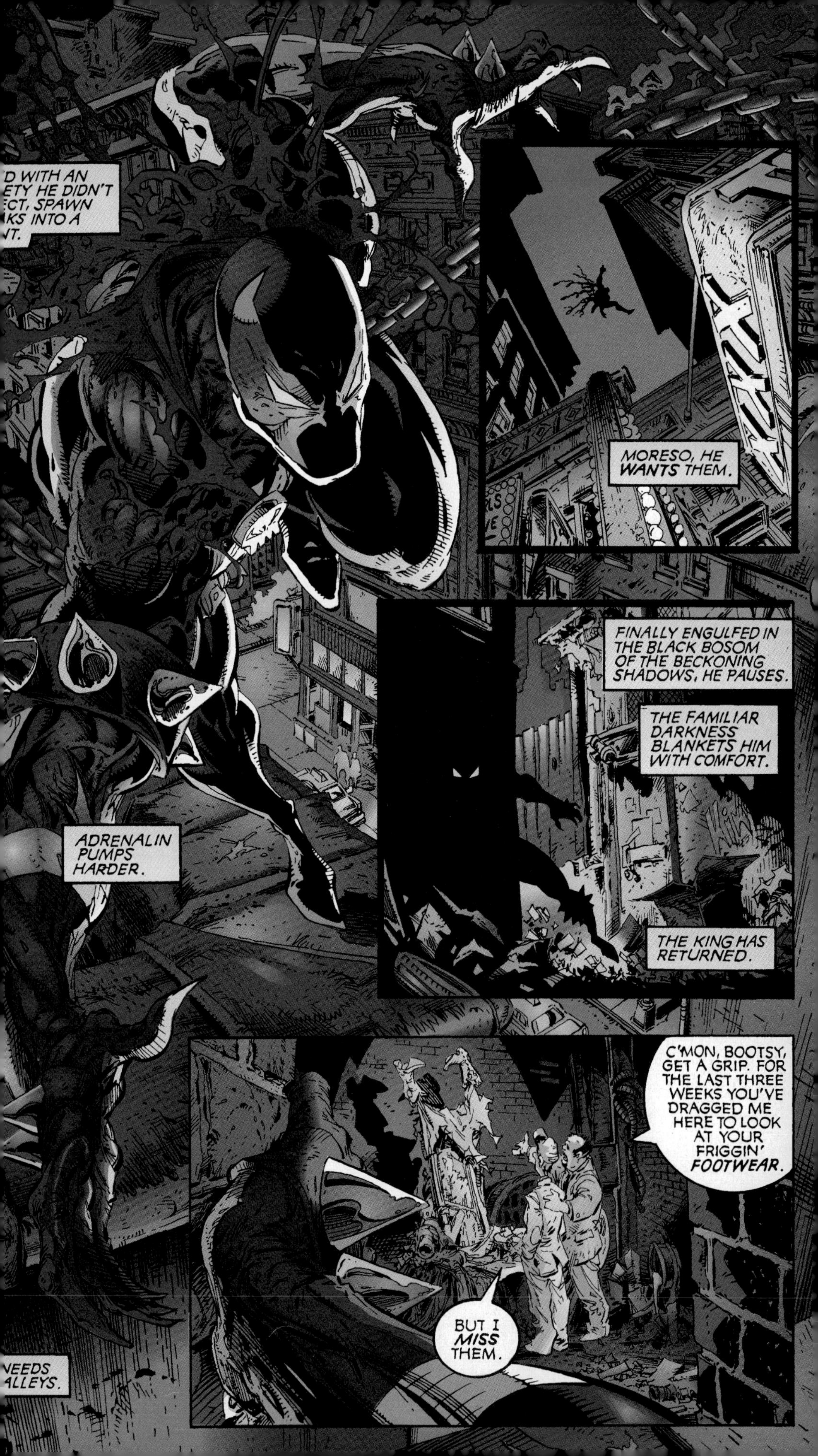

D WITH AN
ETY HE DIDN'T
ECT, SPAWN
KS INTO A
NT.
MORESO, HE WANTS THEM.
ADRENALIN PUMPS HARDER.
FINALLY ENGULFED IN THE BLACK BOSOM OF THE BECKONING SHADOWS, HE PAUSES.
THE FAMILIAR DARKNESS BLANKETS HIM WITH COMFORT.
THE KING HAS RETURNED.
NEEDS
ALLEYS.
C'MON, BOOTSY, GET A GRIP. FOR THE LAST THREE WEEKS YOU'VE DRAGGED ME HERE TO LOOK AT YOUR FRIGGIN' FOOTWEAR.
BUT I MISS THEM.

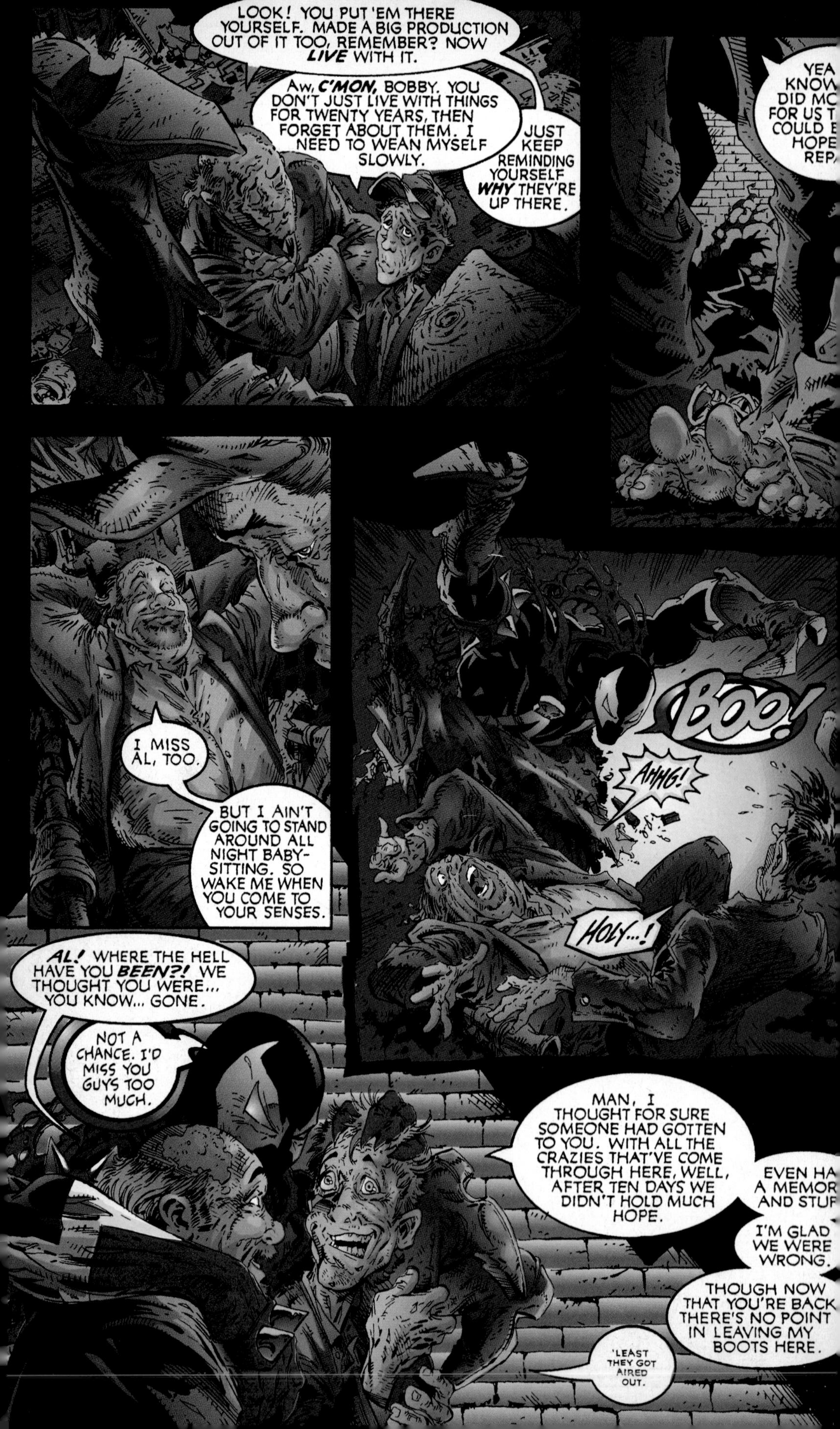
LOOK! YOU PUT 'EM THERE YOURSELF. MADE A BIG PRODUCTION OUT OF IT TOO, REMEMBER? NOW LIVE WITH IT.
Aw, C'MON, BOBBY. YOU DON'T JUST LIVE WITH THINGS FOR TWENTY YEARS, THEN FORGET ABOUT THEM. I NEED TO WEAN MYSELF SLOWLY.
JUST KEEP REMINDING YOURSELF WHY THEY'RE UP THERE.
I MISS AL, TOO.
BUT I AIN'T GOING TO STAND AROUND ALL NIGHT BABY-SITTING. SO WAKE ME WHEN YOU COME TO YOUR SENSES.
BOO!
AHHG!
HOLY...!
AL! WHERE THE HELL HAVE YOU BEEN?! WE THOUGHT YOU WERE... YOU KNOW... GONE.
NOT A CHANCE. I'D MISS YOU GUYS TOO MUCH.
MAN, I THOUGHT FOR SURE SOMEONE HAD GOTTEN TO YOU. WITH ALL THE CRAZIES THAT'VE COME THROUGH HERE, WELL, AFTER TEN DAYS WE DIDN'T HOLD MUCH HOPE.
I'M GLAD WE WERE WRONG.
THOUGH NOW THAT YOU'RE BACK THERE'S NO POINT IN LEAVING MY BOOTS HERE.
'LEAST THEY GOT AIRED OUT.

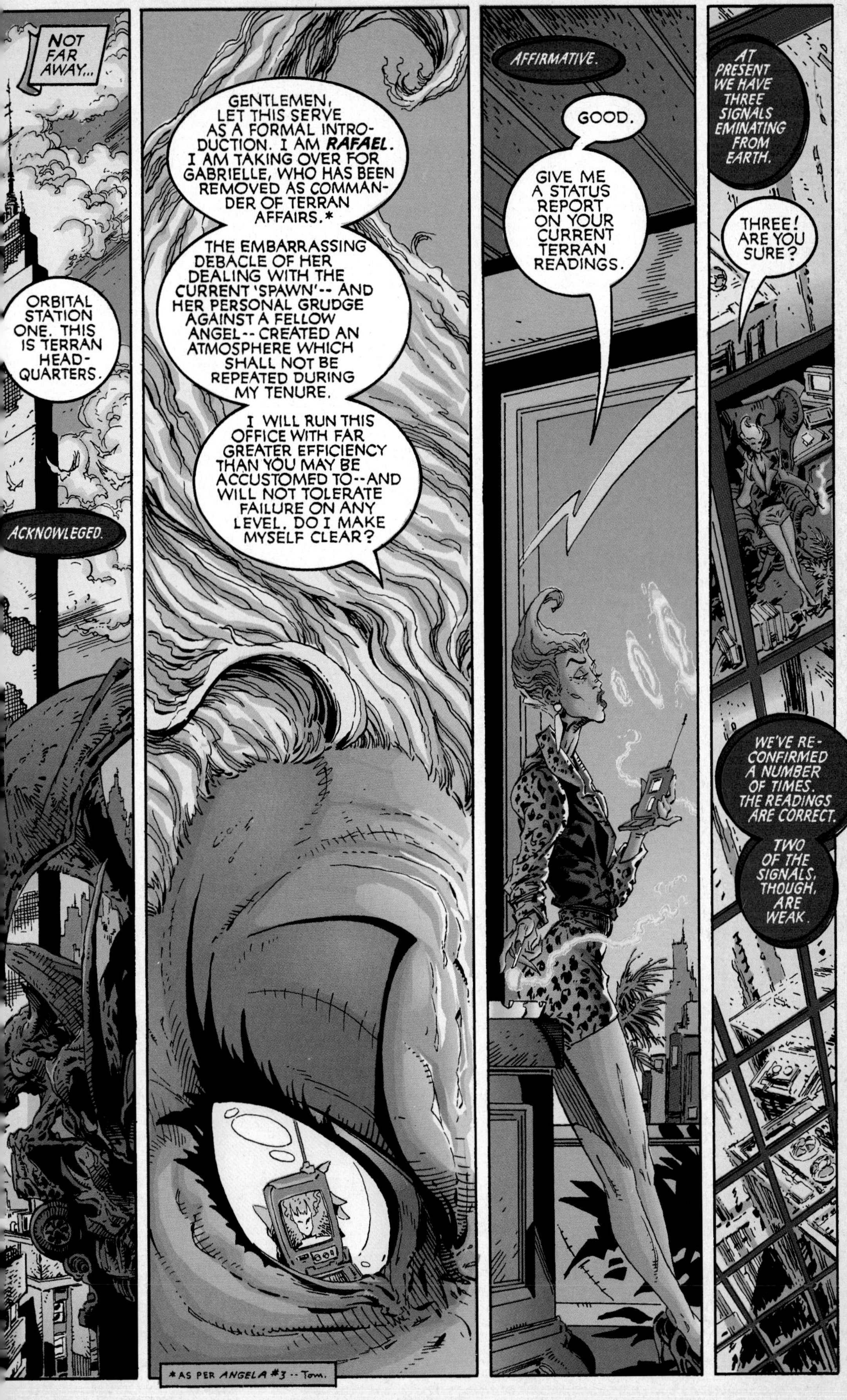

NOT FAR AWAY...
ORBITAL STATION ONE. THIS IS TERRAN HEAD-QUARTERS.
ACKNOWLEGED.
GENTLEMEN, LET THIS SERVE AS A FORMAL INTRO-DUCTION. I AM RAFAEL. I AM TAKING OVER FOR GABRIELLE, WHO HAS BEEN REMOVED AS COMMAN-DER OF TERRAN AFFAIRS.*
THE EMBARRASSING DEBACLE OF HER DEALING WITH THE CURRENT 'SPAWN'-- AND HER PERSONAL GRUDGE AGAINST A FELLOW ANGEL-- CREATED AN ATMOSPHERE WHICH SHALL NOT BE REPEATED DURING MY TENURE.
I WILL RUN THIS OFFICE WITH FAR GREATER EFFICIENCY THAN YOU MAY BE ACCUSTOMED TO--AND WILL NOT TOLERATE FAILURE ON ANY LEVEL. DO I MAKE MYSELF CLEAR?
*AS PER ANGELA #3 -- TOM.
AFFIRMATIVE.
GOOD.
GIVE ME A STATUS REPORT ON YOUR CURRENT TERRAN READINGS.
AT PRESENT WE HAVE THREE SIGNALS EMINATING FROM EARTH.
THREE! ARE YOU SURE?
WE'VE RE-CONFIRMED A NUMBER OF TIMES. THE READINGS ARE CORRECT.
TWO OF THE SIGNALS, THOUGH, ARE WEAK.

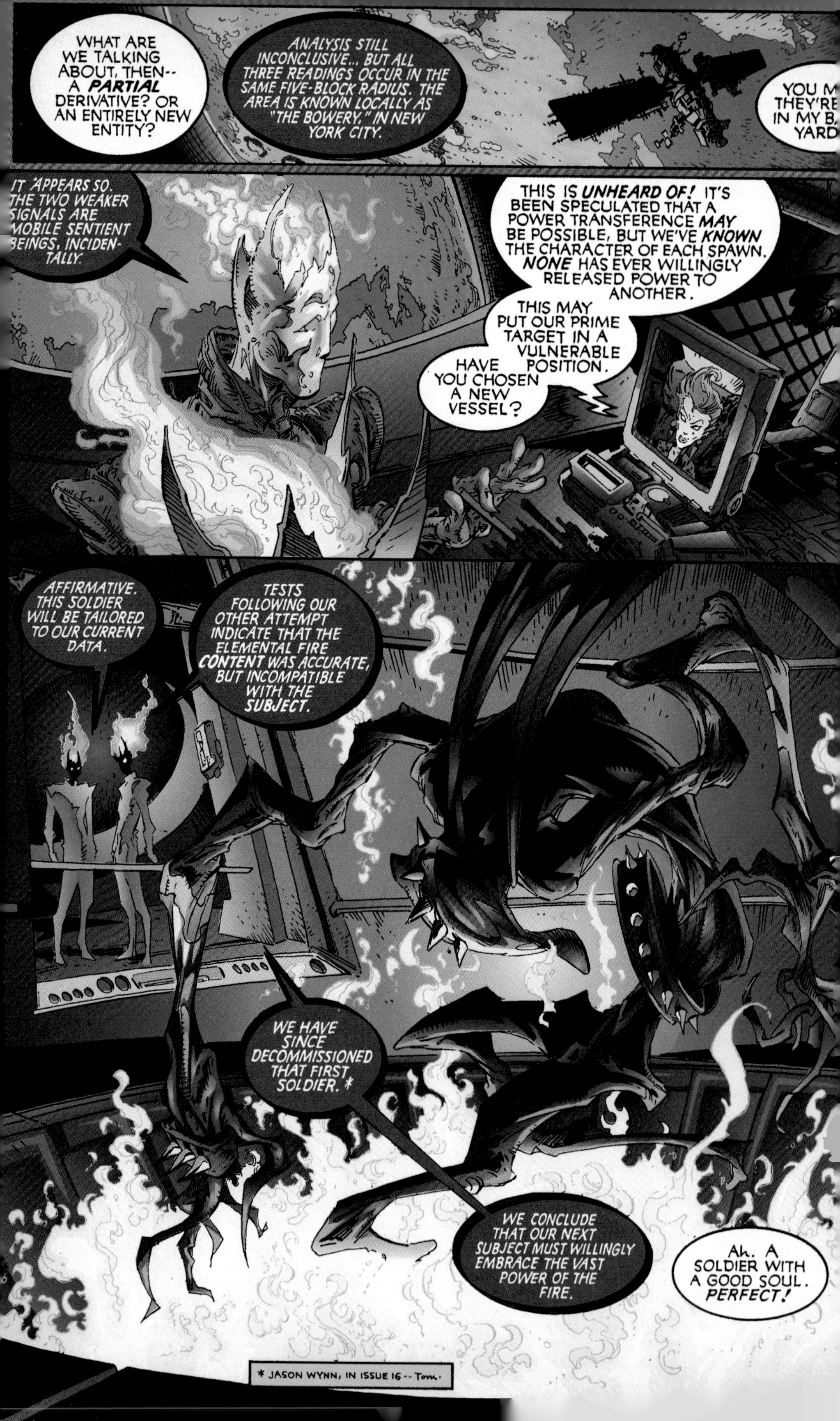
WHAT ARE WE TALKING ABOUT, THEN-- A PARTIAL DERIVATIVE? OR AN ENTIRELY NEW ENTITY?
ANALYSIS STILL INCONCLUSIVE... BUT ALL THREE READINGS OCCUR IN THE SAME FIVE-BLOCK RADIUS. THE AREA IS KNOWN LOCALLY AS "THE BOWERY," IN NEW YORK CITY.
IT APPEARS SO. THE TWO WEAKER SIGNALS ARE MOBILE SENTIENT BEINGS, INCIDENTALLY.
THIS IS UNHEARD OF! IT'S BEEN SPECULATED THAT A POWER TRANSFERENCE MAY BE POSSIBLE, BUT WE'VE KNOWN THE CHARACTER OF EACH SPAWN. NONE HAS EVER WILLINGLY RELEASED POWER TO ANOTHER.
THIS MAY PUT OUR PRIME TARGET IN A VULNERABLE POSITION.
HAVE YOU CHOSEN A NEW VESSEL?
AFFIRMATIVE. THIS SOLDIER WILL BE TAILORED TO OUR CURRENT DATA.
TESTS FOLLOWING OUR OTHER ATTEMPT INDICATE THAT THE ELEMENTAL FIRE CONTENT WAS ACCURATE, BUT INCOMPATIBLE WITH THE SUBJECT.
WE HAVE SINCE DECOMMISSIONED THAT FIRST SOLDIER. *
WE CONCLUDE THAT OUR NEXT SUBJECT MUST WILLINGLY EMBRACE THE VAST POWER OF THE FIRE.
Ah. A SOLDIER WITH A GOOD SOUL. PERFECT!
* JASON WYNN, IN ISSUE 16 -- Tom.

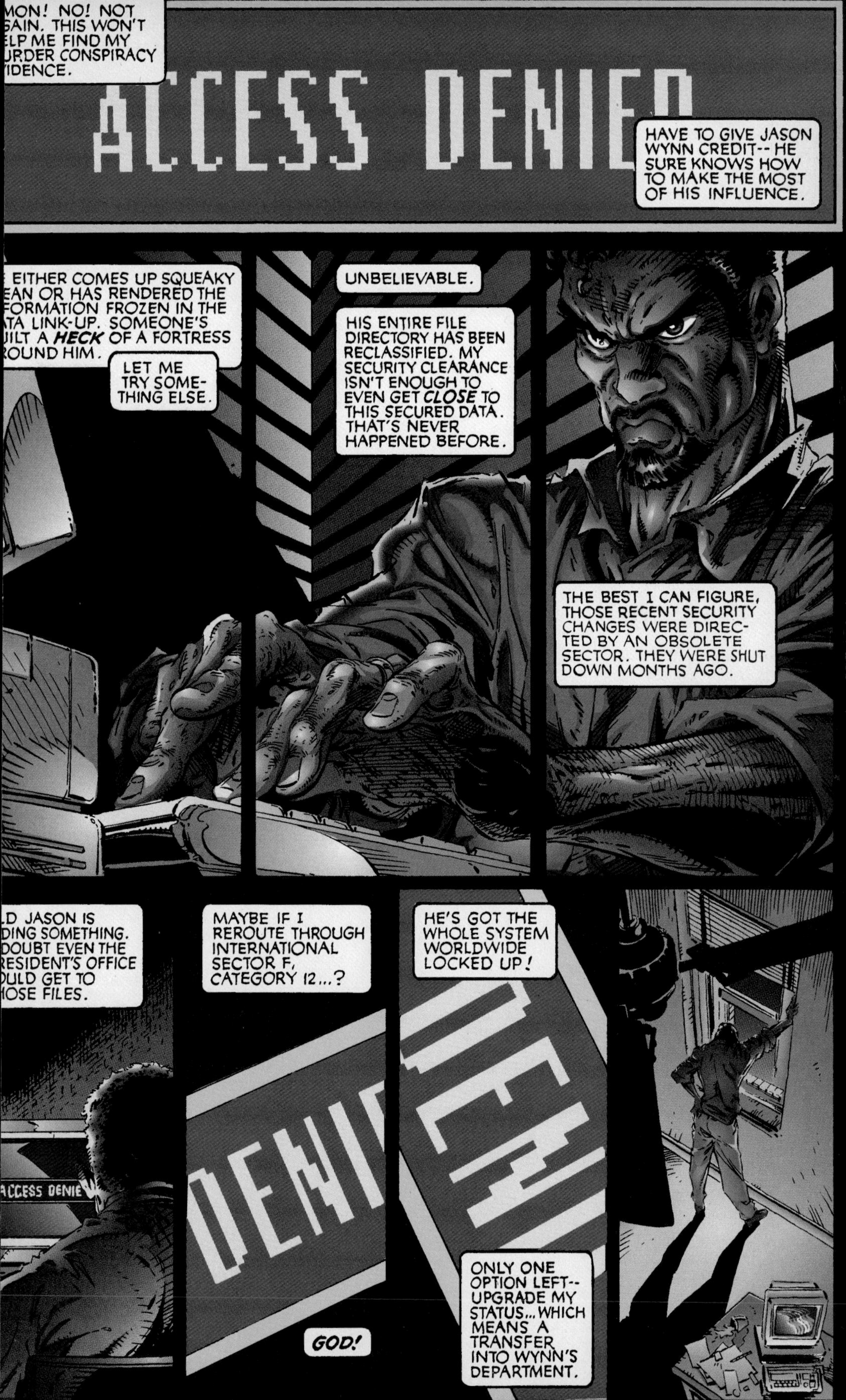

MON! NO! NOT AGAIN. THIS WON'T HELP ME FIND MY MURDER CONSPIRACY EVIDENCE.

ACCESS DENIED

HAVE TO GIVE JASON WYNN CREDIT-- HE SURE KNOWS HOW TO MAKE THE MOST OF HIS INFLUENCE.

IT EITHER COMES UP SQUEAKY CLEAN OR HAS RENDERED THE INFORMATION FROZEN IN THE DATA LINK-UP. SOMEONE'S BUILT A *HECK* OF A FORTRESS AROUND HIM.

LET ME TRY SOMETHING ELSE.

UNBELIEVABLE.

HIS ENTIRE FILE DIRECTORY HAS BEEN RECLASSIFIED. MY SECURITY CLEARANCE ISN'T ENOUGH TO EVEN GET *CLOSE* TO THIS SECURED DATA. THAT'S NEVER HAPPENED BEFORE.

THE BEST I CAN FIGURE, THOSE RECENT SECURITY CHANGES WERE DIRECTED BY AN OBSOLETE SECTOR. THEY WERE SHUT DOWN MONTHS AGO.

OLD JASON IS HIDING SOMETHING. I DOUBT EVEN THE PRESIDENT'S OFFICE COULD GET TO THOSE FILES.

MAYBE IF I REROUTE THROUGH INTERNATIONAL SECTOR F, CATEGORY 12...?

HE'S GOT THE WHOLE SYSTEM WORLDWIDE LOCKED UP!

ACCESS DENIE

GOD!

ONLY ONE OPTION LEFT-- UPGRADE MY STATUS...WHICH MEANS A TRANSFER INTO WYNN'S DEPARTMENT.

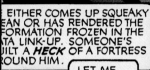

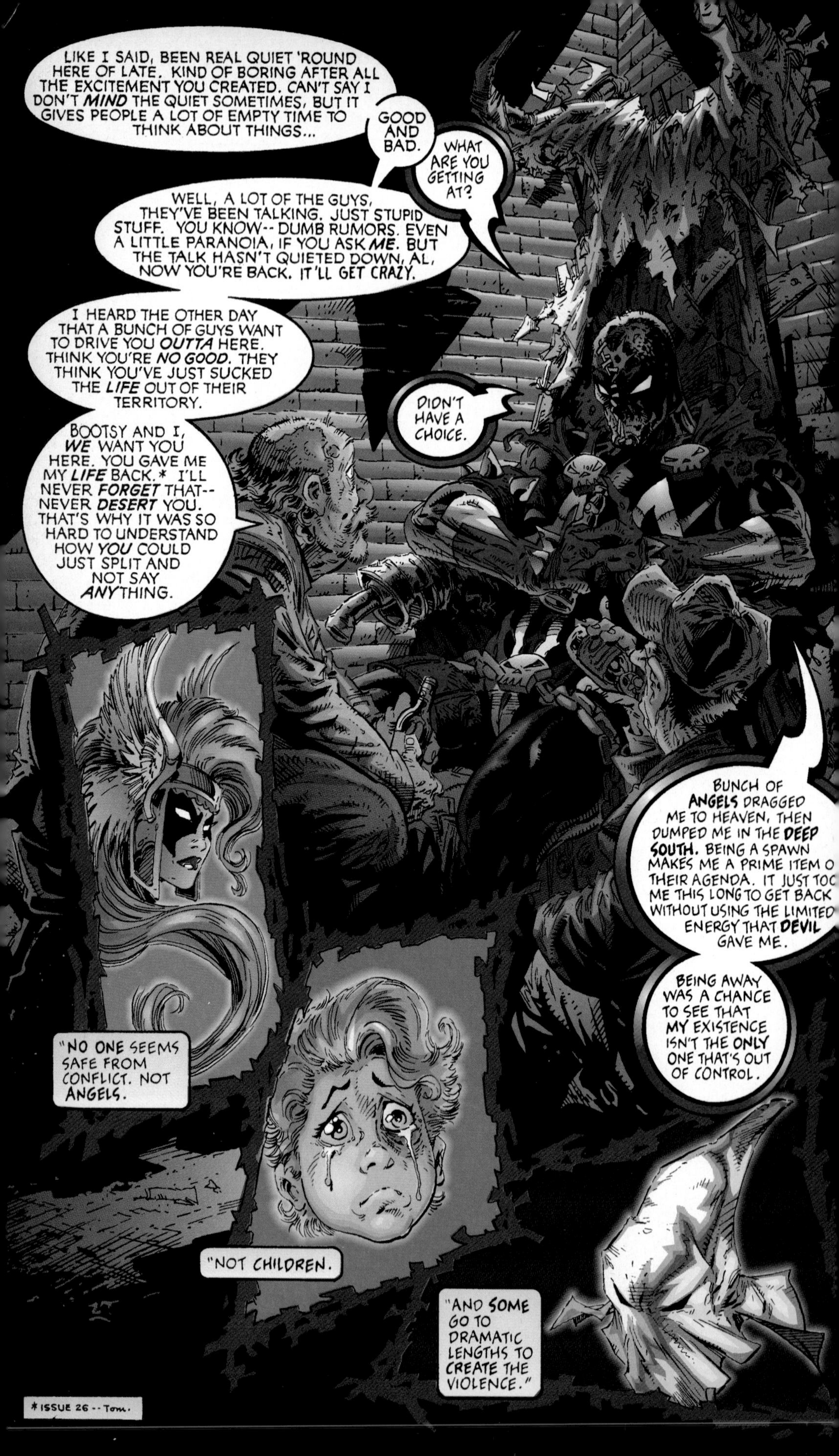
LIKE I SAID, BEEN REAL QUIET 'ROUND HERE OF LATE. KIND OF BORING AFTER ALL THE EXCITEMENT YOU CREATED. CAN'T SAY I DON'T MIND THE QUIET SOMETIMES, BUT IT GIVES PEOPLE A LOT OF EMPTY TIME TO THINK ABOUT THINGS...
GOOD AND BAD.
WHAT ARE YOU GETTING AT?
WELL, A LOT OF THE GUYS, THEY'VE BEEN TALKING. JUST STUPID STUFF. YOU KNOW-- DUMB RUMORS. EVEN A LITTLE PARANOIA, IF YOU ASK ME. BUT THE TALK HASN'T QUIETED DOWN, AL, NOW YOU'RE BACK. IT'LL GET CRAZY.
I HEARD THE OTHER DAY THAT A BUNCH OF GUYS WANT TO DRIVE YOU OUTTA HERE. THINK YOU'RE NO GOOD. THEY THINK YOU'VE JUST SUCKED THE LIFE OUT OF THEIR TERRITORY.
BOOTSY AND I, WE WANT YOU HERE. YOU GAVE ME MY LIFE BACK.* I'LL NEVER FORGET THAT-- NEVER DESERT YOU. THAT'S WHY IT WAS SO HARD TO UNDERSTAND HOW YOU COULD JUST SPLIT AND NOT SAY ANYTHING.
DIDN'T HAVE A CHOICE.
BUNCH OF ANGELS DRAGGED ME TO HEAVEN, THEN DUMPED ME IN THE DEEP SOUTH. BEING A SPAWN MAKES ME A PRIME ITEM O THEIR AGENDA. IT JUST TOC ME THIS LONG TO GET BACK WITHOUT USING THE LIMITED ENERGY THAT DEVIL GAVE ME.
BEING AWAY WAS A CHANCE TO SEE THAT MY EXISTENCE ISN'T THE ONLY ONE THAT'S OUT OF CONTROL.
"NO ONE SEEMS SAFE FROM CONFLICT. NOT ANGELS.
"NOT CHILDREN.
"AND SOME GO TO DRAMATIC LENGTHS TO CREATE THE VIOLENCE."
*ISSUE 26 -- Tom.

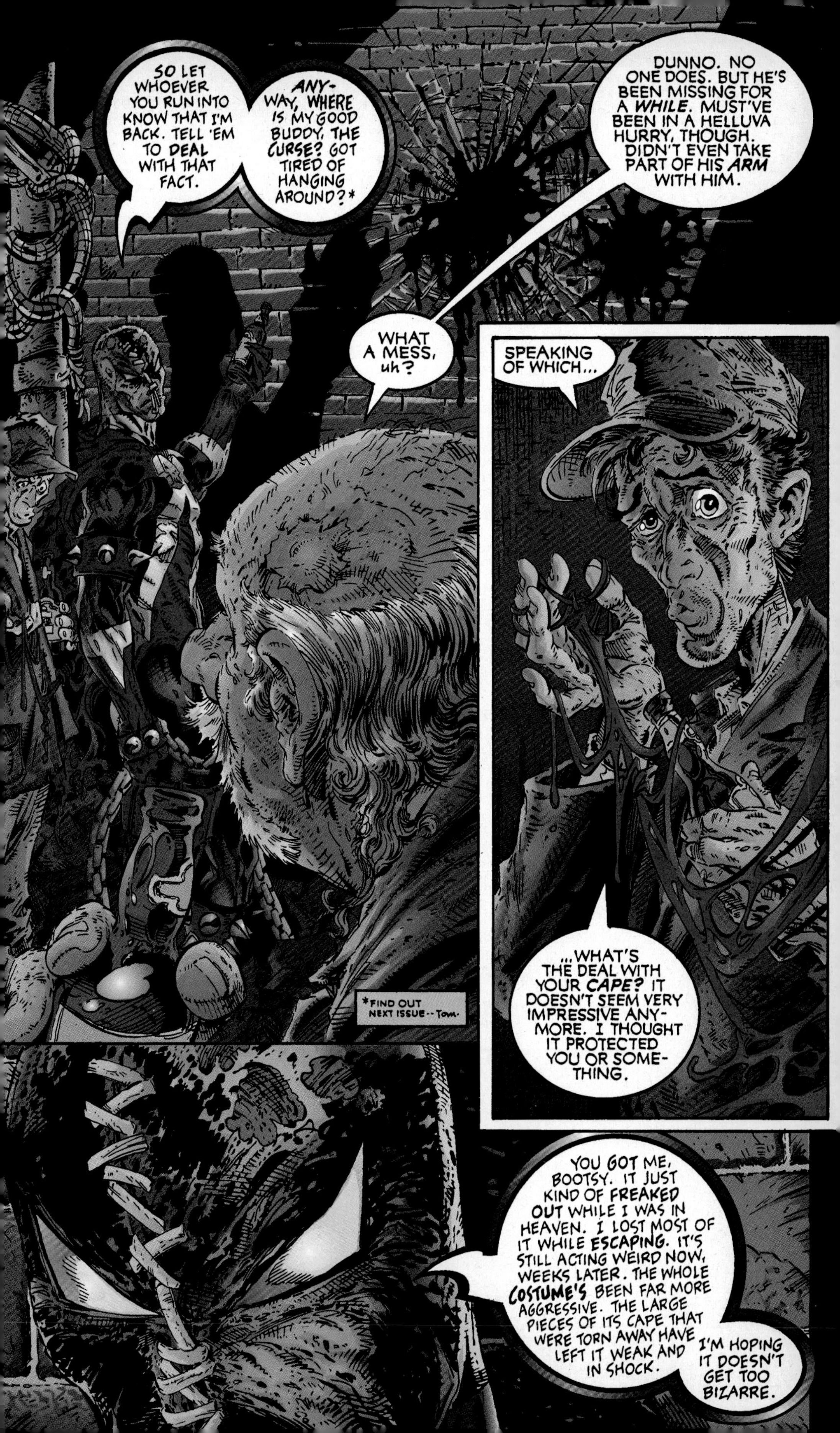
SO LET WHOEVER YOU RUN INTO KNOW THAT I'M BACK. TELL 'EM TO DEAL WITH THAT FACT.
ANY-WAY, WHERE IS MY GOOD BUDDY, THE CURSE? GOT TIRED OF HANGING AROUND?*
DUNNO. NO ONE DOES. BUT HE'S BEEN MISSING FOR A WHILE. MUST'VE BEEN IN A HELLUVA HURRY, THOUGH. DIDN'T EVEN TAKE PART OF HIS ARM WITH HIM.
WHAT A MESS, uh?
*FIND OUT NEXT ISSUE--Tom.
SPEAKING OF WHICH...
...WHAT'S THE DEAL WITH YOUR CAPE? IT DOESN'T SEEM VERY IMPRESSIVE ANY-MORE. I THOUGHT IT PROTECTED YOU OR SOME-THING.
YOU GOT ME, BOOTSY. IT JUST KIND OF FREAKED OUT WHILE I WAS IN HEAVEN. I LOST MOST OF IT WHILE ESCAPING. IT'S STILL ACTING WEIRD NOW, WEEKS LATER. THE WHOLE COSTUME'S BEEN FAR MORE AGGRESSIVE. THE LARGE PIECES OF ITS CAPE THAT WERE TORN AWAY HAVE LEFT IT WEAK AND IN SHOCK.
I'M HOPING IT DOESN'T GET TOO BIZARRE.

"IT HAD BEEN A MIRACLE," HIS MOTHER KEPT TELLING EVERYONE.

21ST STREET MISSION — JESUS SAVES

NO ONE, NOT EVEN HIS PARENTS, EXPECTED SUCH A LIFE CHANGE FROM PHIL TIMPER.

CONSTANTLY IN AND OUT OF JUVENILE DETENTION FROM EARLY ON. FINALLY CONVICTED AND INCARCERATED: TWO YEARS FOR FELONY GRAND THEFT.

IT WAS IN PRISON THAT PHIL GAVE HIMSELF COMPLETELY TO THE LORD'S BIDDING.

NOW HE'S THE MODEL CITIZEN, EVEN TRAINING TO BE A MINISTER AT THE LOCAL CHURCH.

AFTER ELEVEN SOLID YEARS SERVING THE LORD, HE STILL PRAYS EVERY NIGHT THAT HE WILL BE WORTHY OF GOD'S KINGDOM WHEN THE TIME COMES.

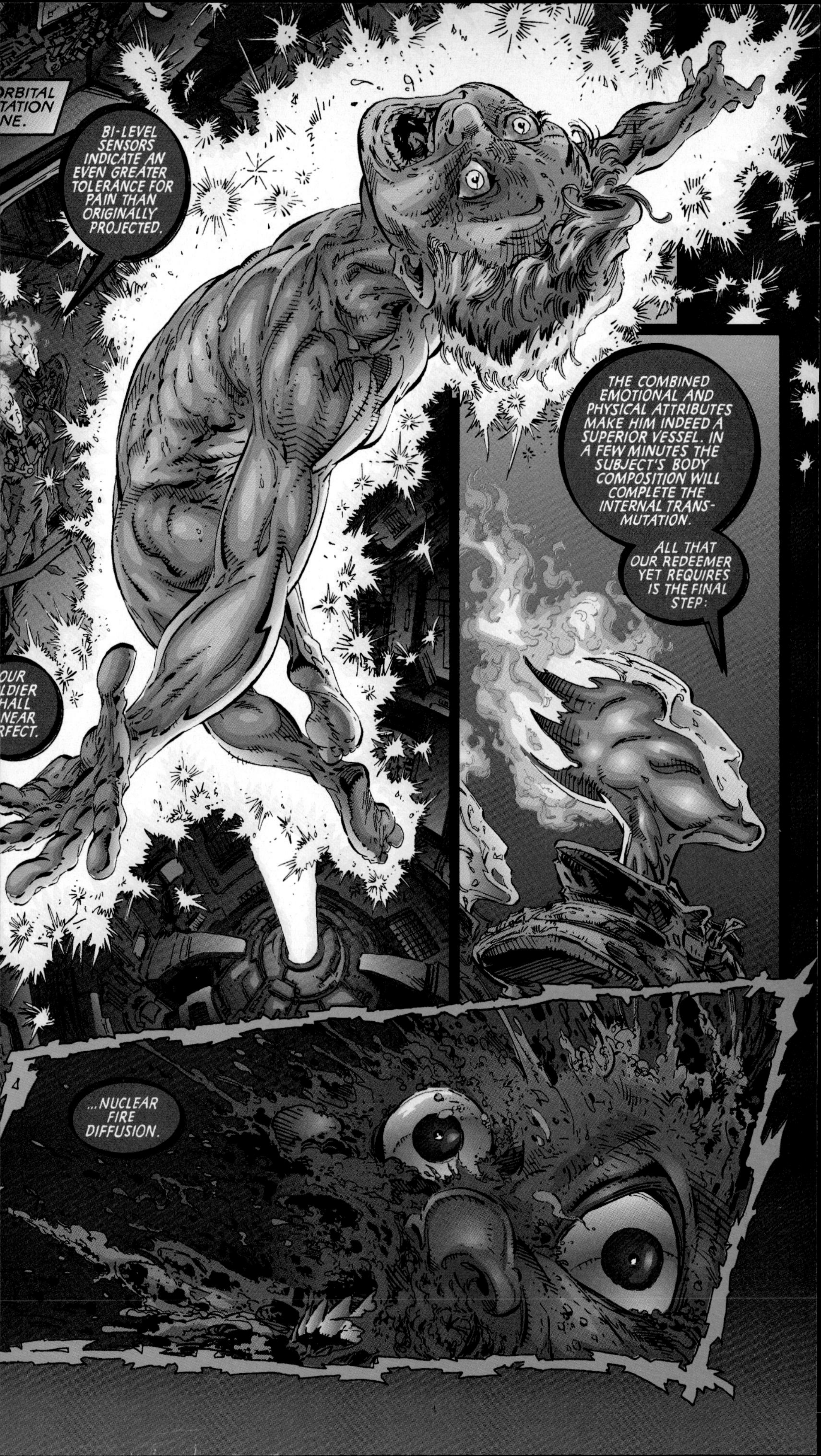

ORBITAL TATION NE.
BI-LEVEL SENSORS INDICATE AN EVEN GREATER TOLERANCE FOR PAIN THAN ORIGINALLY PROJECTED.
OUR LDIER HALL NEAR RFECT.
THE COMBINED EMOTIONAL AND PHYSICAL ATTRIBUTES MAKE HIM INDEED A SUPERIOR VESSEL. IN A FEW MINUTES THE SUBJECT'S BODY COMPOSITION WILL COMPLETE THE INTERNAL TRANS-MUTATION.
ALL THAT OUR REDEEMER YET REQUIRES IS THE FINAL STEP:
...NUCLEAR FIRE DIFFUSION.

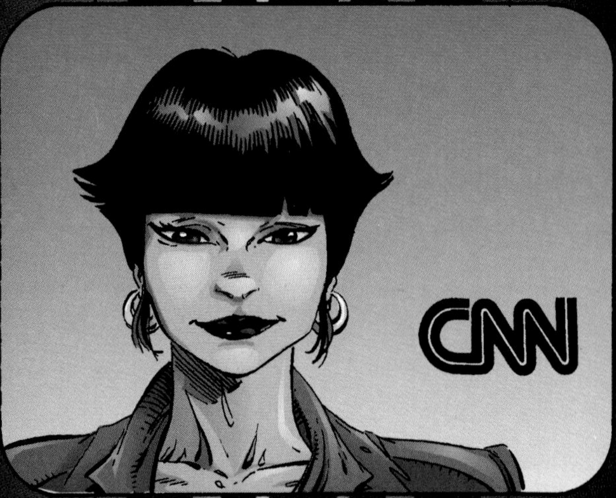
CNN

EARLIER TODAY IN NEW YORK CITY'S
BOWERY, A "MYSTERIOUS LIGHT" WAS
THE CENTER OF THE UNEXPLAINED DISA
PEARANCE OF ONE OF THE AREA'S LEAD
ING CITIZENS. PHIL TIMPER HAD WORKE
WITH THE HOMELESS THROUGH VARIO
CHARITIES AND SHELTERS FOR ELEVEN
YEARS, AND WAS HONORED LAST YEAR
"VOLUNTEER OF THE YEAR" BY THE CIT
MAYOR. NUMEROUS EYEWITNESSES TEL
ESSENTIALLY THE SAME STORY, CNN HA
LEARNED. THEY CLAIM TIMPER WAS STRU
BY WHAT APPEARED TO BE LIGHTNING,
AND VANISHED. HIS GRATEFUL CLIENTS
SCOURED THE AREA IN VAIN. TIMPER IS
OFFICIALLY LISTED AS MISSING, BUT SO
HAVE EXPRESED DOUBT THAT HE COUL
HAVE SURVIVED THE EXPERIENCE.

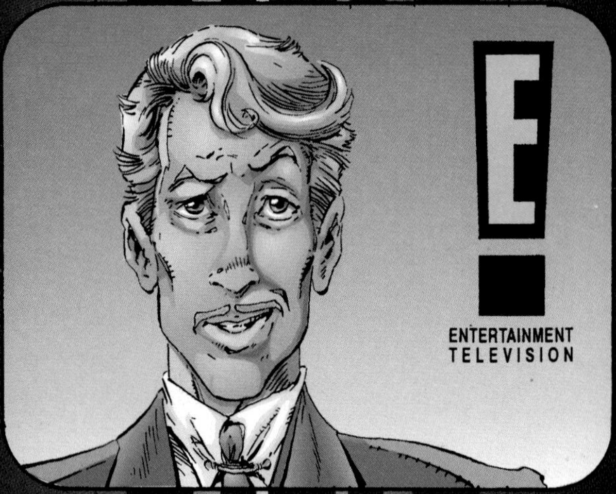
E!
ENTERTAINMENT
TELEVISION

NEW YORK'S FINEST ARE STILL AT A LO
TO EXPLAIN THE DISAPPEARANCE OF A
PROMINENT GOOD SAMARITAN AT THA
BOWERY CHARITY MISSION EARLIER
TODAY. A SOURCE AT THE POLICE
COMMISSIONER'S OFFICE REVEALED TH
THE INVESTIGATION MAY INCLUDE THE
CAPED VIGILANTE KNOWN AS SPAWN.
ELUSIVE MASKED FIGURE HAS BEEN A F
TURE IN THE BOWERY SINCE HIS ARRIVA
SOME MONTHS AGO, AND HAS CON-
TRIBUTED MORE THAN HIS SHARE OF F
AND COMMOTION TO THE SCENE. OUR
CRIMSON AVENGER'S RECENT EXTENDE
UNEXPLAINED ABSENCE HAS LEFT THE
SHABBY LITTLE DISTRICT MUCH AS HE
FOUND IT: DREARIER AND QUIETER THA
ANY RIGHT-THINKING PART OF
MANHATTAN SHOULD EVER BE.

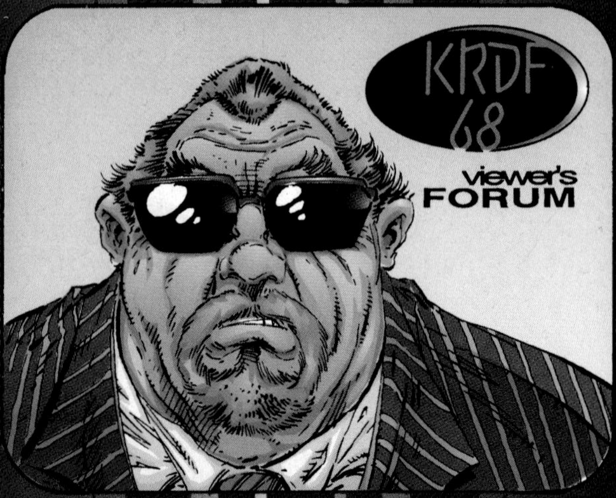
KRDF
68
viewer's
FORUM

NOW, ***BAM!***- OUT OF LEFT FIELD COMES
ANOTHER NEW YORK MOMENT AS A MO
CITIZEN ***VANISHES*** FROM THE MIDDLE OF
SOUP KITCHEN. THIS IS THE SAME WELL-
SCRUBBED CITIZEN WHO WAS SHOWERED
WITH GOLDEN HYPE DURING OUR PREVIO
MAYOR'S FAILED REELECTION BID. COULD
THE SORE LOSER HAVE CALLED IN ONE LA
FAVOR FROM ON HIGH AND HAD THE PO
LAD ***SACRIFIED*** ON THE ALTAR OF ***UNWEL-***
COME AMBITION? THE BOYS IN BLUE,
MEANWHILE, HAVE GIVEN THIS CASE THE
SAME CARE AND ATTENTION THEY WOUL
A STOLEN CAR RADIO IN TIMES SQUARE.
JUST GOES TO SHOW HOW SINCERE OUR
POLITICIANS ARE ABOUT THEIR COMMITT
MENT TO THE LITTLE GUY. PICK OUT AN
"AW-SHUCKS" SOCIAL WORKER, GIVE 'IM
TROPHY AT A PRESS CONFERENCE, THEN L
HIM GO ROT. GOD BLESS US, EVERY ONE

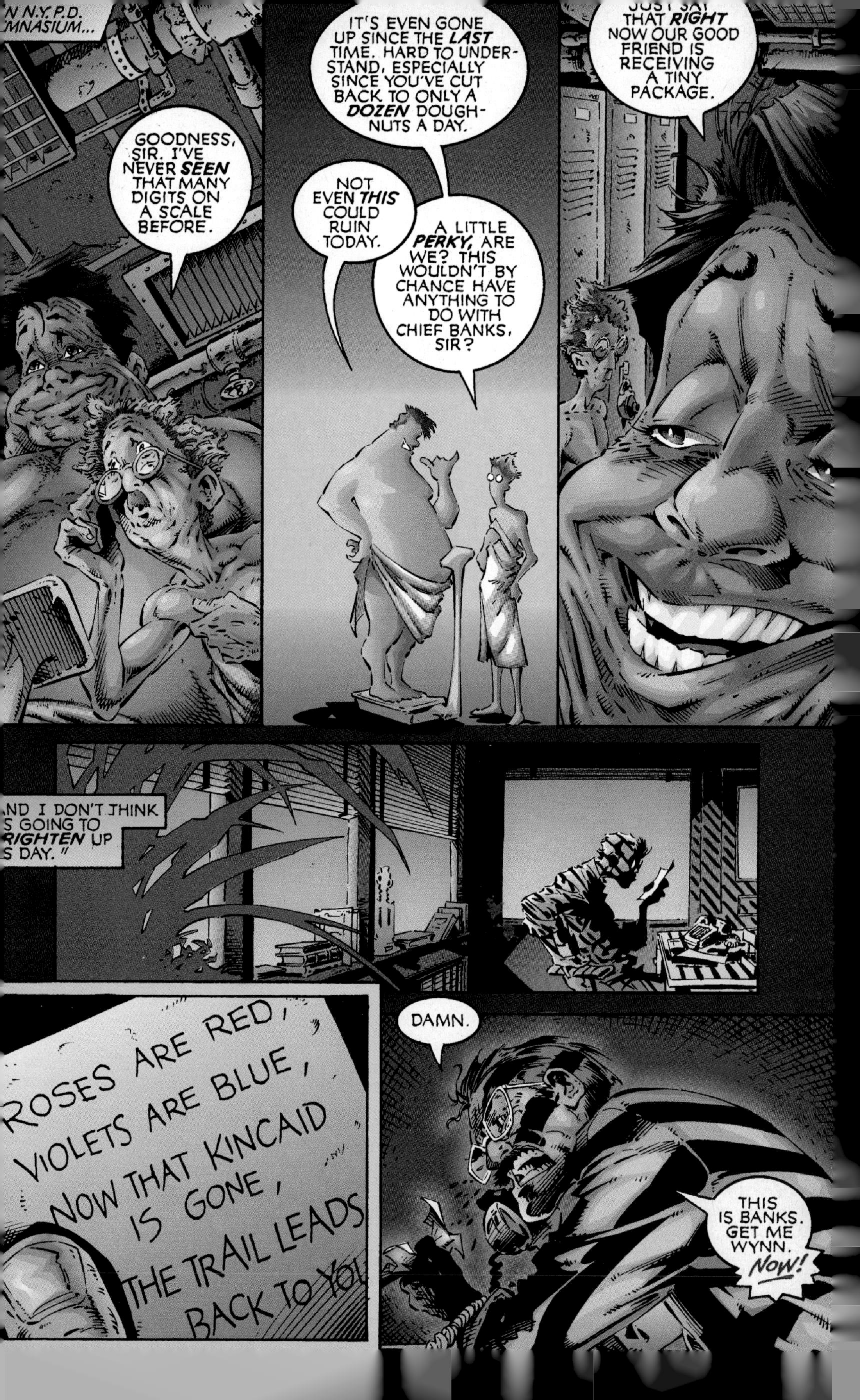

N N.Y.P.D. MNASIUM...
GOODNESS, SIR. I'VE NEVER SEEN THAT MANY DIGITS ON A SCALE BEFORE.
IT'S EVEN GONE UP SINCE THE LAST TIME. HARD TO UNDERSTAND, ESPECIALLY SINCE YOU'VE CUT BACK TO ONLY A DOZEN DOUGHNUTS A DAY.
NOT EVEN THIS COULD RUIN TODAY.
A LITTLE PERKY, ARE WE? THIS WOULDN'T BY CHANCE HAVE ANYTHING TO DO WITH CHIEF BANKS, SIR?
THAT RIGHT NOW OUR GOOD FRIEND IS RECEIVING A TINY PACKAGE.
ND I DON'T THINK S GOING TO RIGHTEN UP S DAY."
ROSES ARE RED, VIOLETS ARE BLUE, NOW THAT KINCAID IS GONE, THE TRAIL LEADS BACK TO YOU
DAMN.
THIS IS BANKS. GET ME WYNN. NOW!

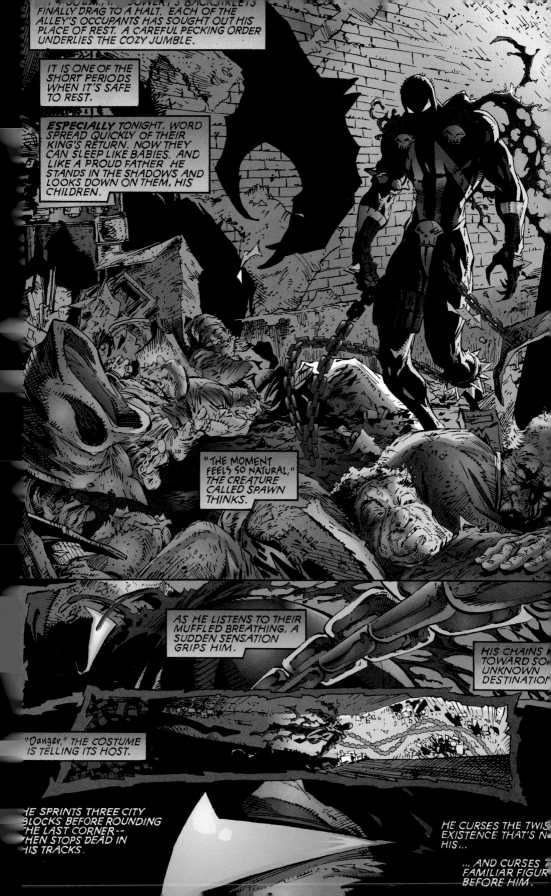

FINALLY DRAG TO A HALT. EACH OF THE ALLEY'S OCCUPANTS HAS SOUGHT OUT HIS PLACE OF REST. A CAREFUL PECKING ORDER UNDERLIES THE COZY JUMBLE.

IT IS ONE OF THE SHORT PERIODS WHEN IT'S SAFE TO REST.

ESPECIALLY TONIGHT. WORD SPREAD QUICKLY OF THEIR KING'S RETURN. NOW THEY CAN SLEEP LIKE BABIES. AND LIKE A PROUD FATHER HE STANDS IN THE SHADOWS AND LOOKS DOWN ON THEM, HIS CHILDREN.

"THE MOMENT FEELS SO NATURAL," THE CREATURE CALLED SPAWN THINKS.

AS HE LISTENS TO THEIR MUFFLED BREATHING, A SUDDEN SENSATION GRIPS HIM.

HIS CHAINS TOWARD SO UNKNOWN DESTINATIO

"Danger," THE COSTUME IS TELLING ITS HOST.

HE SPRINTS THREE CITY BLOCKS BEFORE ROUNDING THE LAST CORNER-- THEN STOPS DEAD IN HIS TRACKS.

HE CURSES THE TWIS EXISTENCE THAT'S N HIS...

... AND CURSES FAMILIAR FIGUR BEFORE HIM.

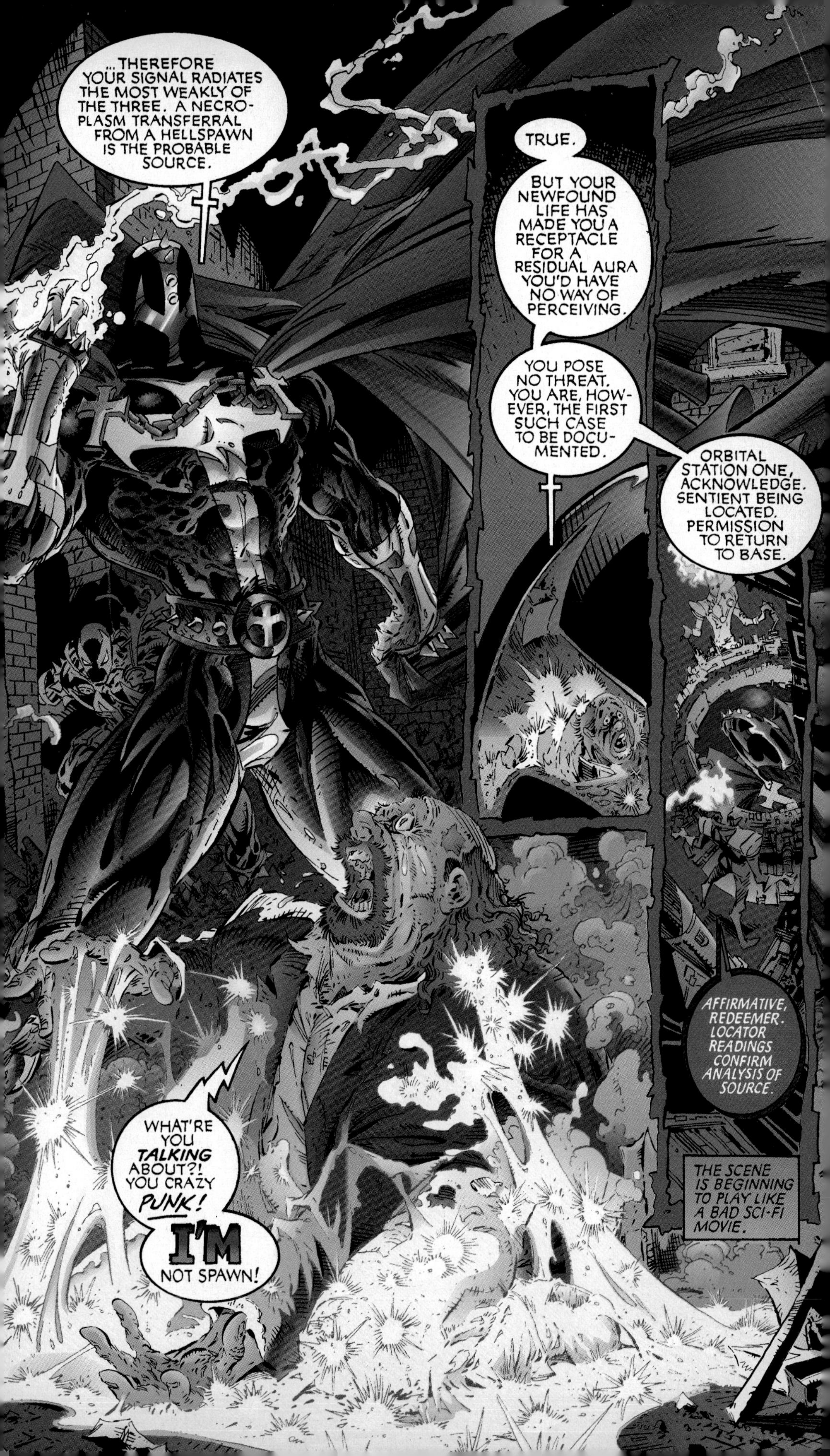
...THEREFORE YOUR SIGNAL RADIATES THE MOST WEAKLY OF THE THREE. A NECRO-PLASM TRANSFERRAL FROM A HELLSPAWN IS THE PROBABLE SOURCE.
TRUE.
BUT YOUR NEWFOUND LIFE HAS MADE YOU A RECEPTACLE FOR A RESIDUAL AURA YOU'D HAVE NO WAY OF PERCEIVING.
YOU POSE NO THREAT. YOU ARE, HOW-EVER, THE FIRST SUCH CASE TO BE DOCU-MENTED.
ORBITAL STATION ONE, ACKNOWLEDGE. SENTIENT BEING LOCATED. PERMISSION TO RETURN TO BASE.
AFFIRMATIVE, REDEEMER. LOCATOR READINGS CONFIRM ANALYSIS OF SOURCE.
WHAT'RE YOU TALKING ABOUT?! YOU CRAZY PUNK!
I'M NOT SPAWN!
THE SCENE IS BEGINNING TO PLAY LIKE A BAD SCI-FI MOVIE.

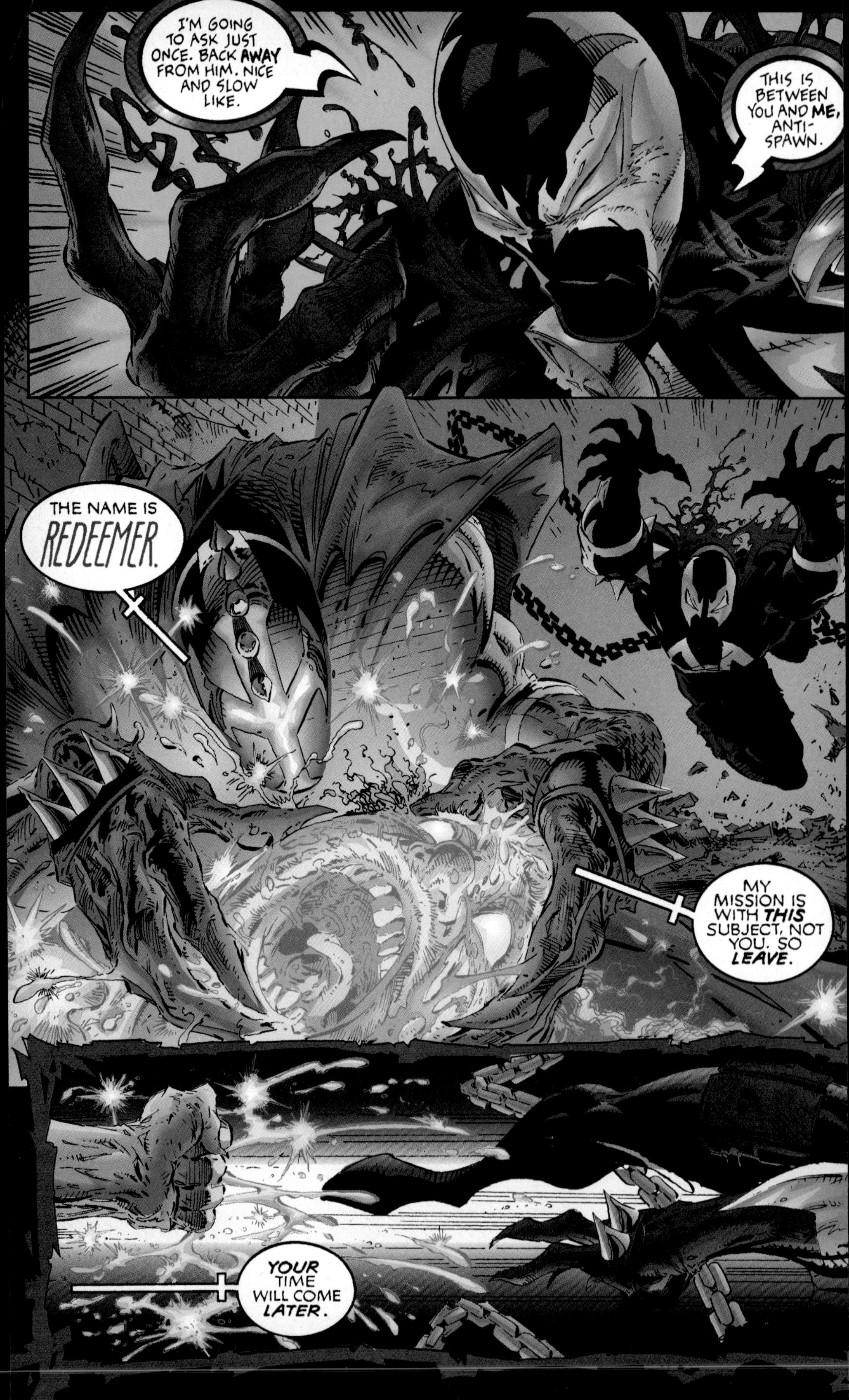

I'M GOING TO ASK JUST ONCE. BACK AWAY FROM HIM. NICE AND SLOW LIKE.
THIS IS BETWEEN YOU AND ME, ANTI-SPAWN.
THE NAME IS REDEEMER.
MY MISSION IS WITH THIS SUBJECT, NOT YOU. SO LEAVE.
YOUR TIME WILL COME LATER.

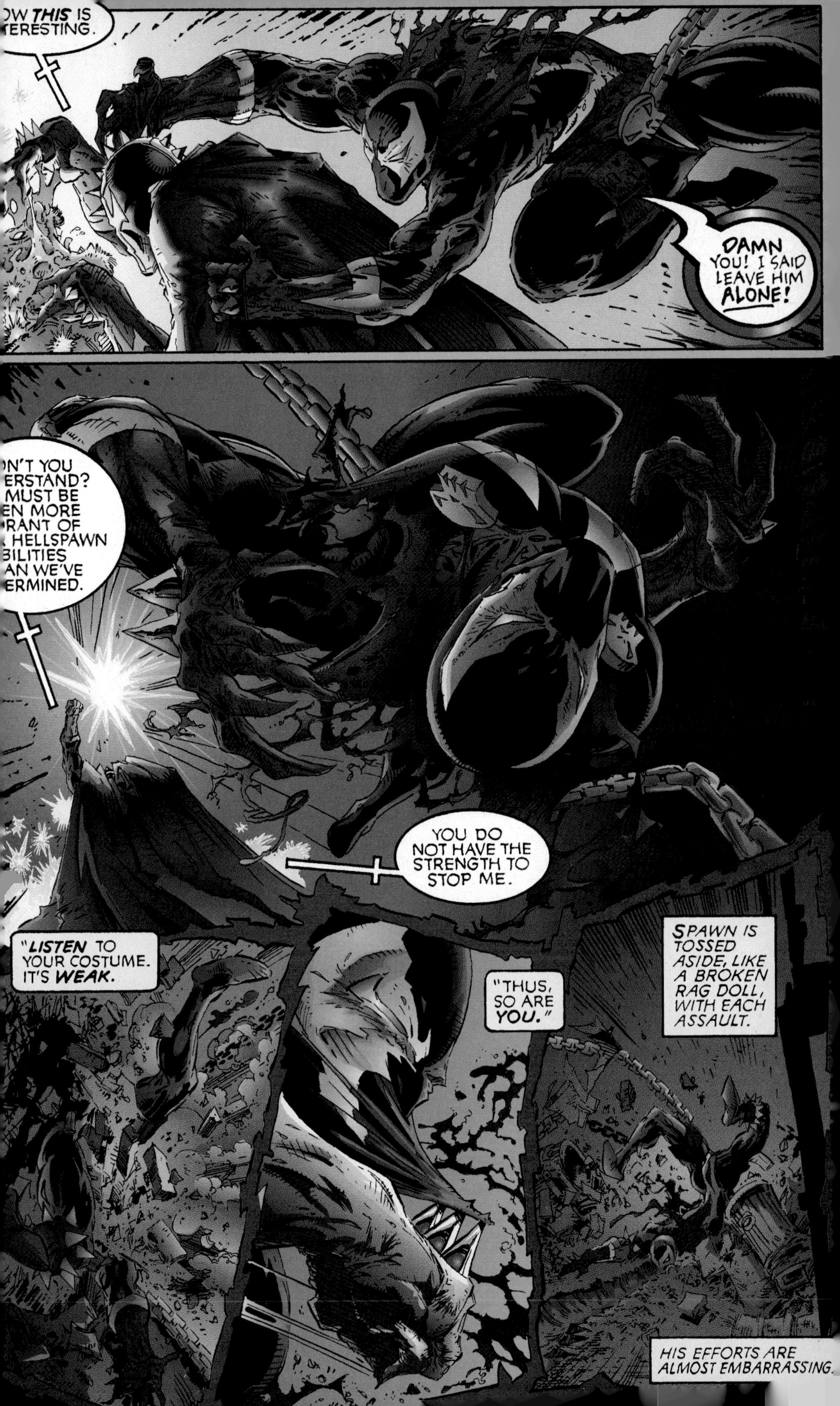
OW THIS IS
TERESTING.
DAMN YOU! I SAID LEAVE HIM ALONE!
N'T YOU ERSTAND? MUST BE EN MORE RANT OF HELLSPAWN BILITIES AN WE'VE ERMINED.
YOU DO NOT HAVE THE STRENGTH TO STOP ME.
"LISTEN TO YOUR COSTUME. IT'S WEAK.
"THUS, SO ARE YOU."
SPAWN IS TOSSED ASIDE, LIKE A BROKEN RAG DOLL, WITH EACH ASSAULT.
HIS EFFORTS ARE ALMOST EMBARRASSING.

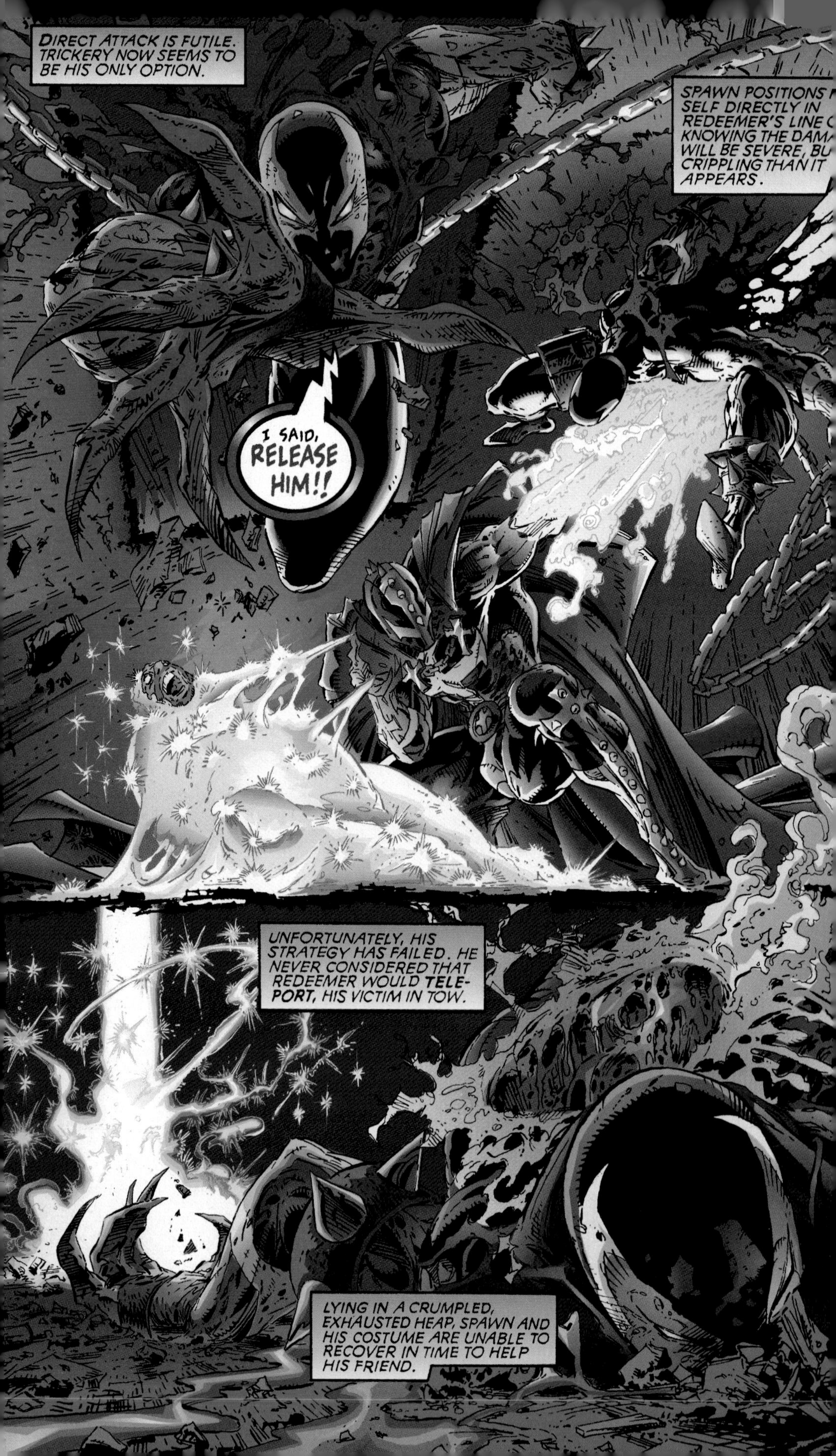
DIRECT ATTACK IS FUTILE. TRICKERY NOW SEEMS TO BE HIS ONLY OPTION.
SPAWN POSITIONS SELF DIRECTLY IN REDEEMER'S LINE KNOWING THE DAMA WILL BE SEVERE, BU CRIPPLING THAN IT APPEARS.
I SAID, RELEASE HIM!!
UNFORTUNATELY, HIS STRATEGY HAS FAILED. HE NEVER CONSIDERED THAT REDEEMER WOULD TELE-PORT, HIS VICTIM IN TOW.
LYING IN A CRUMPLED, EXHAUSTED HEAP, SPAWN AND HIS COSTUME ARE UNABLE TO RECOVER IN TIME TO HELP HIS FRIEND.

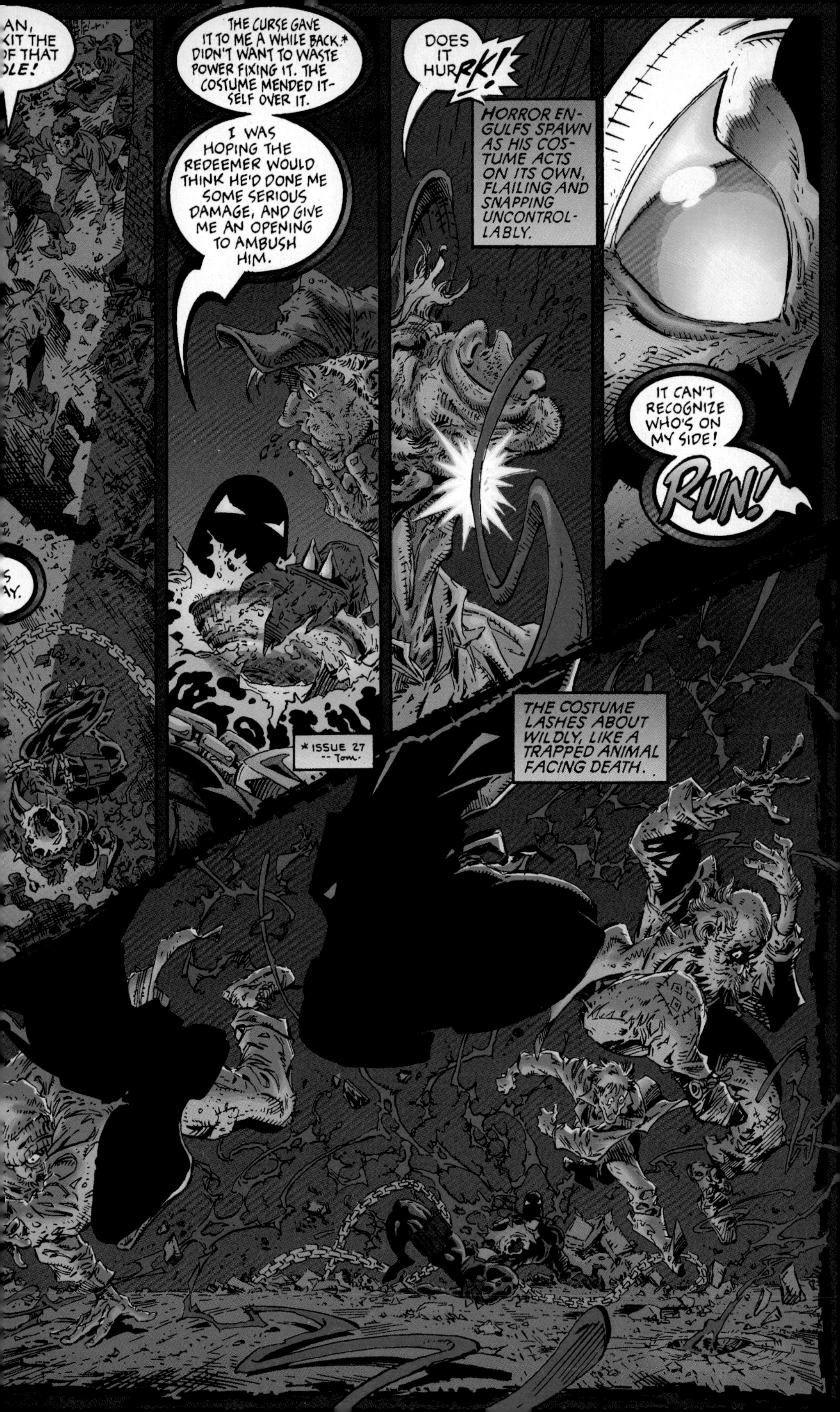
AN, KIT THE OF THAT OLE!
S AY.
THE CURSE GAVE IT TO ME A WHILE BACK.* DIDN'T WANT TO WASTE POWER FIXING IT. THE COSTUME MENDED ITSELF OVER IT.
I WAS HOPING THE REDEEMER WOULD THINK HE'D DONE ME SOME SERIOUS DAMAGE, AND GIVE ME AN OPENING TO AMBUSH HIM.
*ISSUE 27 -- Tom-
DOES IT HURRK!
HORROR ENGULFS SPAWN AS HIS COSTUME ACTS ON ITS OWN, FLAILING AND SNAPPING UNCONTROLLABLY.
IT CAN'T RECOGNIZE WHO'S ON MY SIDE!
RUN!
THE COSTUME LASHES ABOUT WILDLY, LIKE A TRAPPED ANIMAL FACING DEATH.

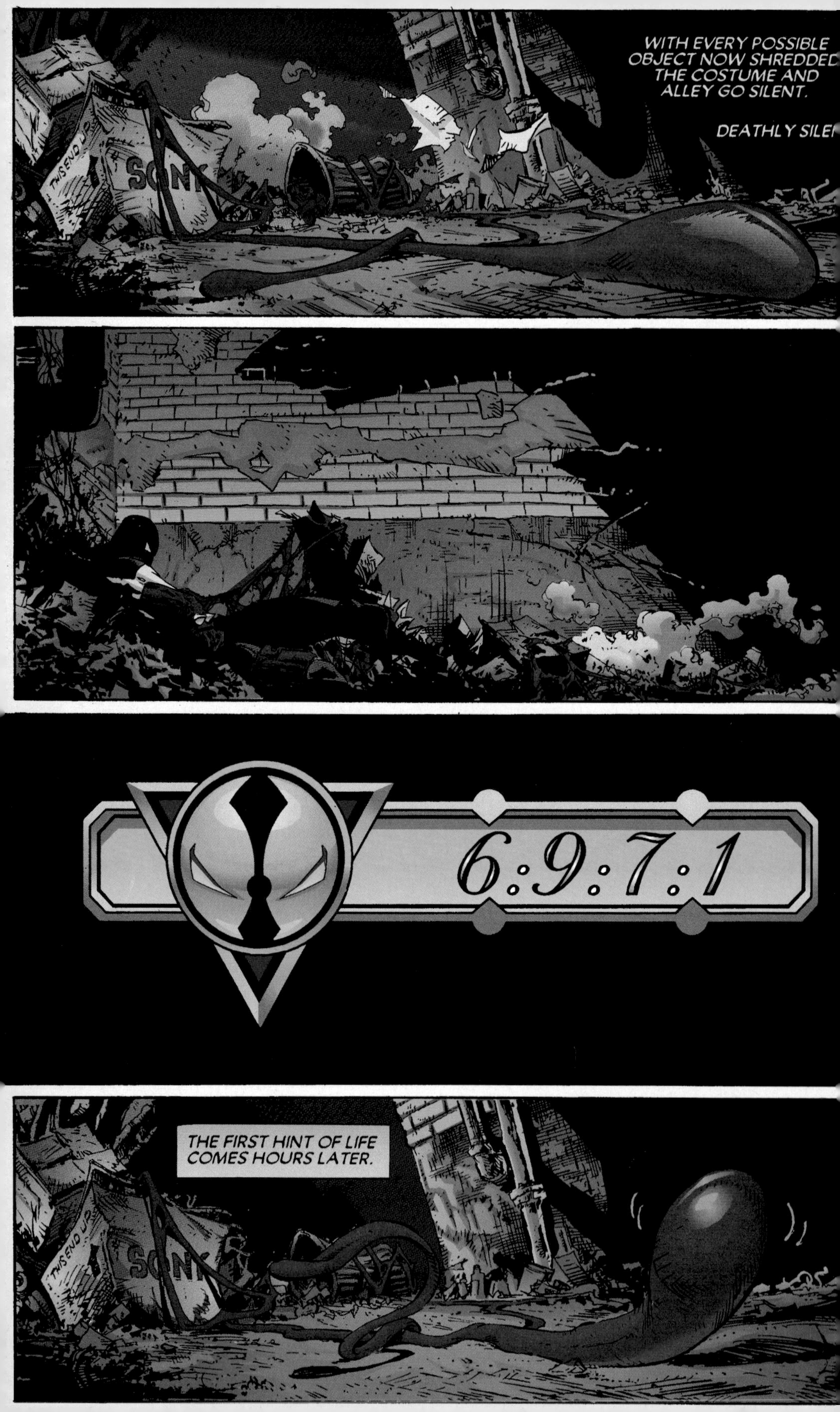

WITH EVERY POSSIBLE OBJECT NOW SHREDDED THE COSTUME AND ALLEY GO SILENT.
DEATHLY SILE
THIS END UP
SONY
6:9:7:1
THE FIRST HINT OF LIFE COMES HOURS LATER.
THIS END UP
SONY

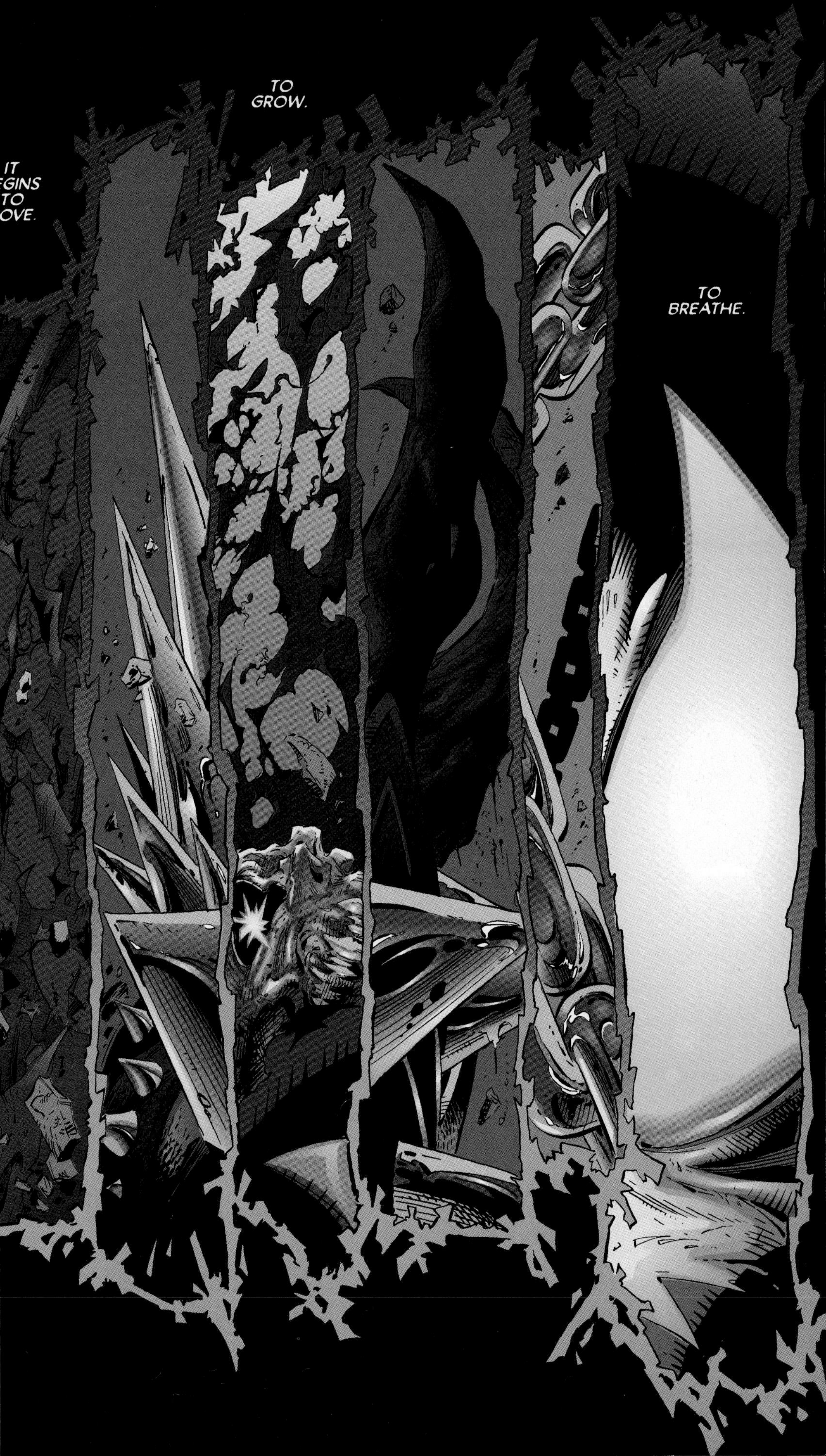
IT
EGINS
TO
OVE.
TO
GROW.
TO
BREATHE.

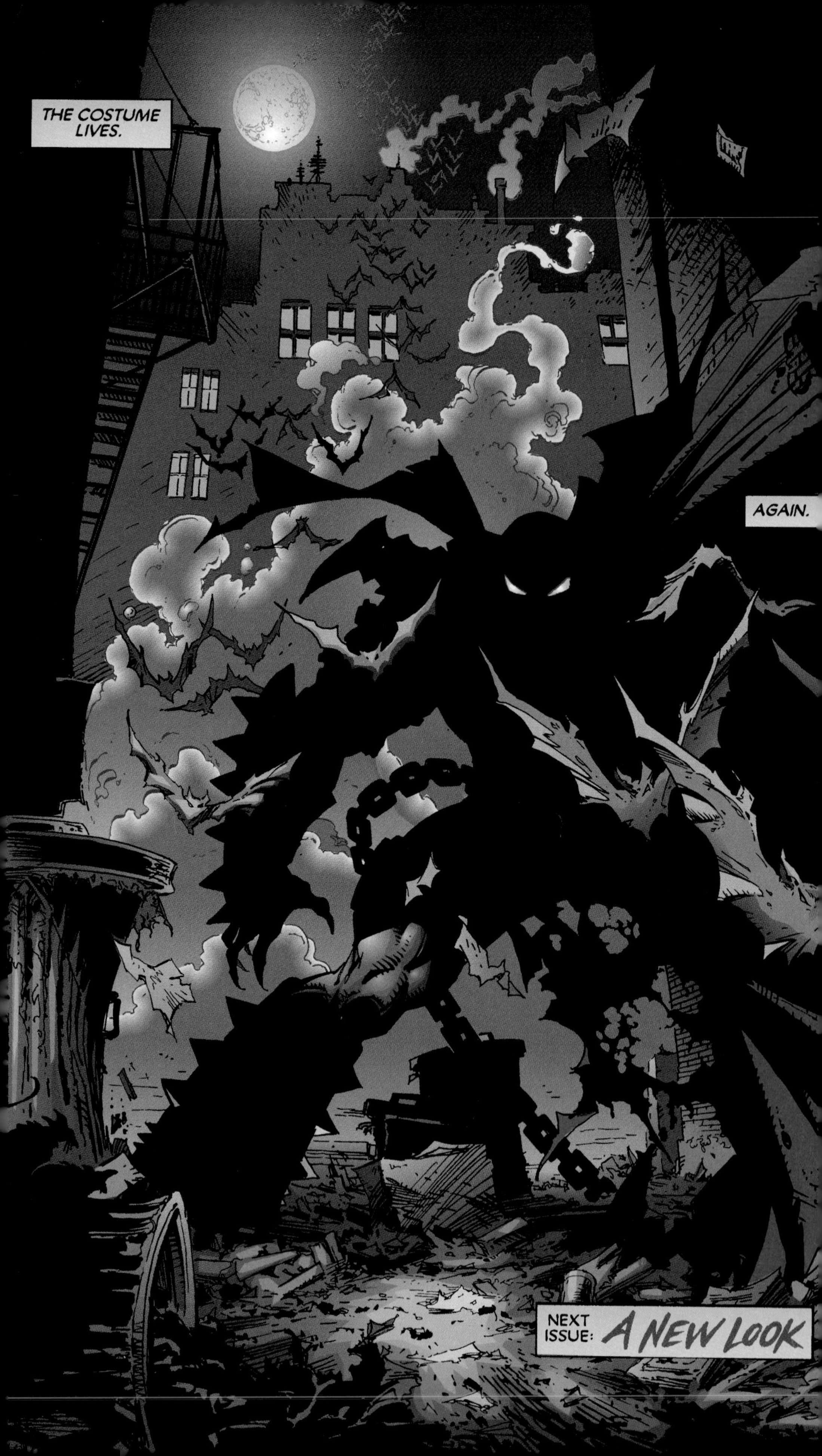
THE COSTUME LIVES.
AGAIN.
NEXT ISSUE: A NEW LOOK

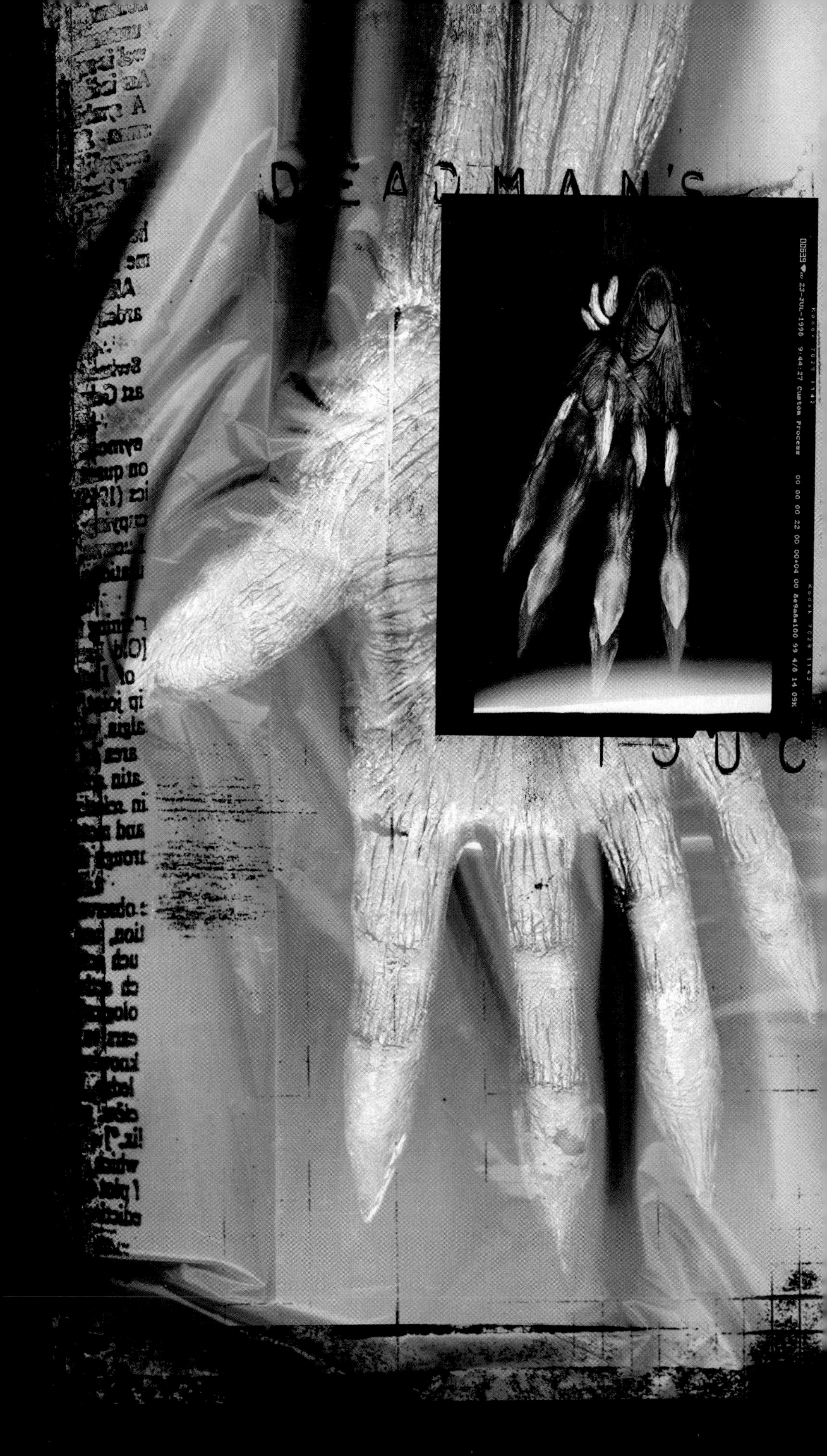
DEADMAN'S

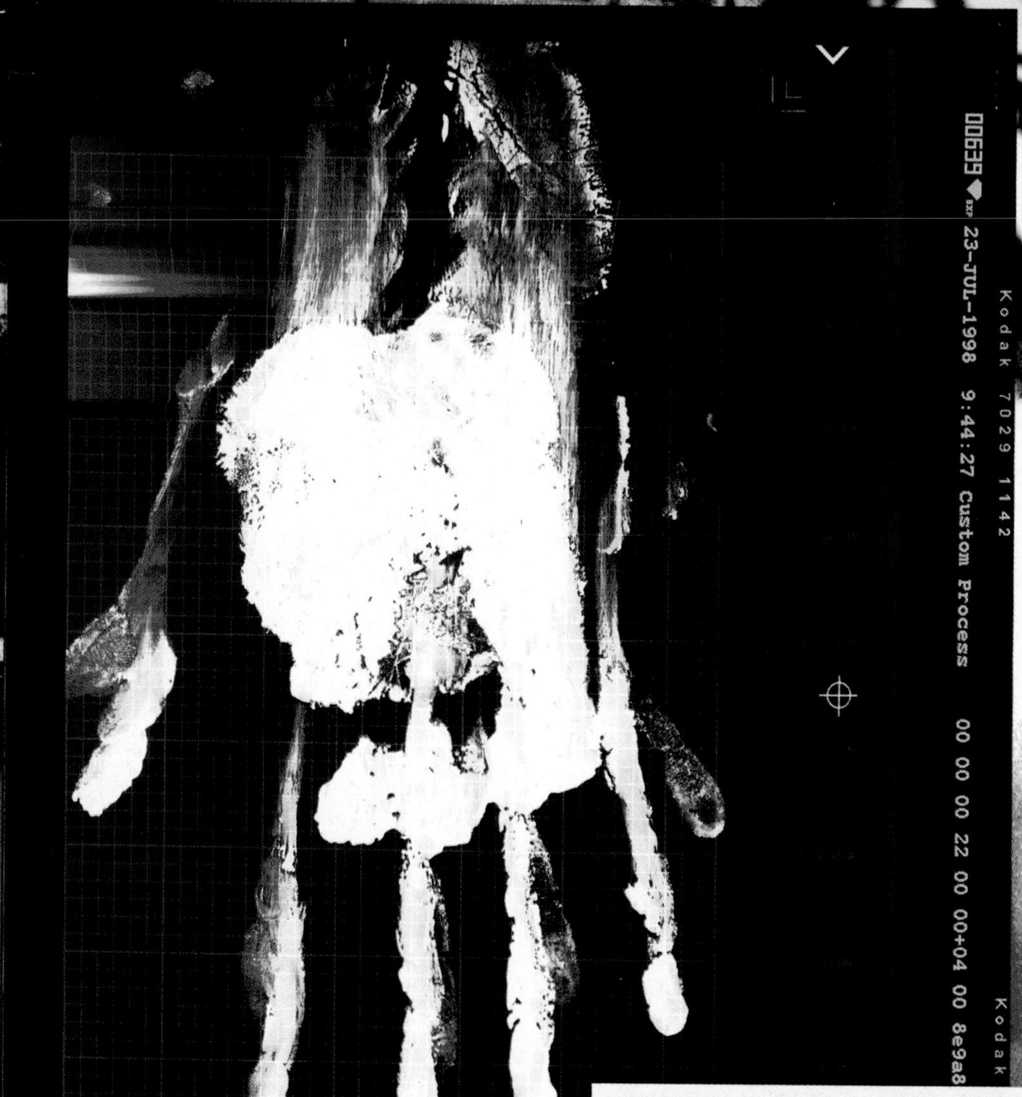
00639
EXP 23-JUL-1998 9:44:27 Custom Process 00 00 00 22 00 00+04 00 8e9a8
Kodak 7029 1142
Kodak

APPEARANCES 32

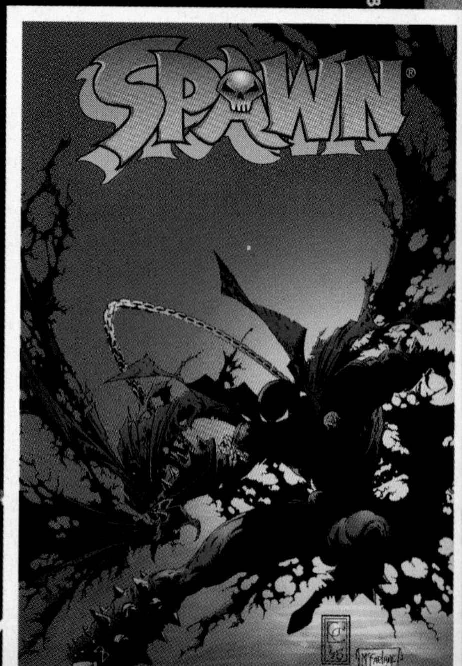
SPAWN

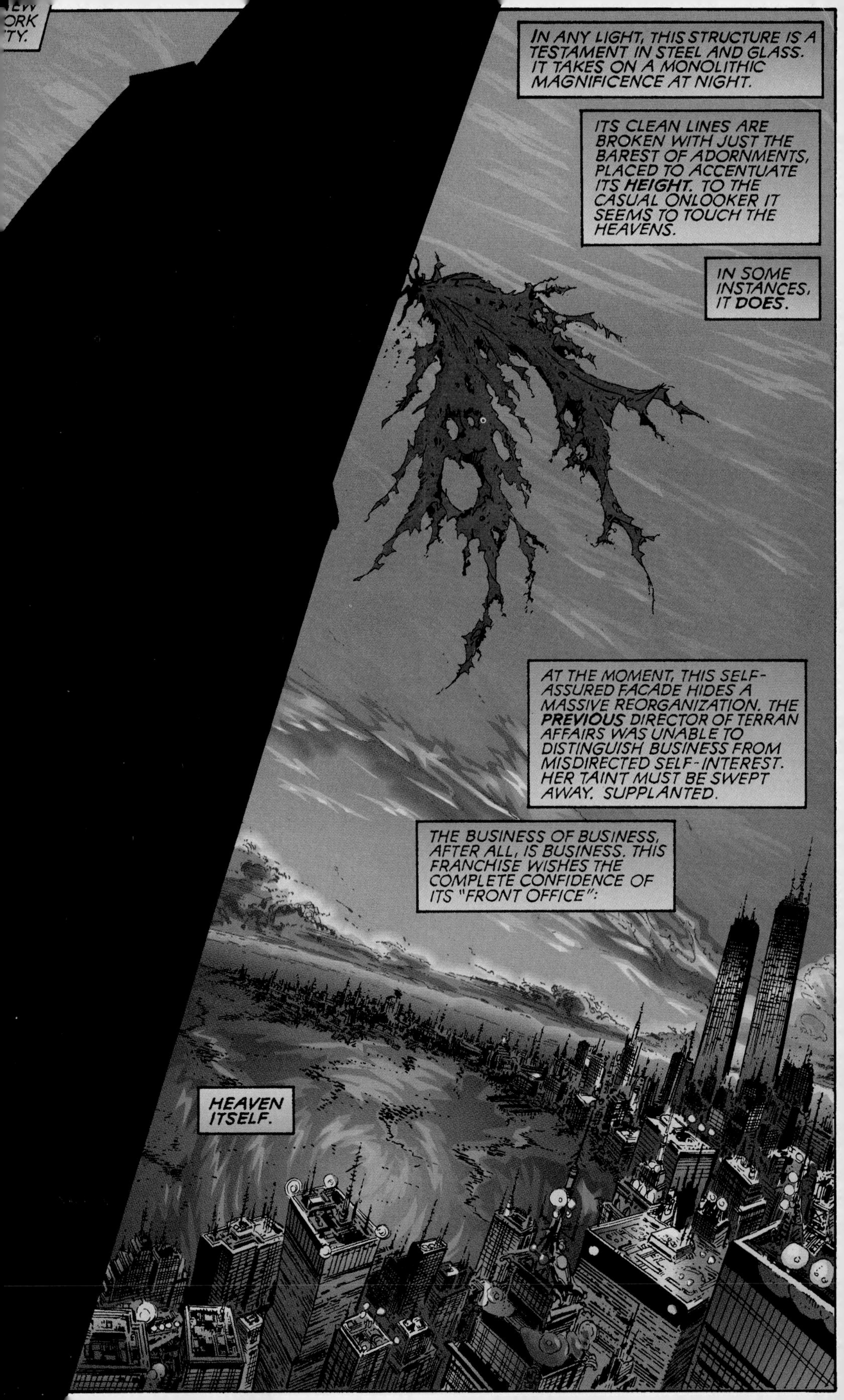
IN ANY LIGHT, THIS STRUCTURE IS A TESTAMENT IN STEEL AND GLASS. IT TAKES ON A MONOLITHIC MAGNIFICENCE AT NIGHT.
ITS CLEAN LINES ARE BROKEN WITH JUST THE BAREST OF ADORNMENTS, PLACED TO ACCENTUATE ITS HEIGHT. TO THE CASUAL ONLOOKER IT SEEMS TO TOUCH THE HEAVENS.
IN SOME INSTANCES, IT DOES.
AT THE MOMENT, THIS SELF-ASSURED FACADE HIDES A MASSIVE REORGANIZATION. THE PREVIOUS DIRECTOR OF TERRAN AFFAIRS WAS UNABLE TO DISTINGUISH BUSINESS FROM MISDIRECTED SELF-INTEREST. HER TAINT MUST BE SWEPT AWAY. SUPPLANTED.
THE BUSINESS OF BUSINESS, AFTER ALL, IS BUSINESS. THIS FRANCHISE WISHES THE COMPLETE CONFIDENCE OF ITS "FRONT OFFICE":
HEAVEN ITSELF.

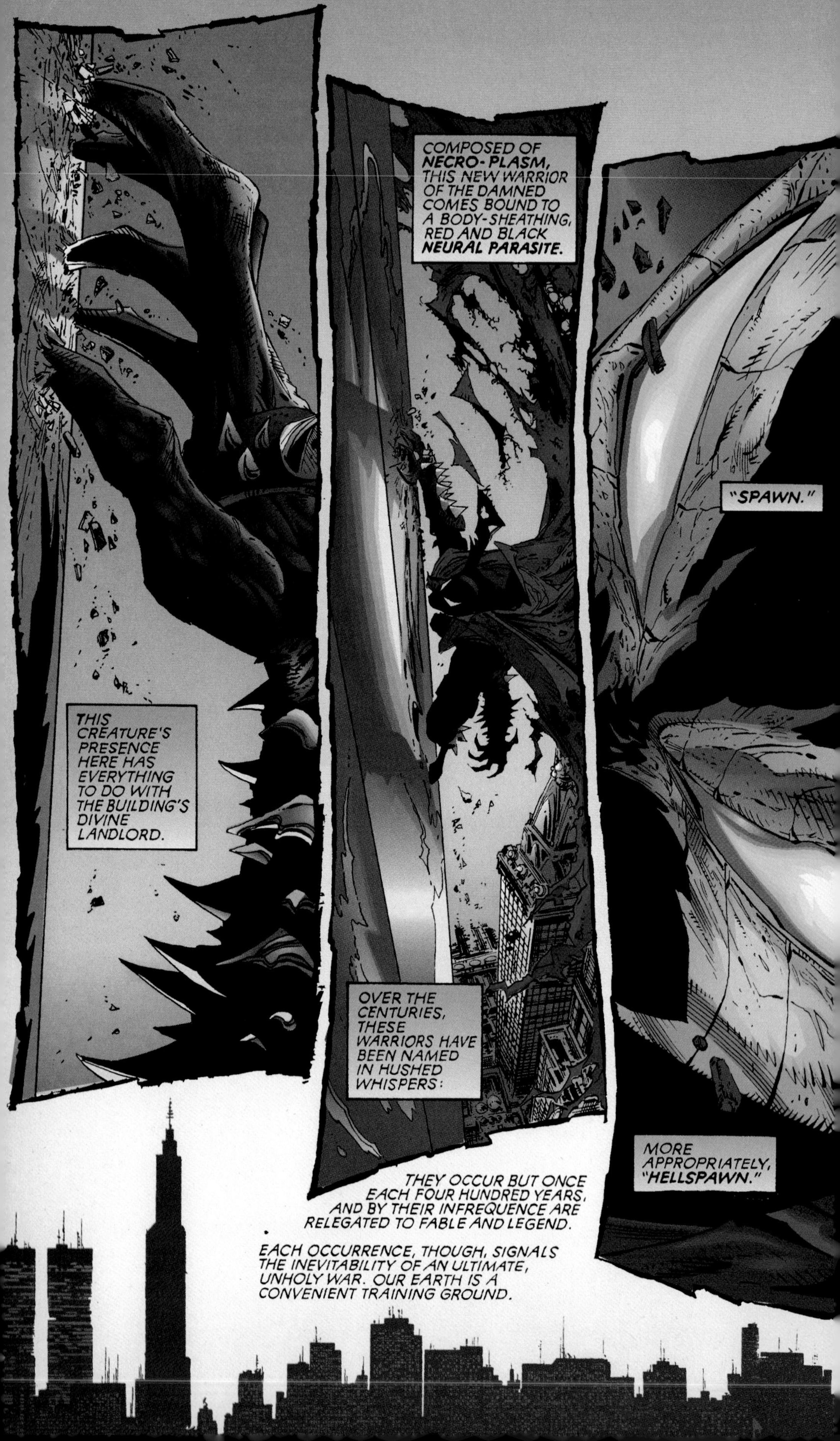

THIS CREATURE'S PRESENCE HERE HAS EVERYTHING TO DO WITH THE BUILDING'S DIVINE LANDLORD.
COMPOSED OF NECRO-PLASM, THIS NEW WARRIOR OF THE DAMNED COMES BOUND TO A BODY-SHEATHING, RED AND BLACK NEURAL PARASITE.
OVER THE CENTURIES, THESE WARRIORS HAVE BEEN NAMED IN HUSHED WHISPERS:
"SPAWN."
MORE APPROPRIATELY, "HELLSPAWN."
THEY OCCUR BUT ONCE EACH FOUR HUNDRED YEARS, AND BY THEIR INFREQUENCE ARE RELEGATED TO FABLE AND LEGEND.
EACH OCCURRENCE, THOUGH, SIGNALS THE INEVITABILITY OF AN ULTIMATE, UNHOLY WAR. OUR EARTH IS A CONVENIENT TRAINING GROUND.

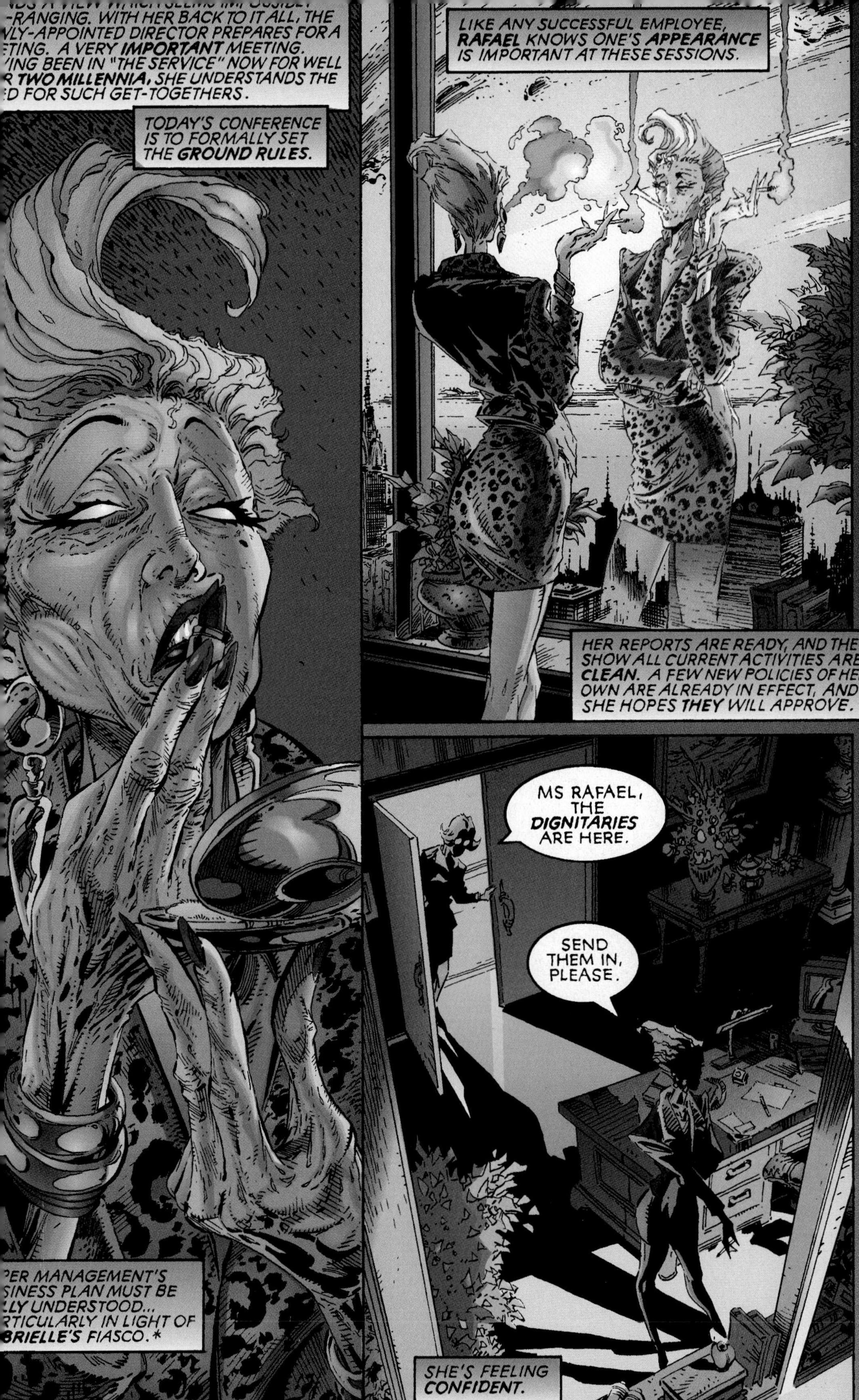
-RANGING. WITH HER BACK TO IT ALL, THE
VLY-APPOINTED DIRECTOR PREPARES FOR A
ETING. A VERY IMPORTANT MEETING.
VING BEEN IN "THE SERVICE" NOW FOR WELL
R TWO MILLENNIA, SHE UNDERSTANDS THE
ED FOR SUCH GET-TOGETHERS.
TODAY'S CONFERENCE IS TO FORMALLY SET THE GROUND RULES.
PER MANAGEMENT'S
SINESS PLAN MUST BE
LLY UNDERSTOOD...
RTICULARLY IN LIGHT OF
BRIELLE'S FIASCO.*
* SEEN IN THE ANGELA MINI-SERIES --Tom.
LIKE ANY SUCCESSFUL EMPLOYEE, RAFAEL KNOWS ONE'S APPEARANCE IS IMPORTANT AT THESE SESSIONS.
HER REPORTS ARE READY, AND THEY SHOW ALL CURRENT ACTIVITIES ARE CLEAN. A FEW NEW POLICIES OF HER OWN ARE ALREADY IN EFFECT, AND SHE HOPES THEY WILL APPROVE.
MS RAFAEL, THE DIGNITARIES ARE HERE.
SEND THEM IN, PLEASE.
SHE'S FEELING CONFIDENT.

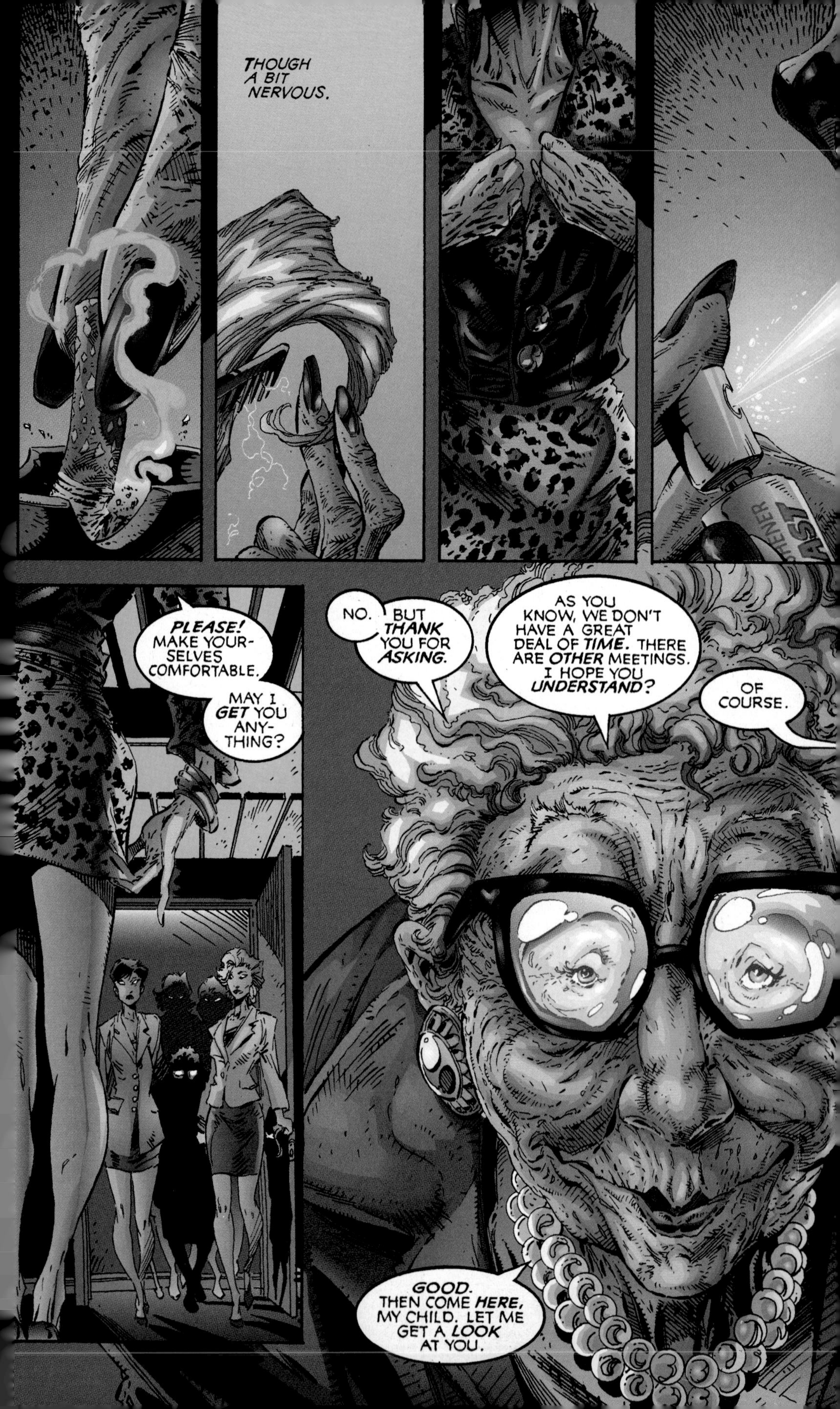
THOUGH A BIT NERVOUS.
PLEASE! MAKE YOURSELVES COMFORTABLE.
MAY I GET YOU ANYTHING?
NO.
BUT THANK YOU FOR ASKING.
AS YOU KNOW, WE DON'T HAVE A GREAT DEAL OF TIME. THERE ARE OTHER MEETINGS. I HOPE YOU UNDERSTAND?
OF COURSE.
GOOD. THEN COME HERE, MY CHILD. LET ME GET A LOOK AT YOU.

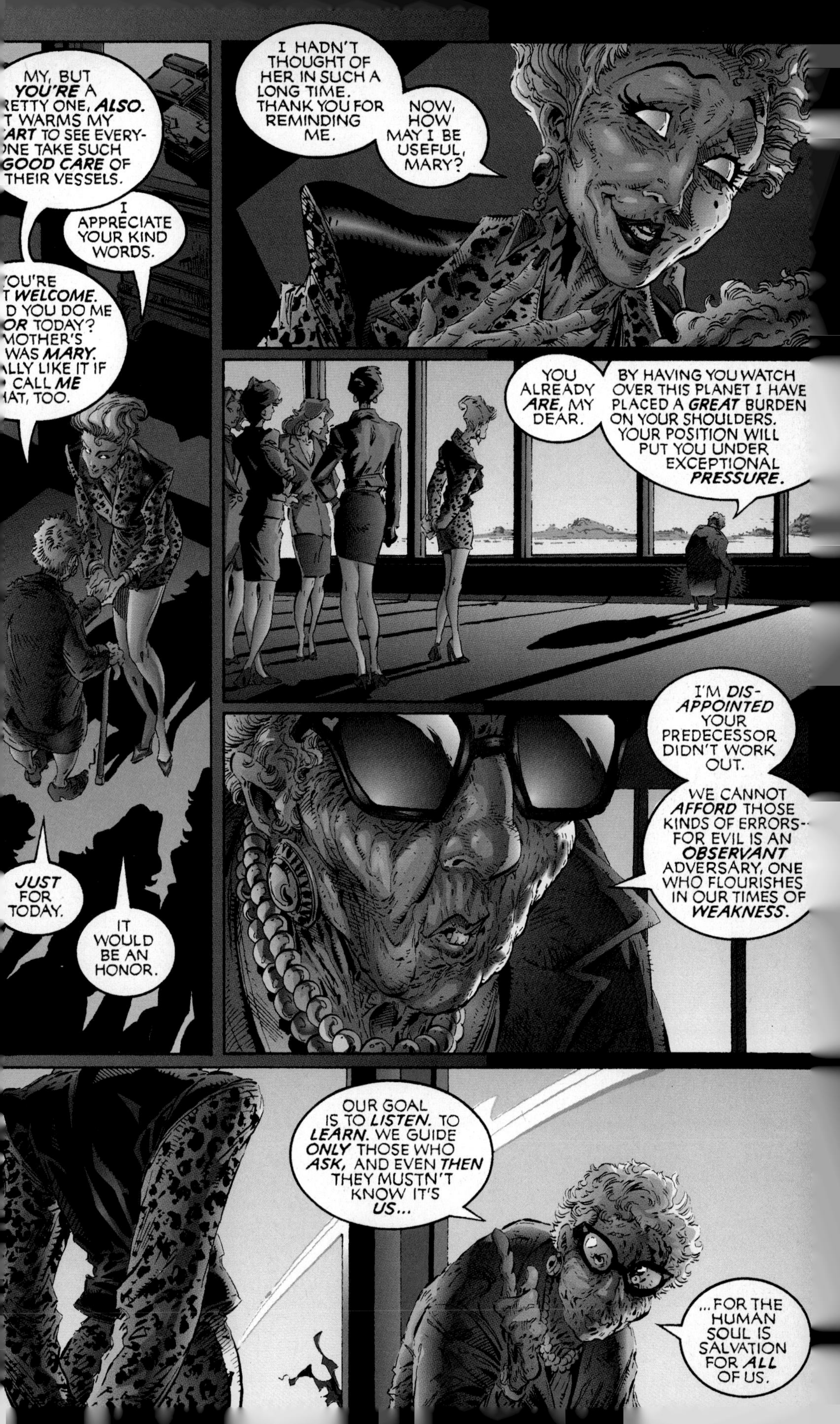
MY, BUT YOU'RE A
RETTY ONE, ALSO.
T WARMS MY
ART TO SEE EVERY-
ONE TAKE SUCH
GOOD CARE OF
THEIR VESSELS.
I APPRECIATE YOUR KIND WORDS.
OU'RE
T WELCOME.
D YOU DO ME
OR TODAY?
MOTHER'S
WAS MARY.
LLY LIKE IT IF
CALL ME
AT, TOO.
I HADN'T THOUGHT OF HER IN SUCH A LONG TIME. THANK YOU FOR REMINDING ME.
NOW, HOW MAY I BE USEFUL, MARY?
JUST FOR TODAY.
IT WOULD BE AN HONOR.
YOU ALREADY ARE, MY DEAR.
BY HAVING YOU WATCH OVER THIS PLANET I HAVE PLACED A GREAT BURDEN ON YOUR SHOULDERS. YOUR POSITION WILL PUT YOU UNDER EXCEPTIONAL PRESSURE.
I'M DIS-APPOINTED YOUR PREDECESSOR DIDN'T WORK OUT.
WE CANNOT AFFORD THOSE KINDS OF ERRORS--FOR EVIL IS AN OBSERVANT ADVERSARY, ONE WHO FLOURISHES IN OUR TIMES OF WEAKNESS.
OUR GOAL IS TO LISTEN. TO LEARN. WE GUIDE ONLY THOSE WHO ASK, AND EVEN THEN THEY MUSTN'T KNOW IT'S US...
...FOR THE HUMAN SOUL IS SALVATION FOR ALL OF US.

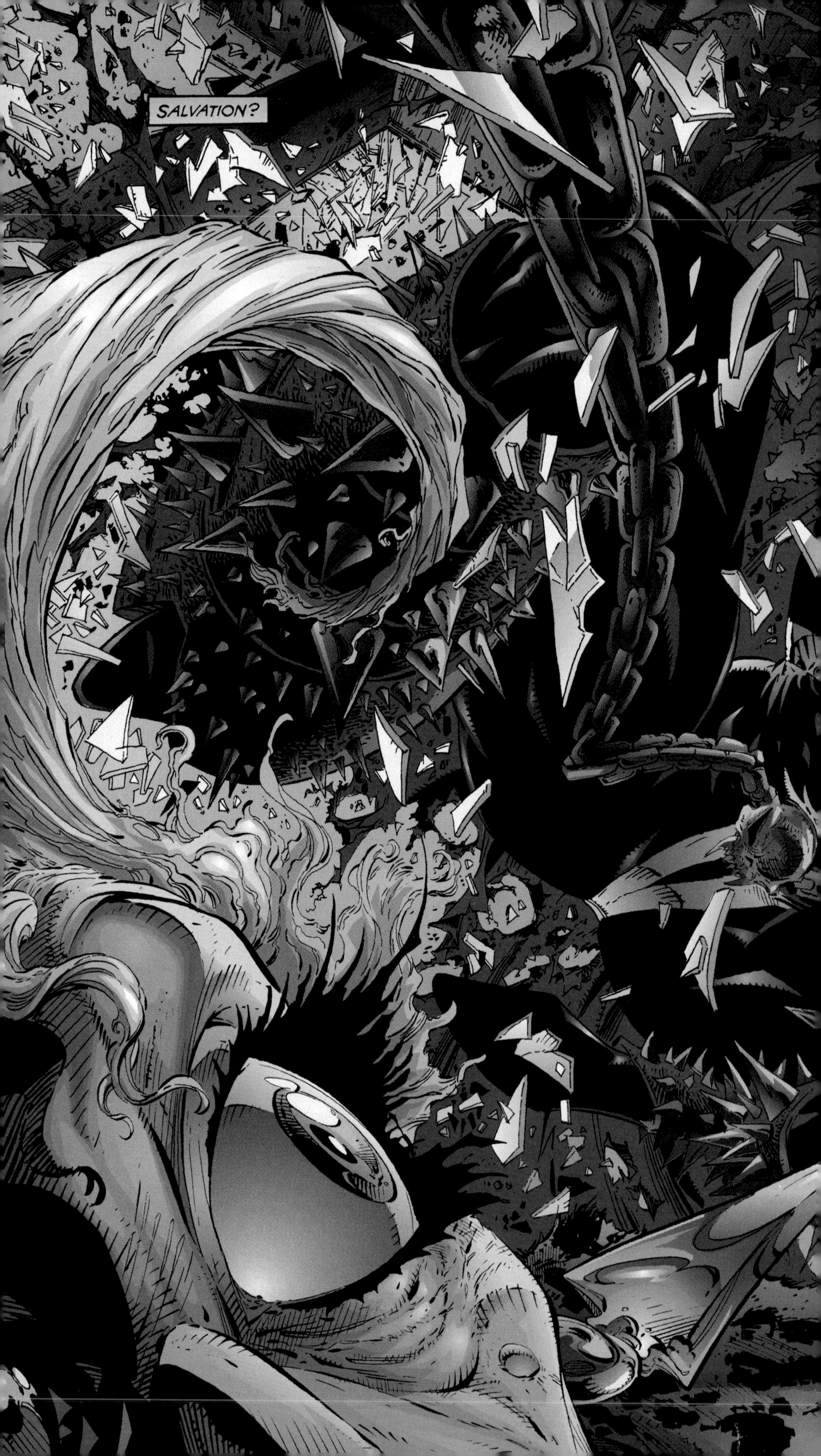
SALVATION?

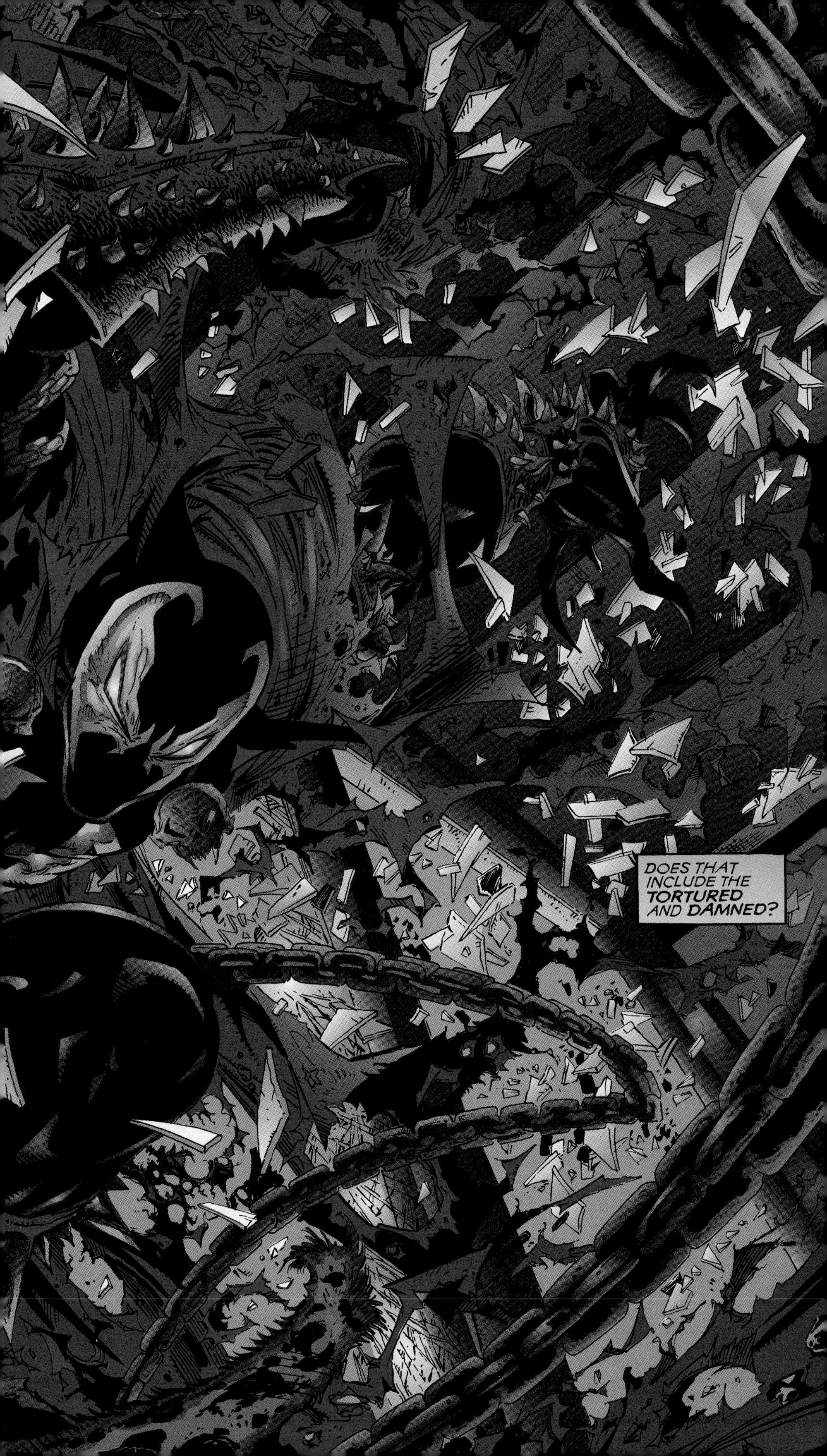
DOES THAT INCLUDE THE TORTURED AND DAMNED?

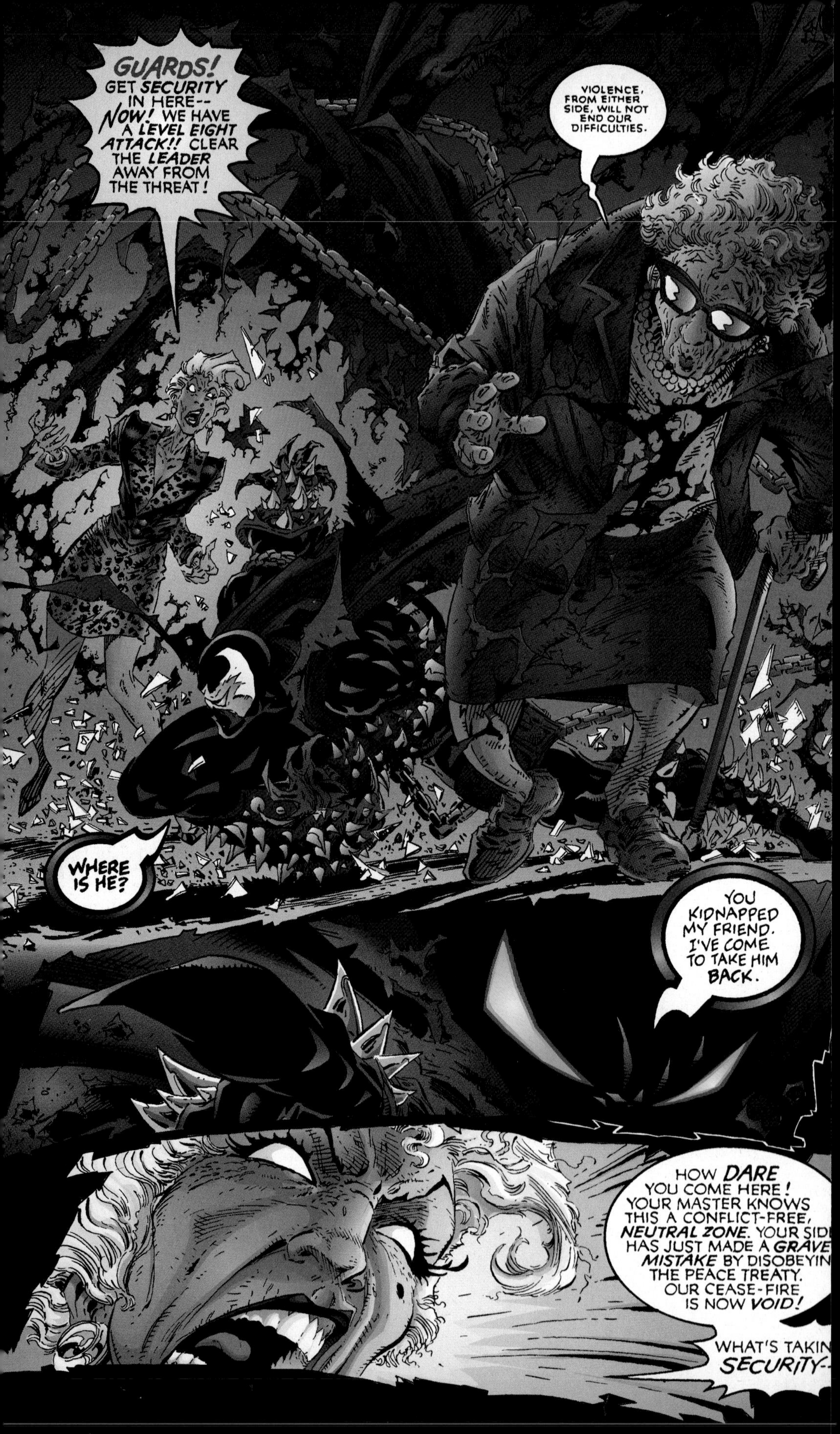
GUARDS! GET SECURITY IN HERE-- NOW! WE HAVE A LEVEL EIGHT ATTACK!! CLEAR THE LEADER AWAY FROM THE THREAT!
VIOLENCE, FROM EITHER SIDE, WILL NOT END OUR DIFFICULTIES.
WHERE IS HE?
YOU KIDNAPPED MY FRIEND. I'VE COME TO TAKE HIM BACK.
HOW DARE YOU COME HERE! YOUR MASTER KNOWS THIS A CONFLICT-FREE, NEUTRAL ZONE. YOUR SID HAS JUST MADE A GRAVE MISTAKE BY DISOBEYIN THE PEACE TREATY. OUR CEASE-FIRE IS NOW VOID!
WHAT'S TAKIN SECURITY--

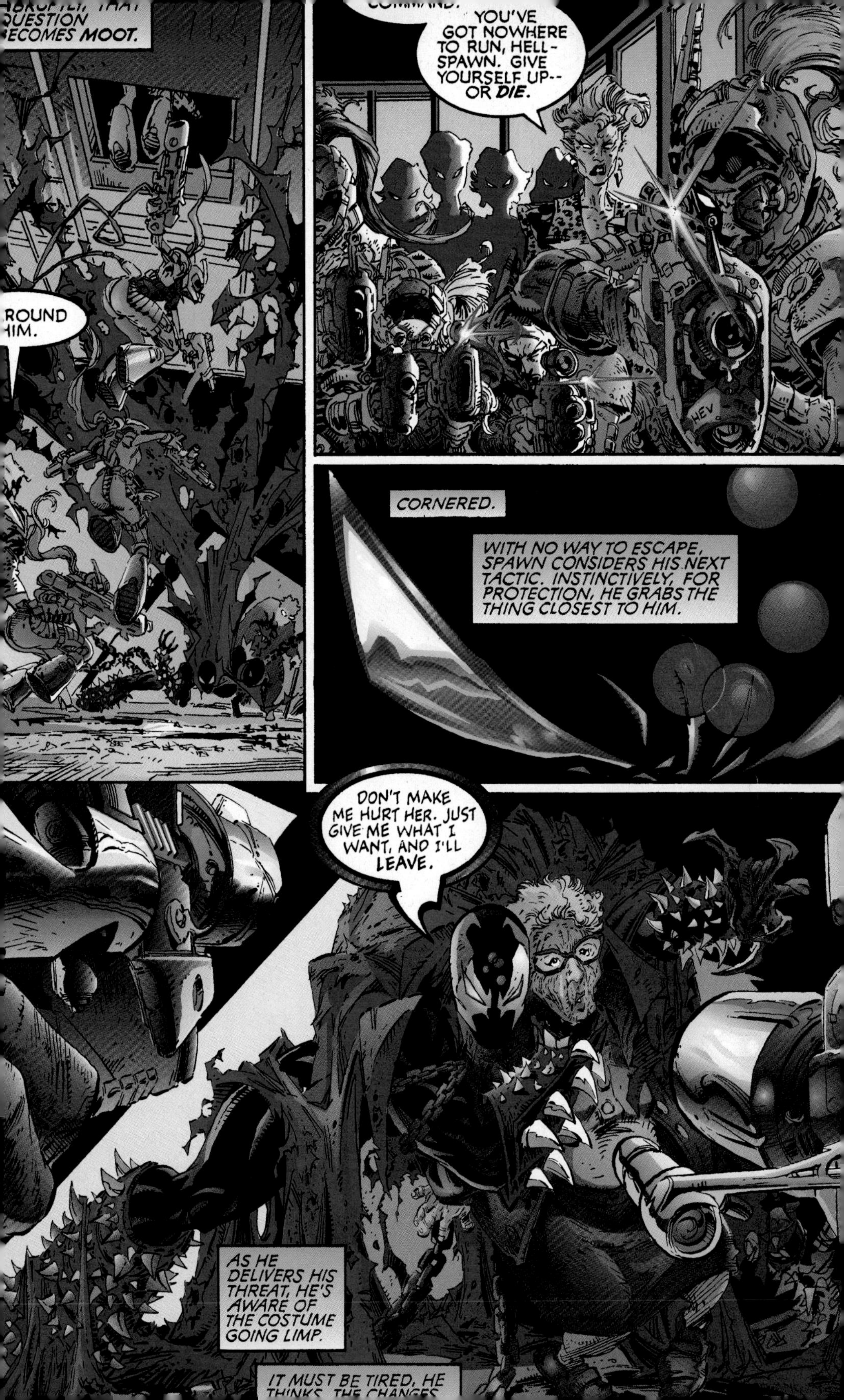

QUESTION
BECOMES MOOT.
ROUND
HIM.
YOU'VE GOT NOWHERE TO RUN, HELL-SPAWN. GIVE YOURSELF UP-- OR DIE.
HEV
CORNERED.
WITH NO WAY TO ESCAPE, SPAWN CONSIDERS HIS NEXT TACTIC. INSTINCTIVELY, FOR PROTECTION, HE GRABS THE THING CLOSEST TO HIM.
DON'T MAKE ME HURT HER. JUST GIVE ME WHAT I WANT, AND I'LL LEAVE.
AS HE DELIVERS HIS THREAT, HE'S AWARE OF THE COSTUME GOING LIMP.
IT MUST BE TIRED, HE

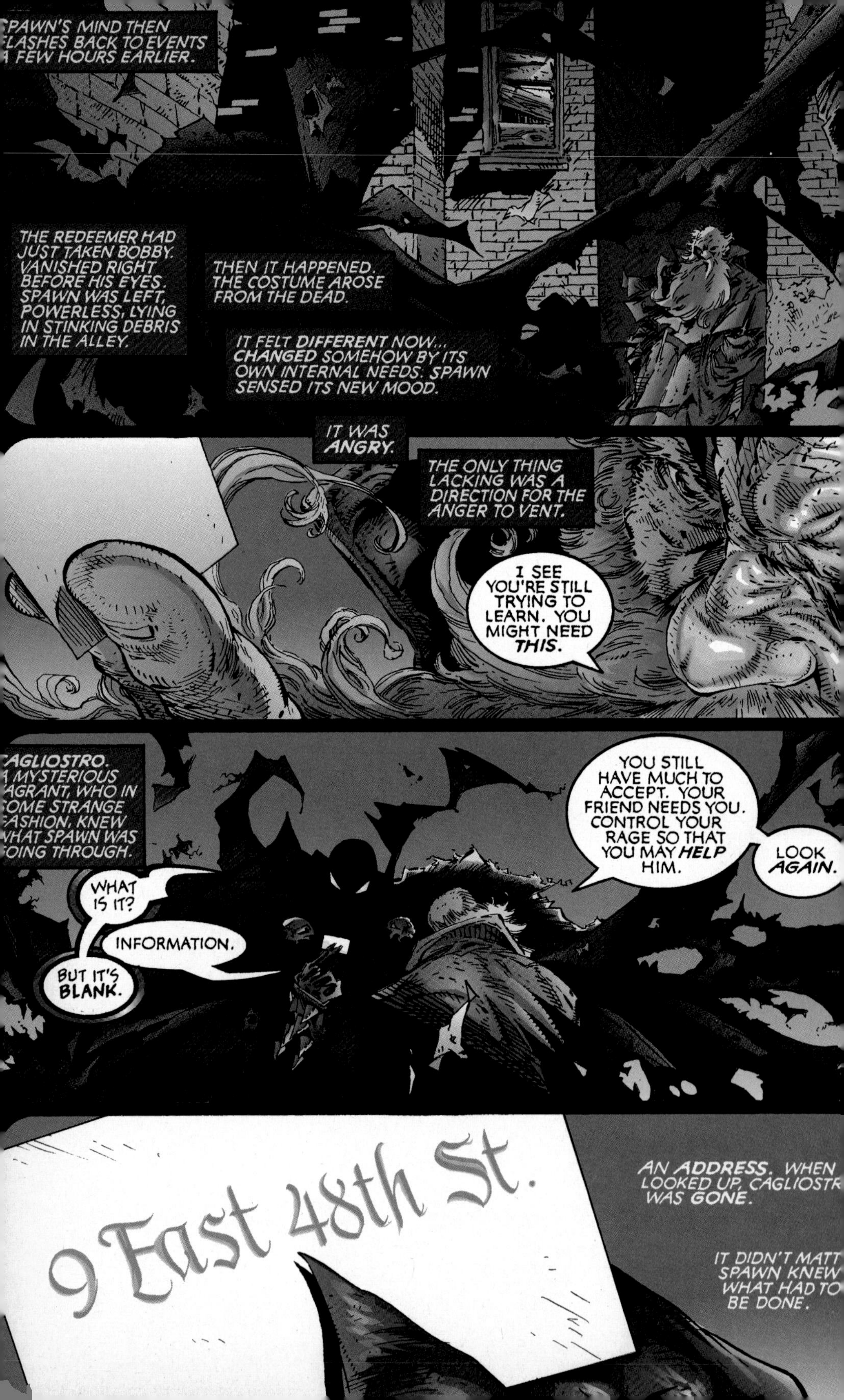

SPAWN'S MIND THEN FLASHES BACK TO EVENTS A FEW HOURS EARLIER.
THE REDEEMER HAD JUST TAKEN BOBBY. VANISHED RIGHT BEFORE HIS EYES. SPAWN WAS LEFT, POWERLESS, LYING IN STINKING DEBRIS IN THE ALLEY.
THEN IT HAPPENED. THE COSTUME AROSE FROM THE DEAD.
IT FELT DIFFERENT NOW... CHANGED SOMEHOW BY ITS OWN INTERNAL NEEDS. SPAWN SENSED ITS NEW MOOD.
IT WAS ANGRY.
THE ONLY THING LACKING WAS A DIRECTION FOR THE ANGER TO VENT.
I SEE YOU'RE STILL TRYING TO LEARN. YOU MIGHT NEED THIS.
CAGLIOSTRO. A MYSTERIOUS VAGRANT, WHO IN SOME STRANGE FASHION, KNEW WHAT SPAWN WAS GOING THROUGH.
WHAT IS IT?
INFORMATION.
BUT IT'S BLANK.
YOU STILL HAVE MUCH TO ACCEPT. YOUR FRIEND NEEDS YOU. CONTROL YOUR RAGE SO THAT YOU MAY HELP HIM.
LOOK AGAIN.
9 East 48th St.
AN ADDRESS. WHEN LOOKED UP, CAGLIOSTR WAS GONE.
IT DIDN'T MATT SPAWN KNEW WHAT HAD TO BE DONE.

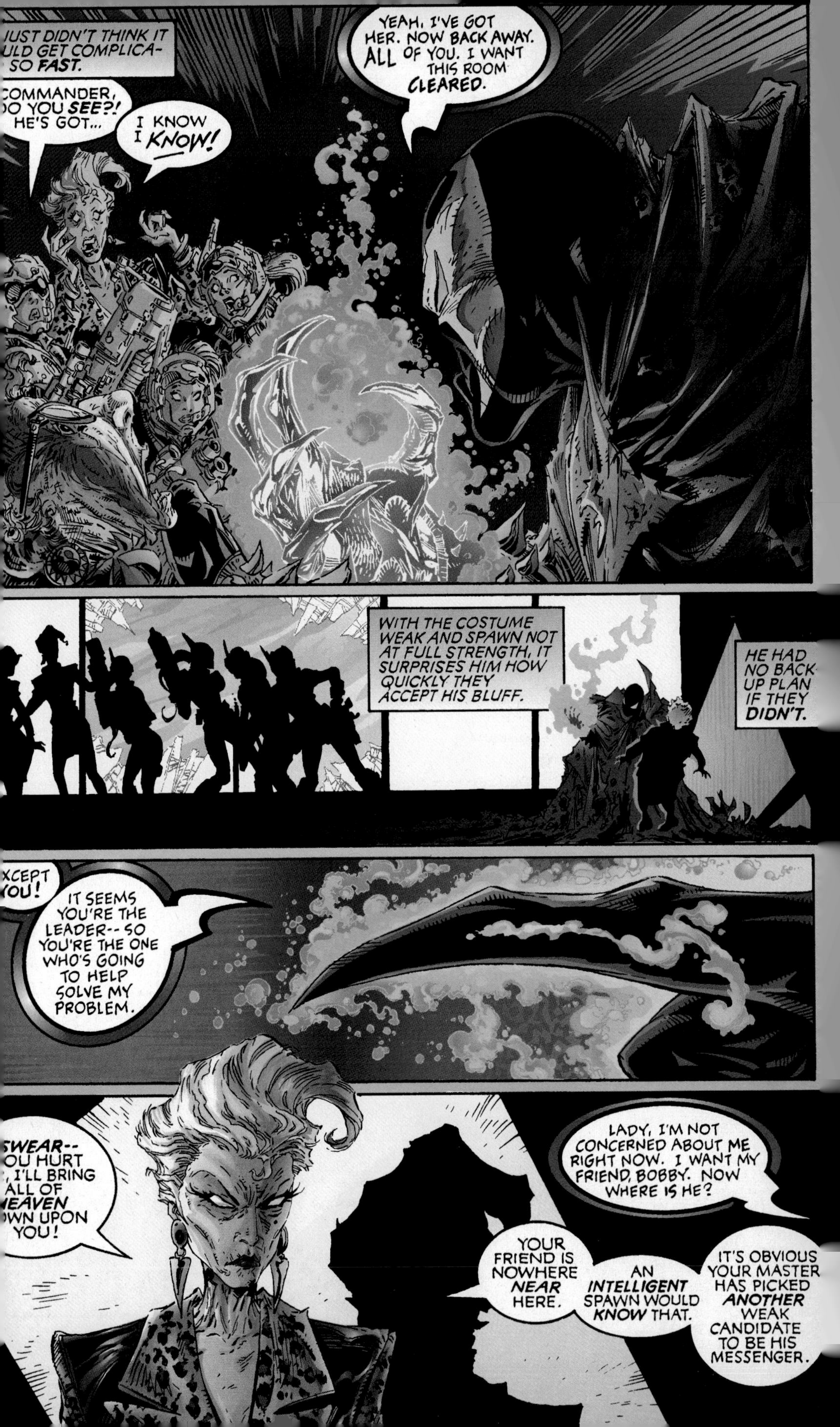

JUST DIDN'T THINK IT
ULD GET COMPLICA-
SO FAST.
COMMANDER,
DO YOU SEE?!
HE'S GOT...
I KNOW
I KNOW!
YEAH, I'VE GOT HER. NOW BACK AWAY. ALL OF YOU. I WANT THIS ROOM CLEARED.
WITH THE COSTUME WEAK AND SPAWN NOT AT FULL STRENGTH, IT SURPRISES HIM HOW QUICKLY THEY ACCEPT HIS BLUFF.
HE HAD NO BACK-UP PLAN IF THEY DIDN'T.
XCEPT
YOU!
IT SEEMS YOU'RE THE LEADER-- SO YOU'RE THE ONE WHO'S GOING TO HELP SOLVE MY PROBLEM.
SWEAR--
OU HURT
, I'LL BRING
ALL OF
HEAVEN
OWN UPON
YOU!
LADY, I'M NOT CONCERNED ABOUT ME RIGHT NOW. I WANT MY FRIEND, BOBBY. NOW WHERE IS HE?
YOUR FRIEND IS NOWHERE NEAR HERE.
AN INTELLIGENT SPAWN WOULD KNOW THAT.
IT'S OBVIOUS YOUR MASTER HAS PICKED ANOTHER WEAK CANDIDATE TO BE HIS MESSENGER.

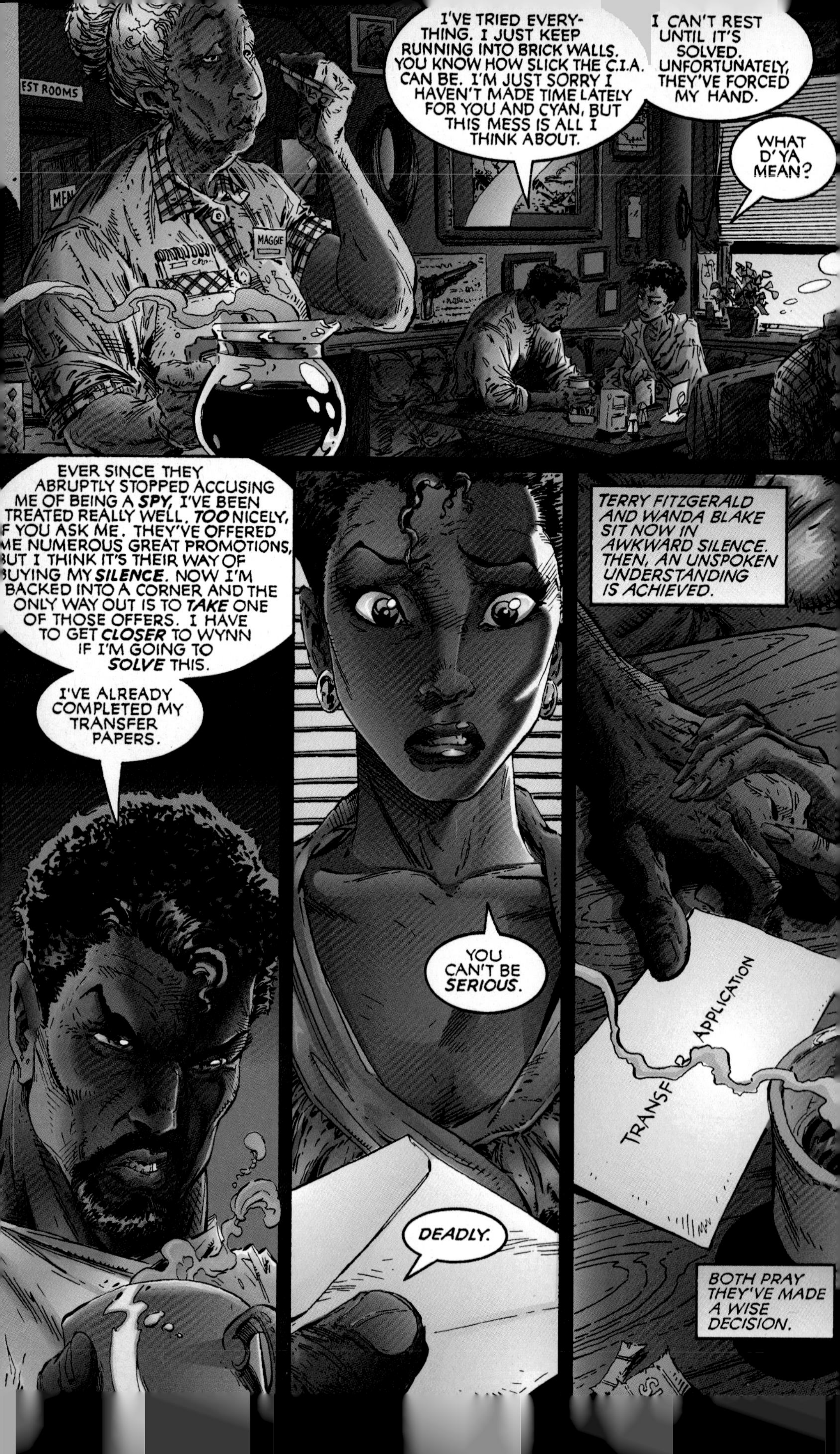
EST ROOMS
MEN
MAGGIE
I'VE TRIED EVERYTHING. I JUST KEEP RUNNING INTO BRICK WALLS. YOU KNOW HOW SLICK THE C.I.A. CAN BE. I'M JUST SORRY I HAVEN'T MADE TIME LATELY FOR YOU AND CYAN, BUT THIS MESS IS ALL I THINK ABOUT.
I CAN'T REST UNTIL IT'S SOLVED. UNFORTUNATELY, THEY'VE FORCED MY HAND.
WHAT D'YA MEAN?
EVER SINCE THEY ABRUPTLY STOPPED ACCUSING ME OF BEING A SPY, I'VE BEEN TREATED REALLY WELL. TOO NICELY, IF YOU ASK ME. THEY'VE OFFERED ME NUMEROUS GREAT PROMOTIONS, BUT I THINK IT'S THEIR WAY OF BUYING MY SILENCE. NOW I'M BACKED INTO A CORNER AND THE ONLY WAY OUT IS TO TAKE ONE OF THOSE OFFERS. I HAVE TO GET CLOSER TO WYNN IF I'M GOING TO SOLVE THIS.
I'VE ALREADY COMPLETED MY TRANSFER PAPERS.
YOU CAN'T BE SERIOUS.
DEADLY.
TERRY FITZGERALD AND WANDA BLAKE SIT NOW IN AWKWARD SILENCE. THEN, AN UNSPOKEN UNDERSTANDING IS ACHIEVED.
TRANSFER APPLICATION
BOTH PRAY THEY'VE MADE A WISE DECISION.

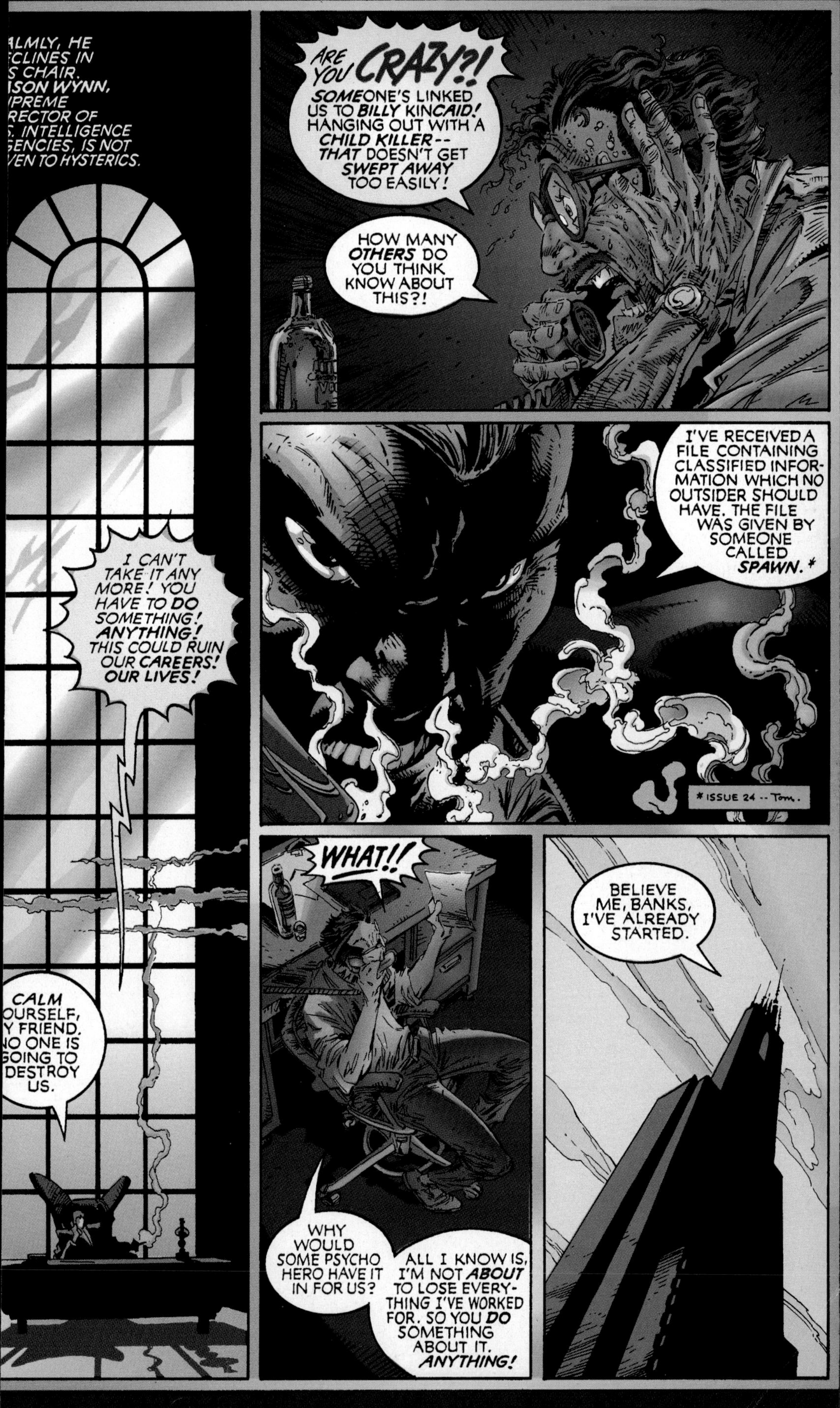

ALMLY, HE ECLINES IN S CHAIR. ASON WYNN, UPREME RECTOR OF S. INTELLIGENCE GENCIES, IS NOT VEN TO HYSTERICS.
ARE YOU CRAZY?! SOMEONE'S LINKED US TO BILLY KINCAID! HANGING OUT WITH A CHILD KILLER-- THAT DOESN'T GET SWEPT AWAY TOO EASILY!
HOW MANY OTHERS DO YOU THINK KNOW ABOUT THIS?!
I CAN'T TAKE IT ANY MORE! YOU HAVE TO DO SOMETHING! ANYTHING! THIS COULD RUIN OUR CAREERS! OUR LIVES!
CALM OURSELF, Y FRIEND. NO ONE IS GOING TO DESTROY US.
I'VE RECEIVED A FILE CONTAINING CLASSIFIED INFORMATION WHICH NO OUTSIDER SHOULD HAVE. THE FILE WAS GIVEN BY SOMEONE CALLED SPAWN.*
*ISSUE 24 -- Tom.
WHAT!!
WHY WOULD SOME PSYCHO HERO HAVE IT IN FOR US?
ALL I KNOW IS, I'M NOT ABOUT TO LOSE EVERYTHING I'VE WORKED FOR. SO YOU DO SOMETHING ABOUT IT. ANYTHING!
BELIEVE ME, BANKS, I'VE ALREADY STARTED.

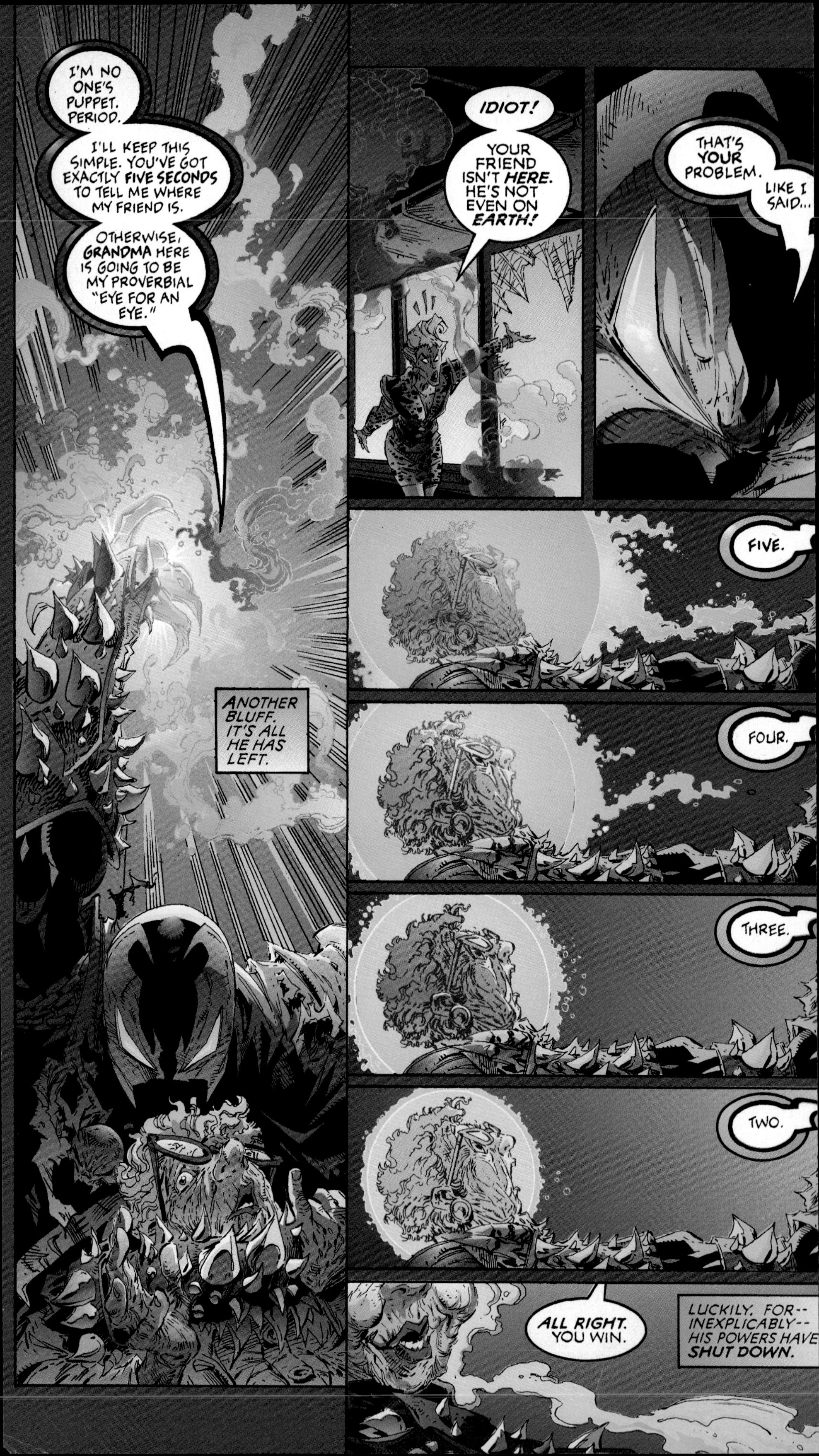
I'M NO ONE'S PUPPET. PERIOD.
I'LL KEEP THIS SIMPLE. YOU'VE GOT EXACTLY FIVE SECONDS TO TELL ME WHERE MY FRIEND IS.
OTHERWISE, GRANDMA HERE IS GOING TO BE MY PROVERBIAL "EYE FOR AN EYE."
ANOTHER BLUFF. IT'S ALL HE HAS LEFT.
IDIOT!
YOUR FRIEND ISN'T HERE. HE'S NOT EVEN ON EARTH!
THAT'S YOUR PROBLEM.
LIKE I SAID...
FIVE.
FOUR.
THREE.
TWO.
ALL RIGHT. YOU WIN.
LUCKILY, FOR-- INEXPLICABLY-- HIS POWERS HAVE SHUT DOWN.

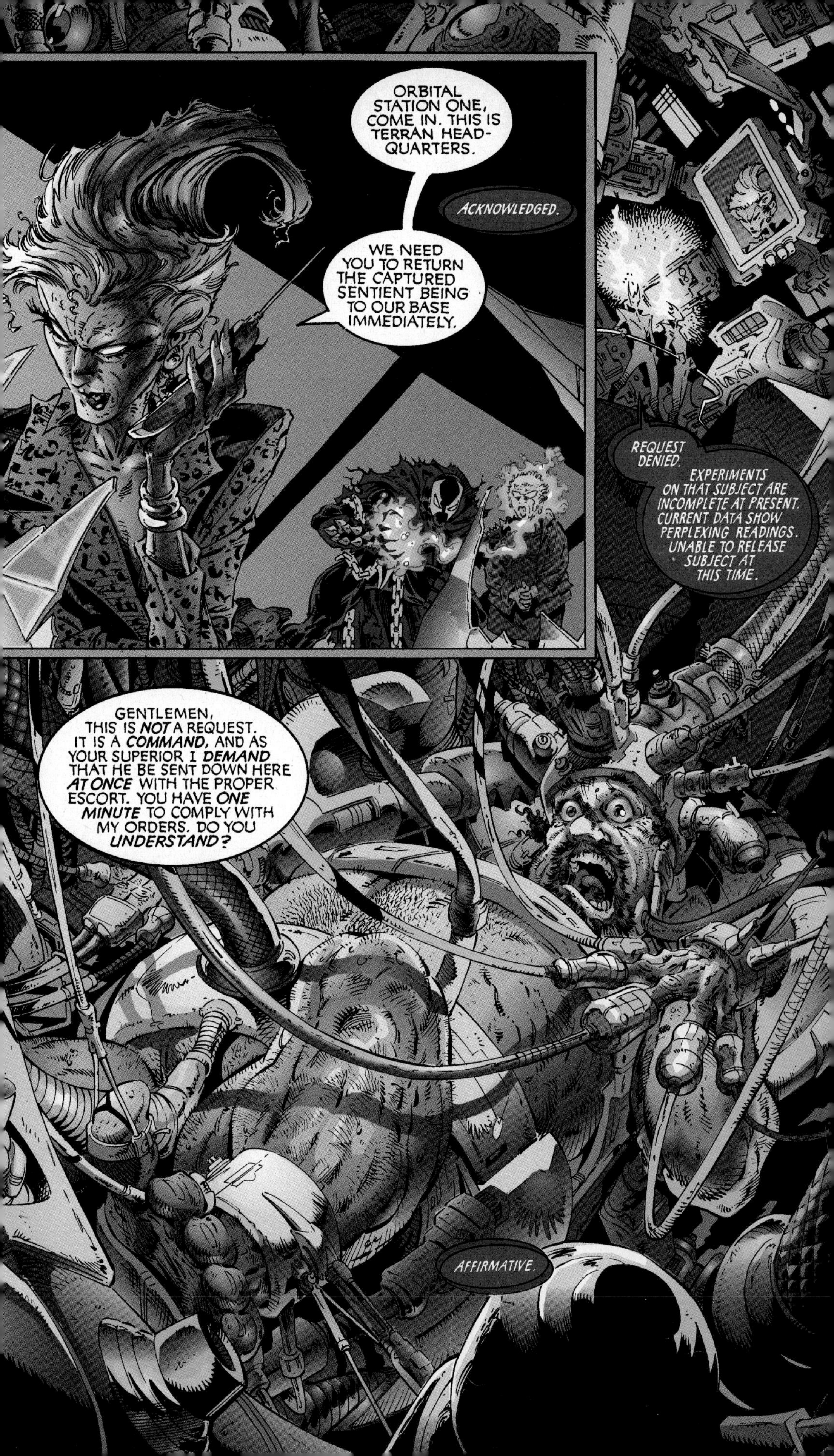
ORBITAL STATION ONE, COME IN. THIS IS TERRAN HEAD-QUARTERS.
ACKNOWLEDGED.
WE NEED YOU TO RETURN THE CAPTURED SENTIENT BEING TO OUR BASE IMMEDIATELY.
REQUEST DENIED.
EXPERIMENTS ON THAT SUBJECT ARE INCOMPLETE AT PRESENT. CURRENT DATA SHOW PERPLEXING READINGS. UNABLE TO RELEASE SUBJECT AT THIS TIME.
GENTLEMEN, THIS IS NOT A REQUEST. IT IS A COMMAND, AND AS YOUR SUPERIOR I DEMAND THAT HE BE SENT DOWN HERE AT ONCE WITH THE PROPER ESCORT. YOU HAVE ONE MINUTE TO COMPLY WITH MY ORDERS. DO YOU UNDERSTAND?
AFFIRMATIVE.

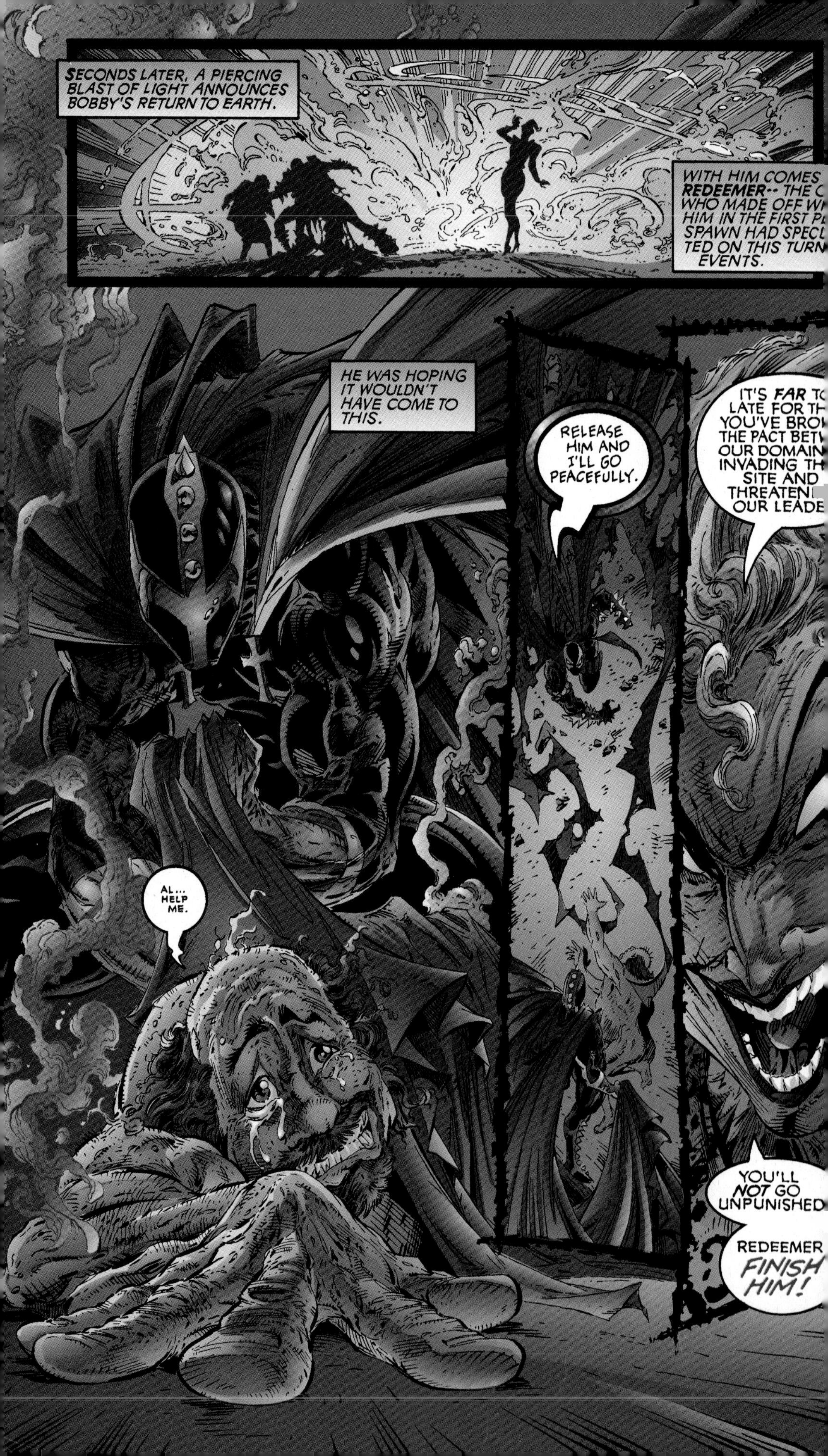
SECONDS LATER, A PIERCING BLAST OF LIGHT ANNOUNCES BOBBY'S RETURN TO EARTH.
WITH HIM COMES REDEEMER-- THE C WHO MADE OFF WI HIM IN THE FIRST PL SPAWN HAD SPECL TED ON THIS TURN EVENTS.
HE WAS HOPING IT WOULDN'T HAVE COME TO THIS.
AL... HELP ME.
RELEASE HIM AND I'LL GO PEACEFULLY.
IT'S FAR TO LATE FOR TH YOU'VE BRO THE PACT BETV OUR DOMAIN INVADING TH SITE AND THREATENI OUR LEADE
YOU'LL NOT GO UNPUNISHED
REDEEMER FINISH HIM!

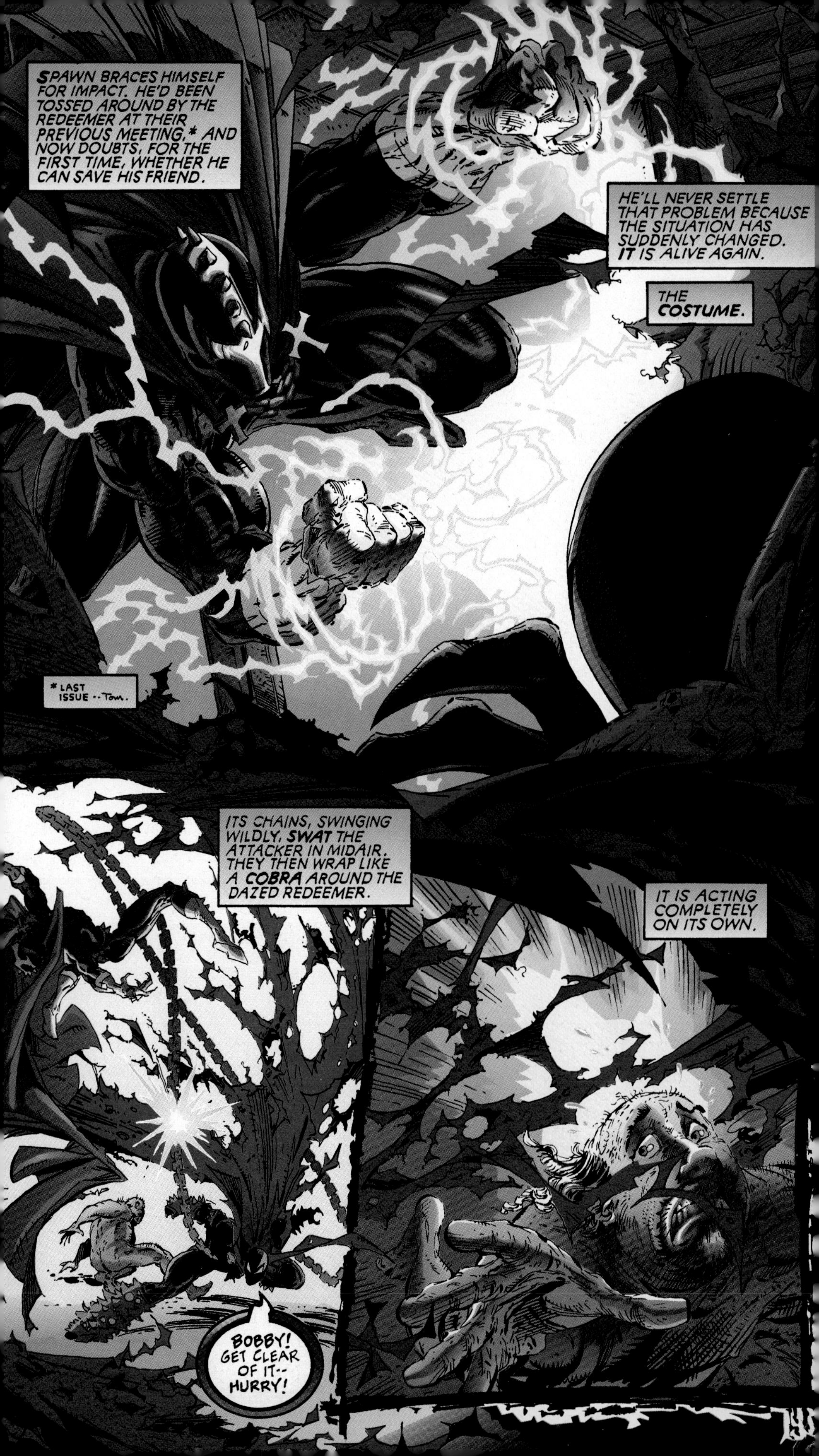
SPAWN BRACES HIMSELF FOR IMPACT. HE'D BEEN TOSSED AROUND BY THE REDEEMER AT THEIR PREVIOUS MEETING,* AND NOW DOUBTS, FOR THE FIRST TIME, WHETHER HE CAN SAVE HIS FRIEND.
HE'LL NEVER SETTLE THAT PROBLEM BECAUSE THE SITUATION HAS SUDDENLY CHANGED. IT IS ALIVE AGAIN.
THE COSTUME.
* LAST ISSUE -- Tom.
ITS CHAINS, SWINGING WILDLY, SWAT THE ATTACKER IN MIDAIR. THEY THEN WRAP LIKE A COBRA AROUND THE DAZED REDEEMER.
IT IS ACTING COMPLETELY ON ITS OWN.
BOBBY! GET CLEAR OF IT-- HURRY!

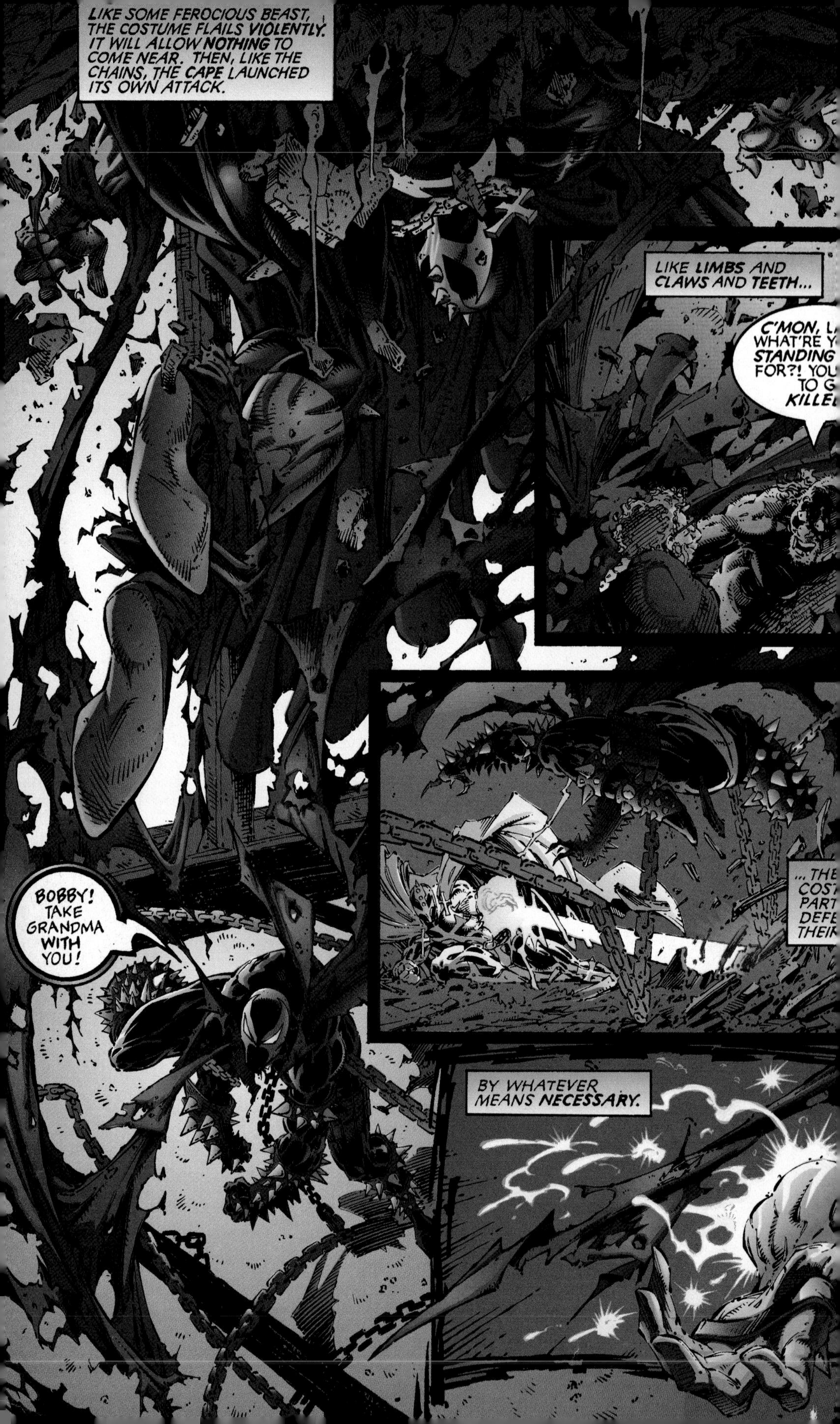
LIKE SOME FEROCIOUS BEAST, THE COSTUME FLAILS VIOLENTLY. IT WILL ALLOW NOTHING TO COME NEAR. THEN, LIKE THE CHAINS, THE CAPE LAUNCHED ITS OWN ATTACK.
LIKE LIMBS AND CLAWS AND TEETH...
C'MON, L WHAT'RE Y STANDING FOR?! YOU TO G KILLE
BOBBY! TAKE GRANDMA WITH YOU!
...THE COST PART DEFE THEIR
BY WHATEVER MEANS NECESSARY.

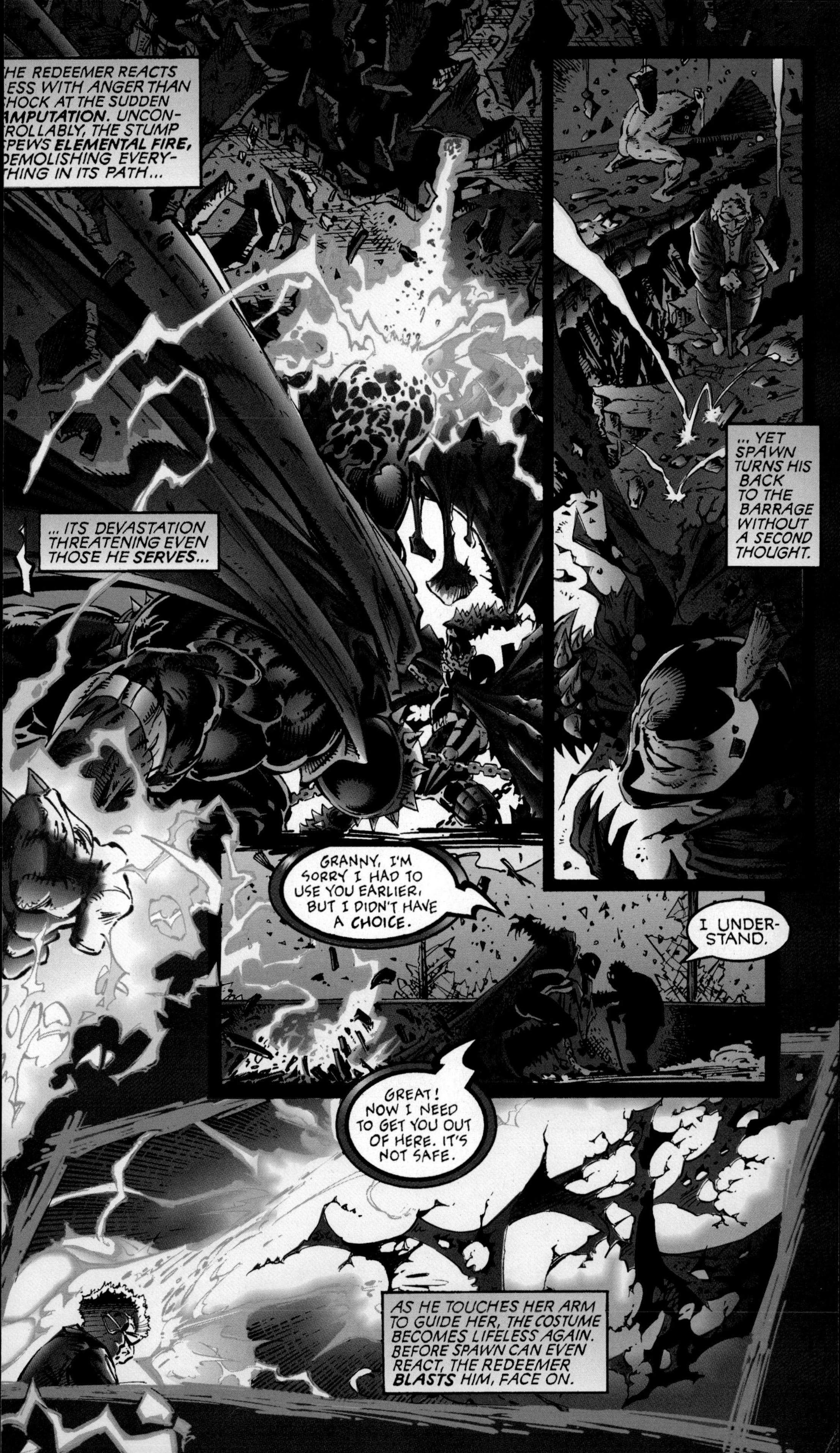

HE REDEEMER REACTS ESS WITH ANGER THAN HOCK AT THE SUDDEN AMPUTATION. UNCON-ROLLABLY, THE STUMP PEWS ELEMENTAL FIRE, DEMOLISHING EVERY-THING IN ITS PATH...
... ITS DEVASTATION THREATENING EVEN THOSE HE SERVES...
... YET SPAWN TURNS HIS BACK TO THE BARRAGE WITHOUT A SECOND THOUGHT.
GRANNY, I'M SORRY I HAD TO USE YOU EARLIER, BUT I DIDN'T HAVE A CHOICE.
I UNDER-STAND.
GREAT! NOW I NEED TO GET YOU OUT OF HERE. IT'S NOT SAFE.
AS HE TOUCHES HER ARM TO GUIDE HER, THE COSTUME BECOMES LIFELESS AGAIN. BEFORE SPAWN CAN EVEN REACT, THE REDEEMER BLASTS HIM, FACE ON.

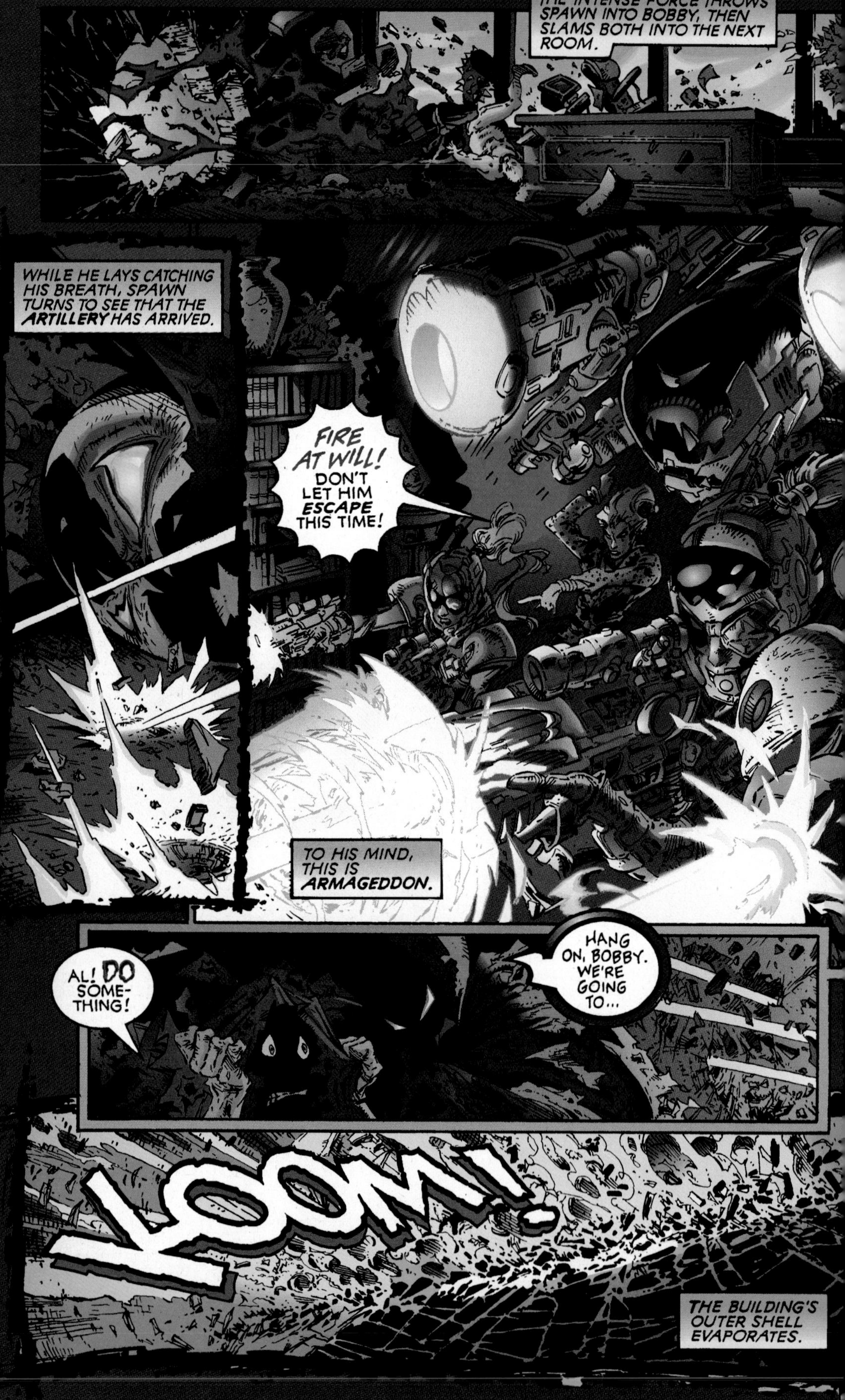

THE INTENSE FORCE THROWS SPAWN INTO BOBBY, THEN SLAMS BOTH INTO THE NEXT ROOM.
WHILE HE LAYS CATCHING HIS BREATH, SPAWN TURNS TO SEE THAT THE ARTILLERY HAS ARRIVED.
FIRE AT WILL! DON'T LET HIM ESCAPE THIS TIME!
TO HIS MIND, THIS IS ARMAGEDDON.
AL! DO SOME-THING!
HANG ON, BOBBY. WE'RE GOING TO...
KOOM!
THE BUILDING'S OUTER SHELL EVAPORATES.

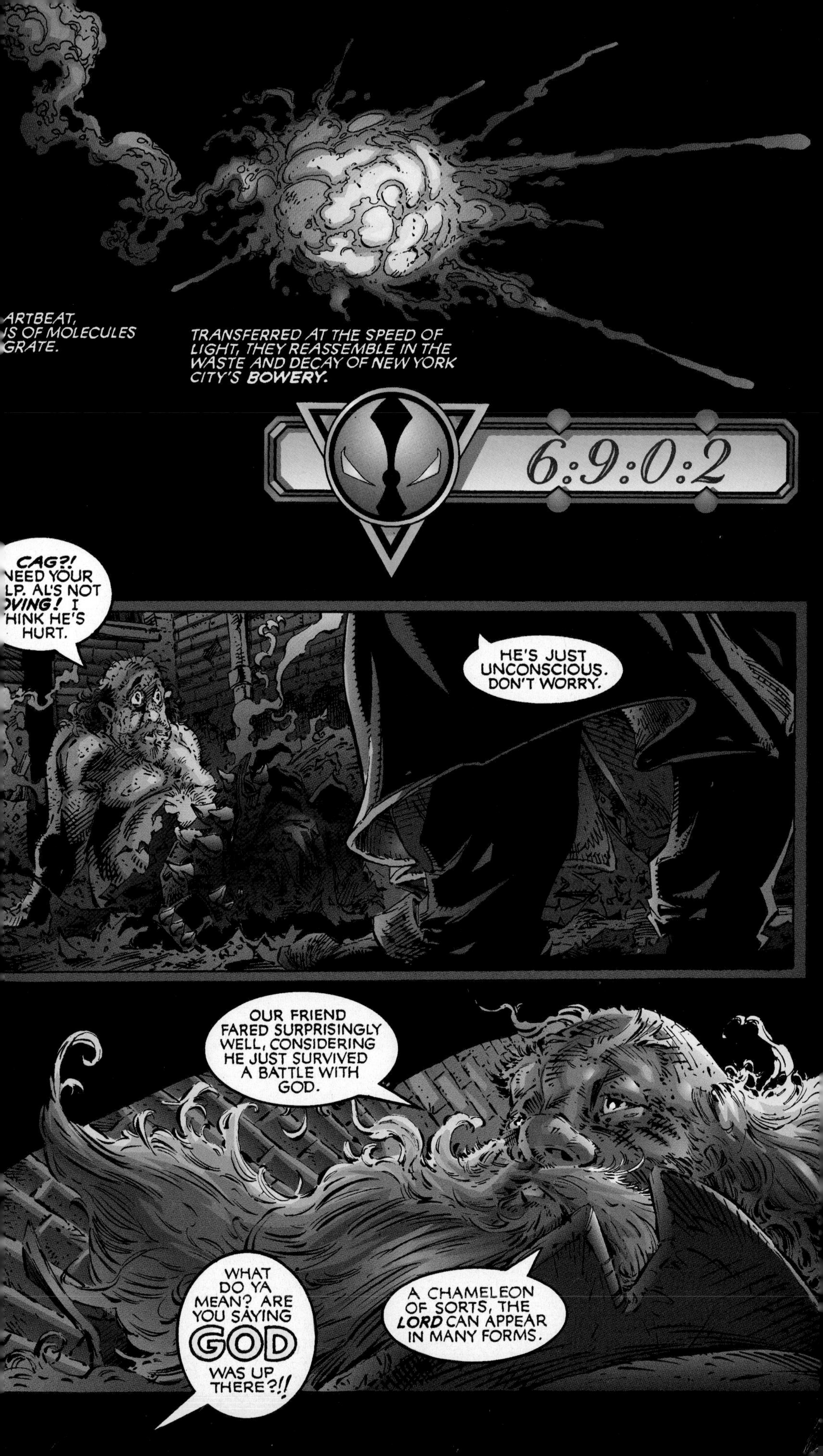
ARTBEAT, IS OF MOLECULES GRATE.
TRANSFERRED AT THE SPEED OF LIGHT, THEY REASSEMBLE IN THE WASTE AND DECAY OF NEW YORK CITY'S **BOWERY.**
6:9:0:2
CAG?! NEED YOUR LP. AL'S NOT VING! I HINK HE'S HURT.
HE'S JUST UNCONSCIOUS. DON'T WORRY.
OUR FRIEND FARED SURPRISINGLY WELL, CONSIDERING HE JUST SURVIVED A BATTLE WITH GOD.
WHAT DO YA MEAN? ARE YOU SAYING GOD WAS UP THERE?!!
A CHAMELEON OF SORTS, THE **LORD** CAN APPEAR IN MANY FORMS.

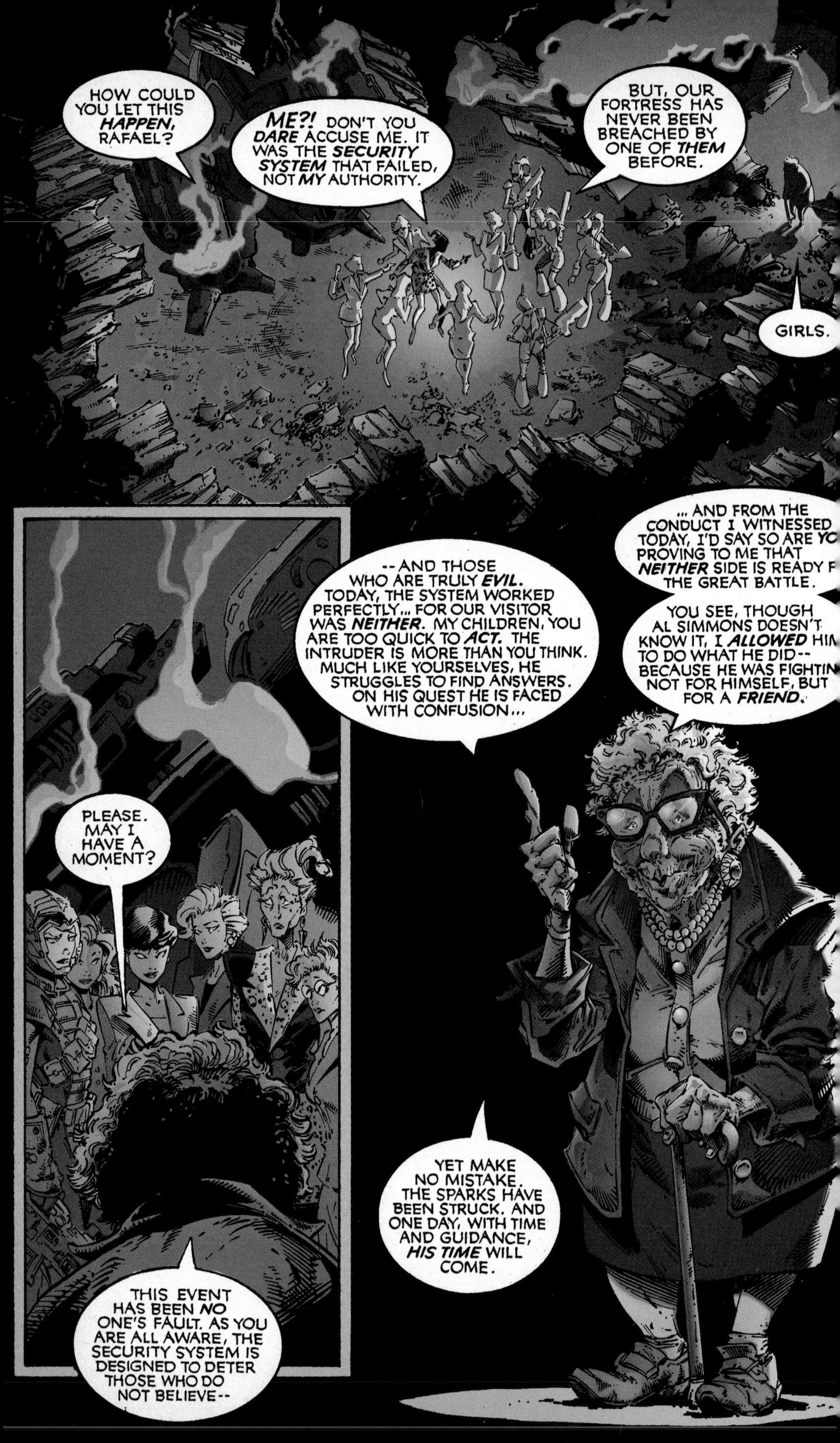

HOW COULD YOU LET THIS HAPPEN, RAFAEL?
ME?! DON'T YOU DARE ACCUSE ME. IT WAS THE SECURITY SYSTEM THAT FAILED, NOT MY AUTHORITY.
BUT, OUR FORTRESS HAS NEVER BEEN BREACHED BY ONE OF THEM BEFORE.
GIRLS.
PLEASE. MAY I HAVE A MOMENT?
THIS EVENT HAS BEEN NO ONE'S FAULT. AS YOU ARE ALL AWARE, THE SECURITY SYSTEM IS DESIGNED TO DETER THOSE WHO DO NOT BELIEVE--
--AND THOSE WHO ARE TRULY EVIL. TODAY, THE SYSTEM WORKED PERFECTLY... FOR OUR VISITOR WAS NEITHER. MY CHILDREN, YOU ARE TOO QUICK TO ACT. THE INTRUDER IS MORE THAN YOU THINK. MUCH LIKE YOURSELVES, HE STRUGGLES TO FIND ANSWERS. ON HIS QUEST HE IS FACED WITH CONFUSION...
YET MAKE NO MISTAKE. THE SPARKS HAVE BEEN STRUCK. AND ONE DAY, WITH TIME AND GUIDANCE, HIS TIME WILL COME.
... AND FROM THE CONDUCT I WITNESSED TODAY, I'D SAY SO ARE YO PROVING TO ME THAT NEITHER SIDE IS READY F THE GREAT BATTLE.
YOU SEE, THOUGH AL SIMMONS DOESN'T KNOW IT, I ALLOWED HIM TO DO WHAT HE DID-- BECAUSE HE WAS FIGHTIN NOT FOR HIMSELF, BUT FOR A FRIEND.

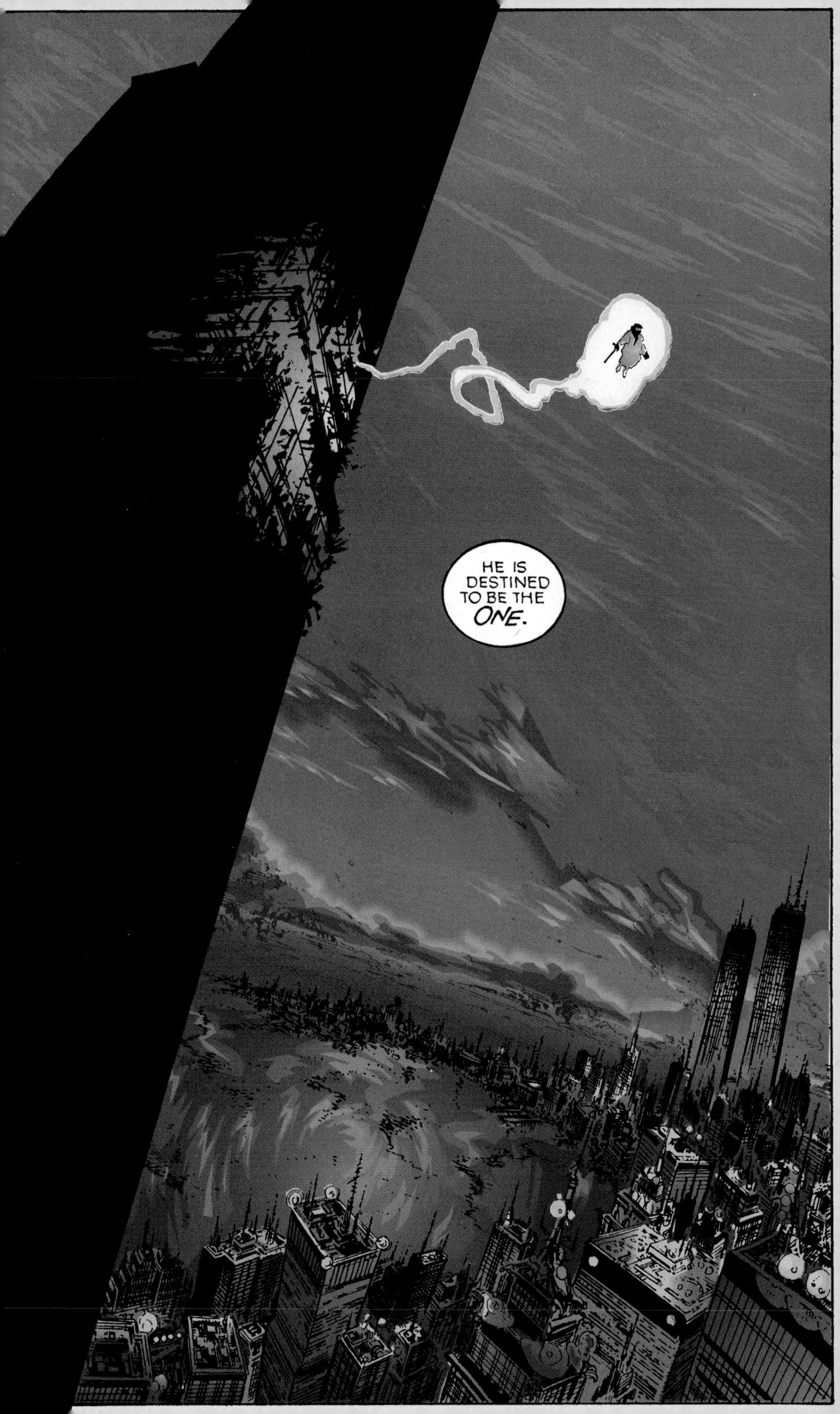
HE IS DESTINED TO BE THE *ONE*.

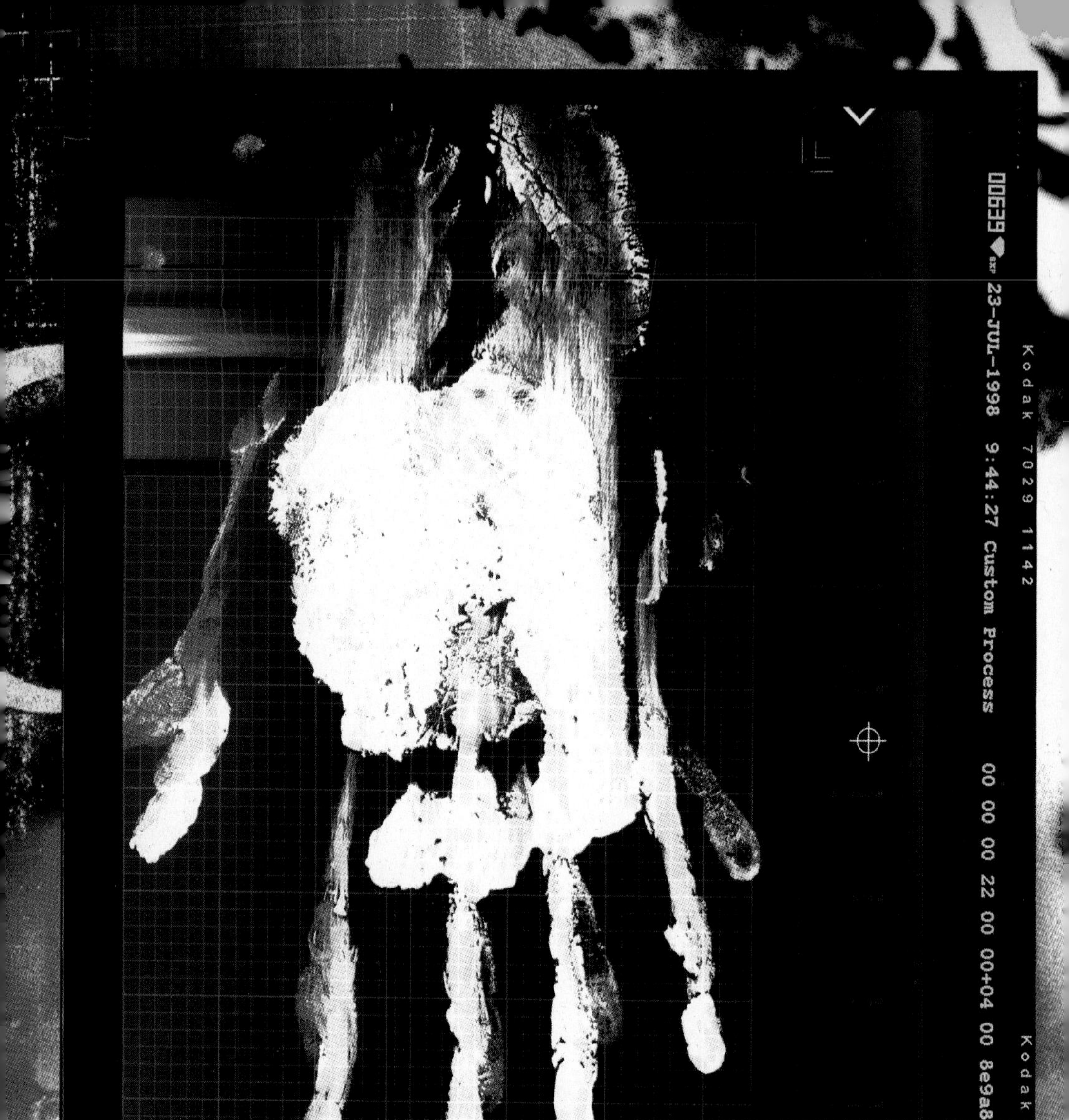
00639
23-JUL-1998 9:44:27 Custom Process 00 00 00 22 00 00+04 00 8e9a8
Kodak 7029 1142
Kodak

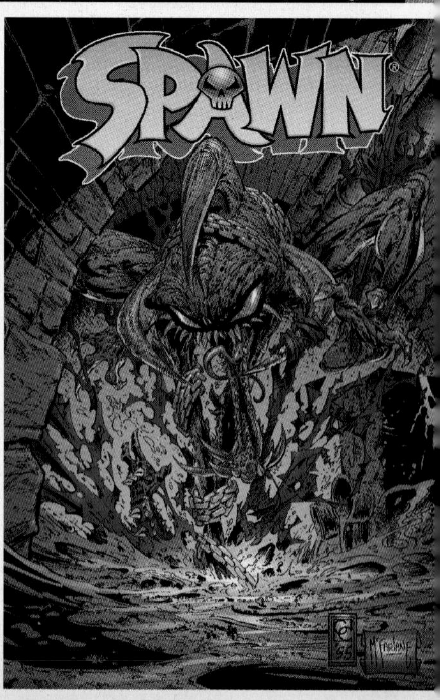
SPAWN

SHADOWS PART 1 33

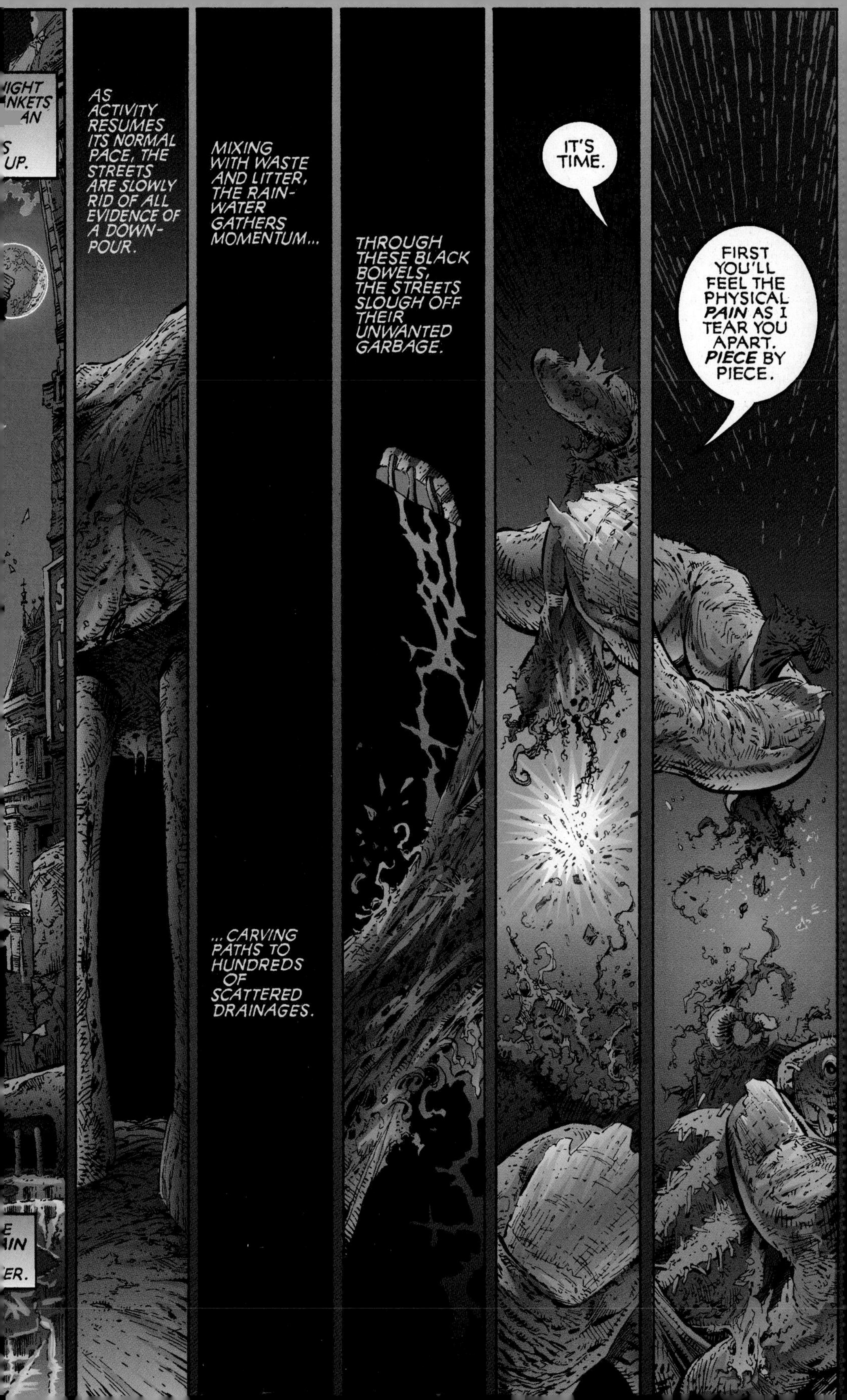
AS ACTIVITY RESUMES ITS NORMAL PACE, THE STREETS ARE SLOWLY RID OF ALL EVIDENCE OF A DOWN-POUR.
MIXING WITH WASTE AND LITTER, THE RAIN-WATER GATHERS MOMENTUM...
...CARVING PATHS TO HUNDREDS OF SCATTERED DRAINAGES.
THROUGH THESE BLACK BOWELS, THE STREETS SLOUGH OFF THEIR UNWANTED GARBAGE.
IT'S TIME.
FIRST YOU'LL FEEL THE PHYSICAL PAIN AS I TEAR YOU APART. PIECE BY PIECE.

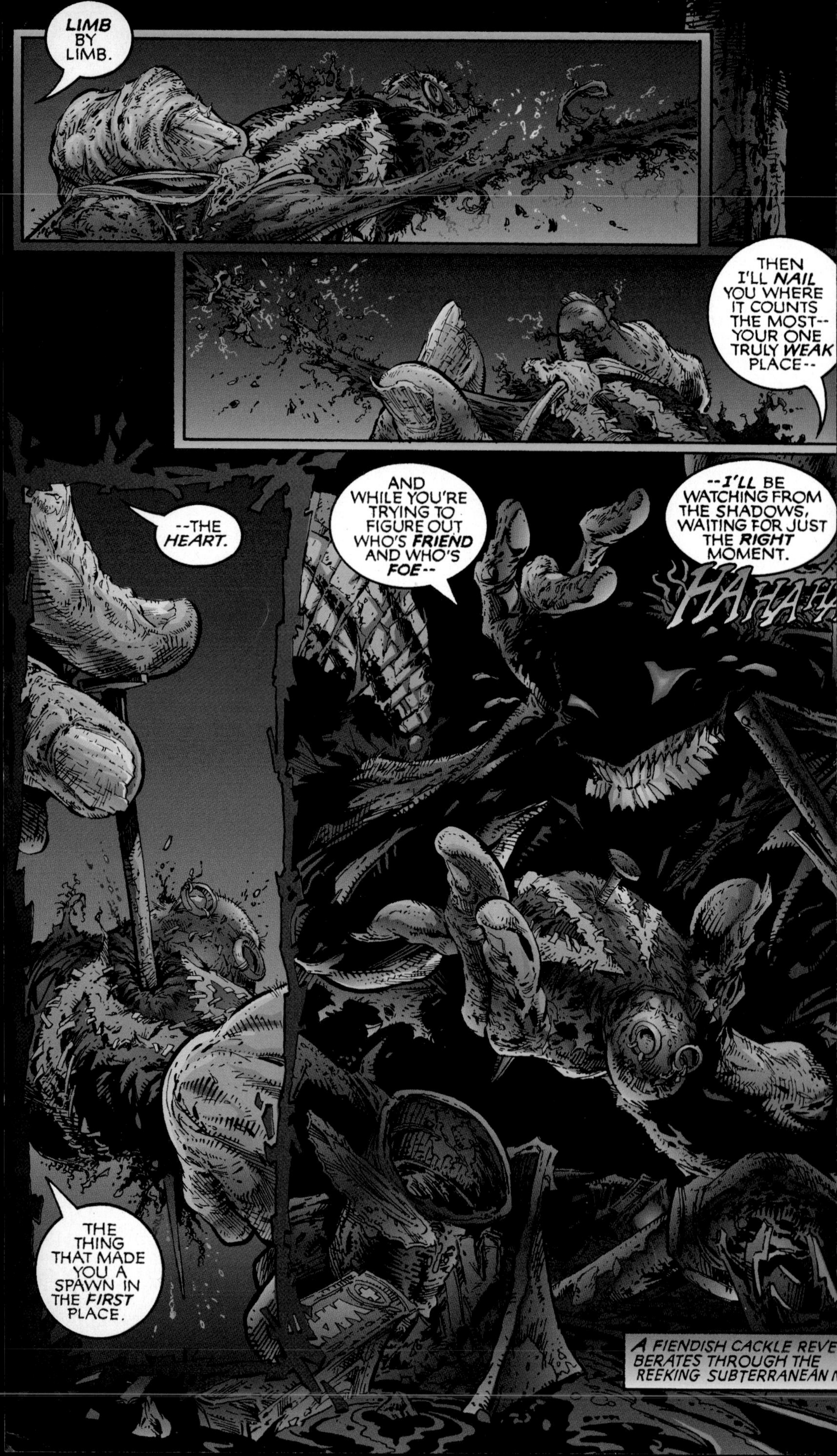
LIMB BY LIMB.
THEN I'LL NAIL YOU WHERE IT COUNTS THE MOST-- YOUR ONE TRULY WEAK PLACE--
--THE HEART.
THE THING THAT MADE YOU A SPAWN IN THE FIRST PLACE.
AND WHILE YOU'RE TRYING TO FIGURE OUT WHO'S FRIEND AND WHO'S FOE--
--I'LL BE WATCHING FROM THE SHADOWS, WAITING FOR JUST THE RIGHT MOMENT.
HAHAHA
A FIENDISH CACKLE REVE BERATES THROUGH THE REEKING SUBTERRANEAN

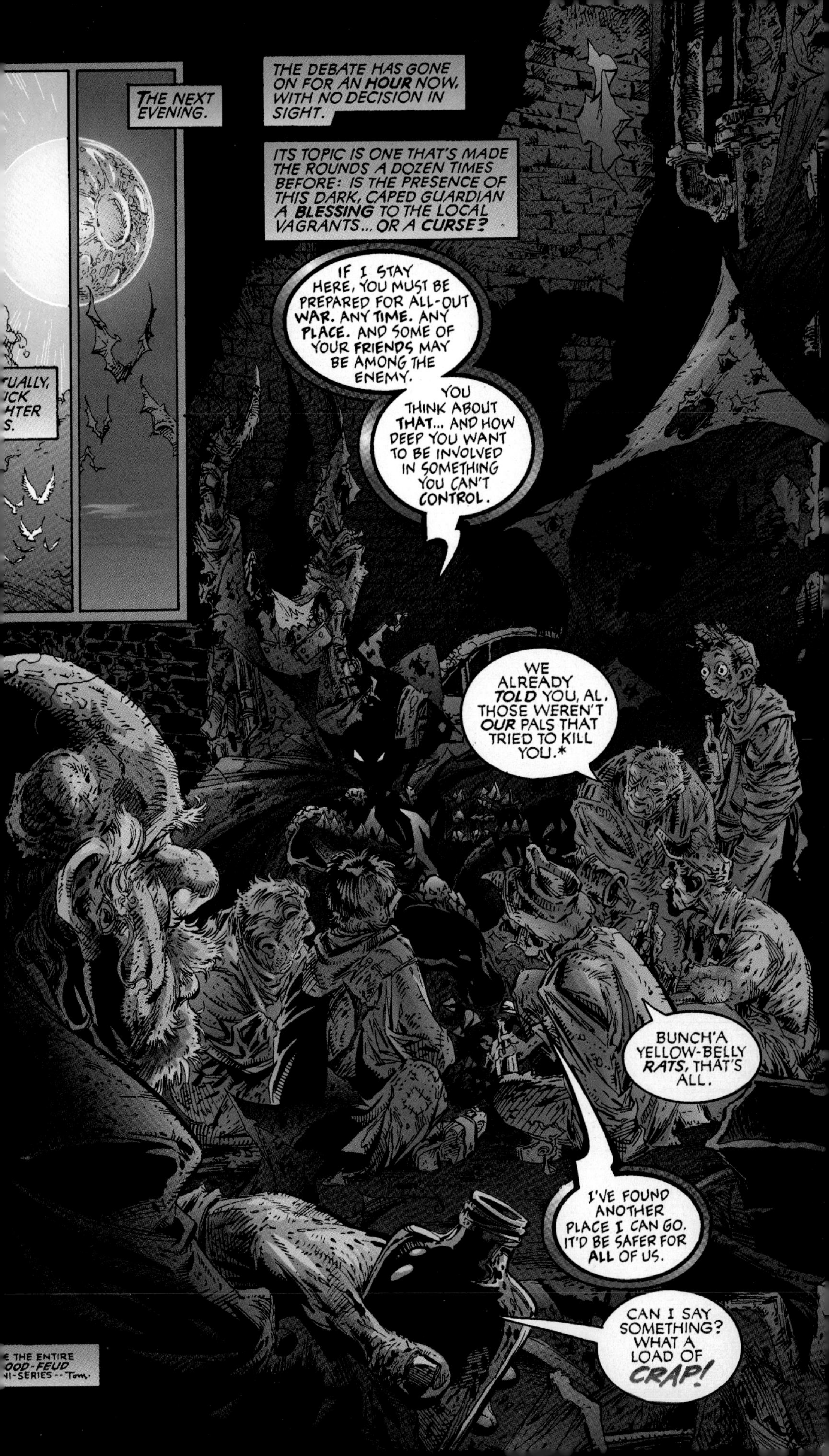
THE NEXT EVENING.
THE DEBATE HAS GONE ON FOR AN HOUR NOW, WITH NO DECISION IN SIGHT.
ITS TOPIC IS ONE THAT'S MADE THE ROUNDS A DOZEN TIMES BEFORE: IS THE PRESENCE OF THIS DARK, CAPED GUARDIAN A BLESSING TO THE LOCAL VAGRANTS... OR A CURSE?
IF I STAY HERE, YOU MUST BE PREPARED FOR ALL-OUT WAR. ANY TIME. ANY PLACE. AND SOME OF YOUR FRIENDS MAY BE AMONG THE ENEMY.
YOU THINK ABOUT THAT... AND HOW DEEP YOU WANT TO BE INVOLVED IN SOMETHING YOU CAN'T CONTROL.
WE ALREADY TOLD YOU, AL. THOSE WEREN'T OUR PALS THAT TRIED TO KILL YOU.*
BUNCH'A YELLOW-BELLY RATS, THAT'S ALL.
I'VE FOUND ANOTHER PLACE I CAN GO. IT'D BE SAFER FOR ALL OF US.
CAN I SAY SOMETHING? WHAT A LOAD OF CRAP!

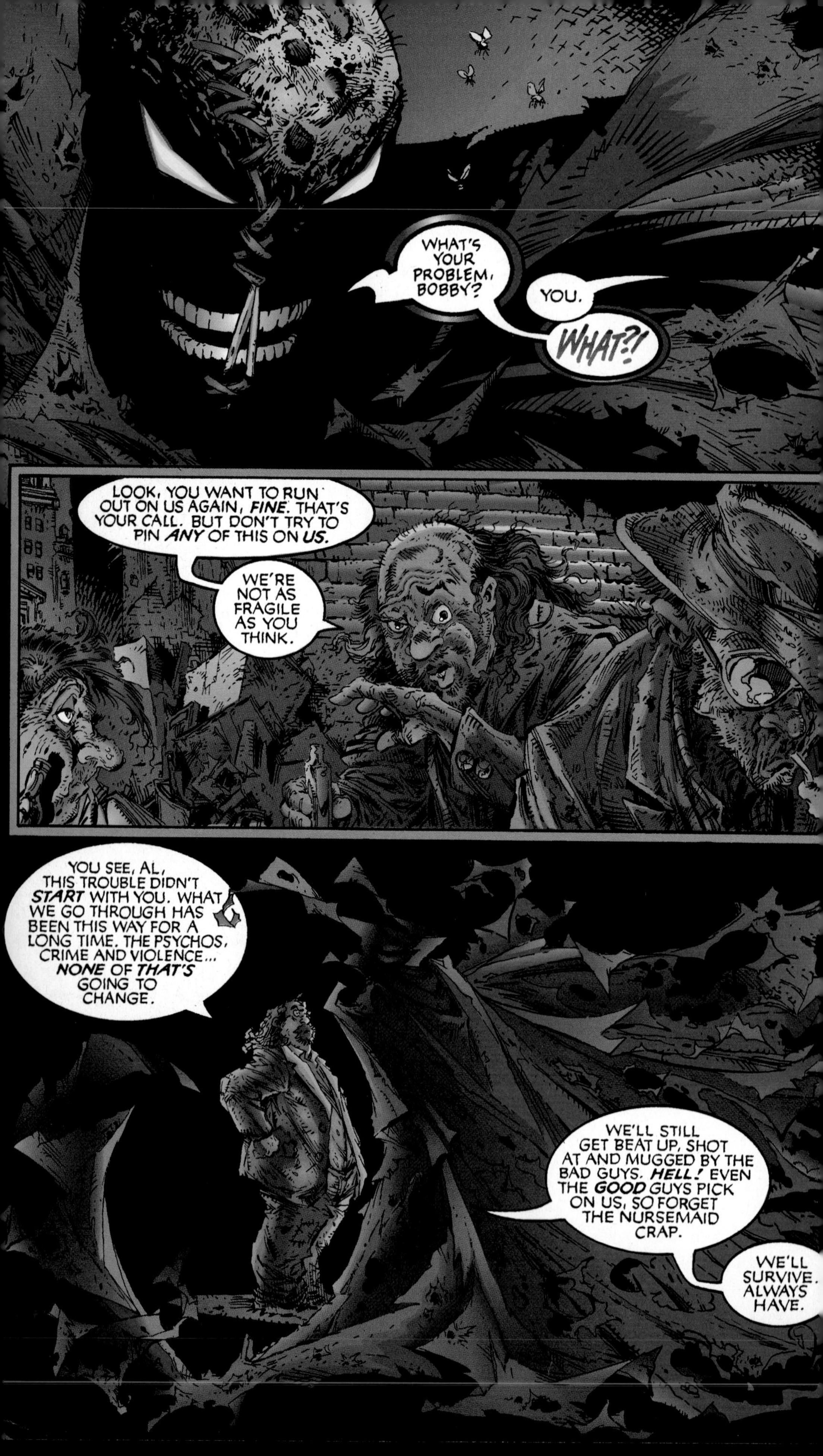
WHAT'S YOUR PROBLEM, BOBBY?
YOU.
WHAT?!
LOOK, YOU WANT TO RUN OUT ON US AGAIN, *FINE*. THAT'S YOUR CALL. BUT DON'T TRY TO PIN *ANY* OF THIS ON *US*.
WE'RE NOT AS FRAGILE AS YOU THINK.
YOU SEE, AL, THIS TROUBLE DIDN'T *START* WITH YOU. WHAT WE GO THROUGH HAS BEEN THIS WAY FOR A LONG TIME. THE PSYCHOS, CRIME AND VIOLENCE... *NONE* OF *THAT'S* GOING TO CHANGE.
WE'LL STILL GET BEAT UP, SHOT AT AND MUGGED BY THE BAD GUYS. *HELL!* EVEN THE *GOOD* GUYS PICK ON US, SO FORGET THE NURSEMAID CRAP.
WE'LL SURVIVE. ALWAYS HAVE.

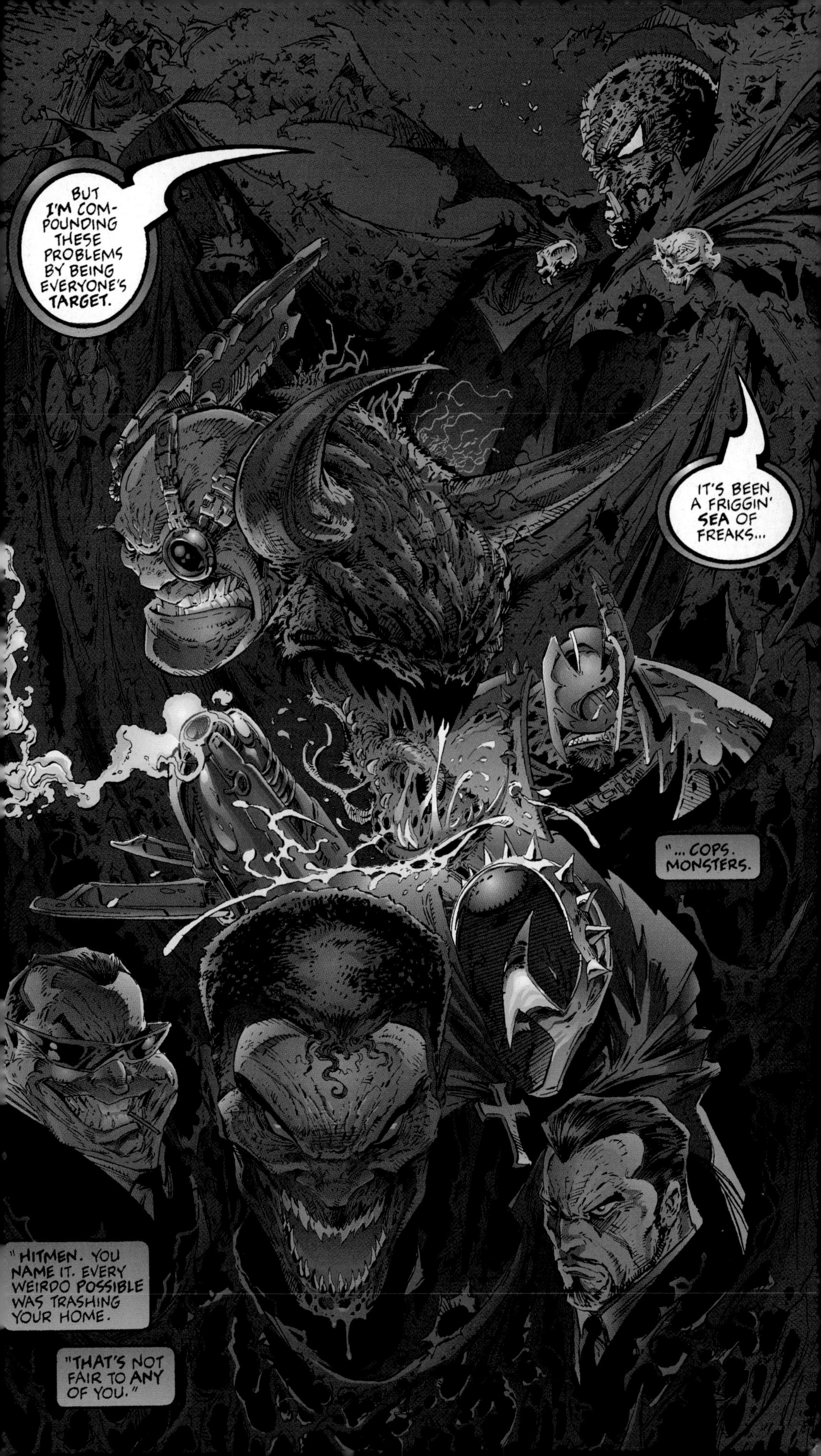
BUT I'M COMPOUNDING THESE PROBLEMS BY BEING EVERYONE'S TARGET.
IT'S BEEN A FRIGGIN' SEA OF FREAKS...
"...COPS. MONSTERS.
"HITMEN. YOU NAME IT. EVERY WEIRDO POSSIBLE WAS TRASHING YOUR HOME.
"THAT'S NOT FAIR TO ANY OF YOU."

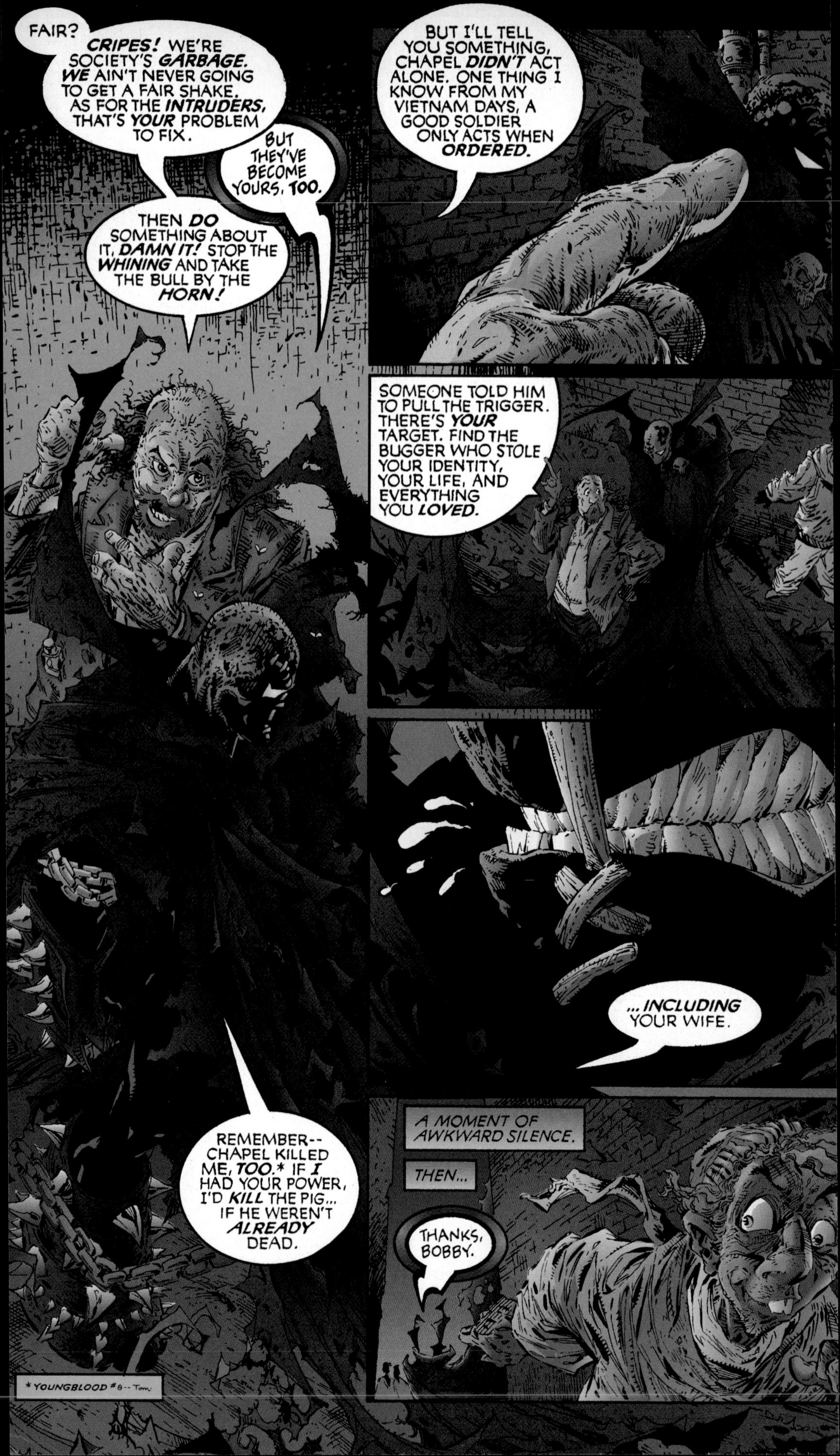
FAIR?
CRIPES! WE'RE SOCIETY'S GARBAGE. WE AIN'T NEVER GOING TO GET A FAIR SHAKE. AS FOR THE INTRUDERS, THAT'S YOUR PROBLEM TO FIX.
BUT THEY'VE BECOME YOURS, TOO.
THEN DO SOMETHING ABOUT IT, DAMN IT! STOP THE WHINING AND TAKE THE BULL BY THE HORN!
BUT I'LL TELL YOU SOMETHING, CHAPEL DIDN'T ACT ALONE. ONE THING I KNOW FROM MY VIETNAM DAYS, A GOOD SOLDIER ONLY ACTS WHEN ORDERED.
SOMEONE TOLD HIM TO PULL THE TRIGGER. THERE'S YOUR TARGET. FIND THE BUGGER WHO STOLE YOUR IDENTITY, YOUR LIFE, AND EVERYTHING YOU LOVED.
...INCLUDING YOUR WIFE.
REMEMBER-- CHAPEL KILLED ME, TOO.* IF I HAD YOUR POWER, I'D KILL THE PIG... IF HE WEREN'T ALREADY DEAD.
A MOMENT OF AWKWARD SILENCE.
THEN...
THANKS, BOBBY.
*YOUNGBLOOD #8-- Tom

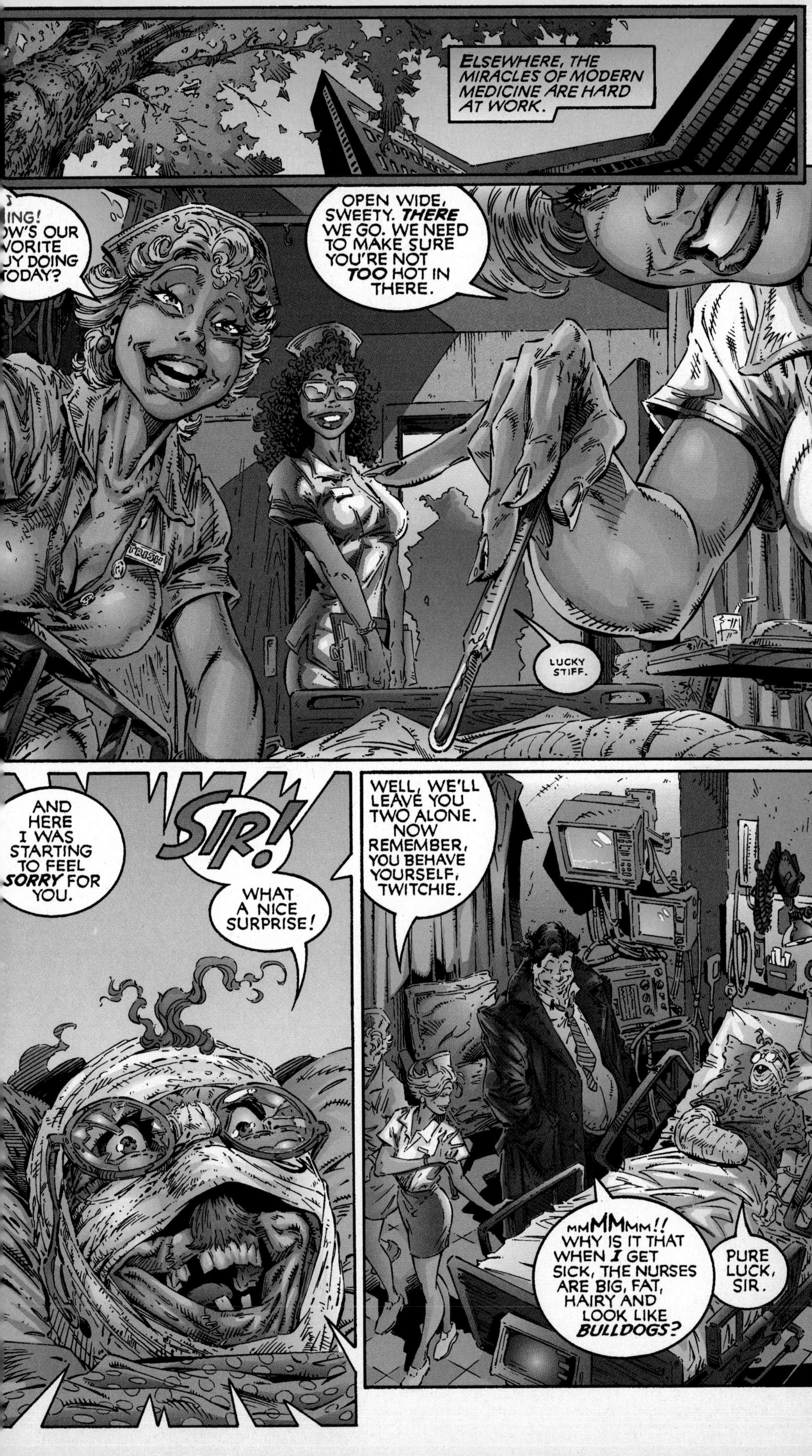
ELSEWHERE, THE MIRACLES OF MODERN MEDICINE ARE HARD AT WORK.
ING! OW'S OUR VORITE UY DOING TODAY?
OPEN WIDE, SWEETY. THERE WE GO. WE NEED TO MAKE SURE YOU'RE NOT TOO HOT IN THERE.
LUCKY STIFF.
AND HERE I WAS STARTING TO FEEL SORRY FOR YOU.
SIR!
WHAT A NICE SURPRISE!
WELL, WE'LL LEAVE YOU TWO ALONE. NOW REMEMBER, YOU BEHAVE YOURSELF, TWITCHIE.
mmMMmm!! WHY IS IT THAT WHEN I GET SICK, THE NURSES ARE BIG, FAT, HAIRY AND LOOK LIKE BULLDOGS?
PURE LUCK, SIR.

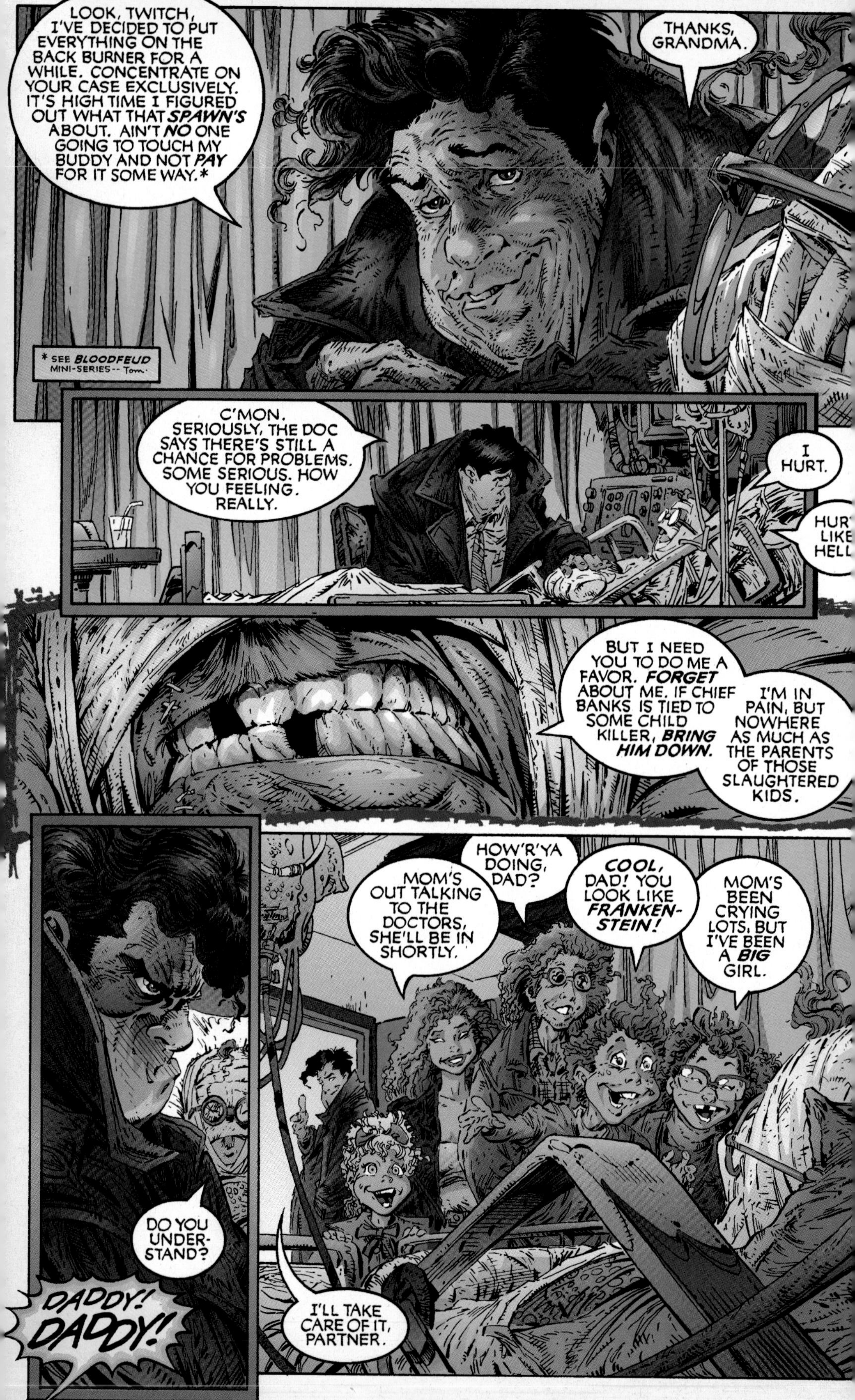
LOOK, TWITCH, I'VE DECIDED TO PUT EVERYTHING ON THE BACK BURNER FOR A WHILE. CONCENTRATE ON YOUR CASE EXCLUSIVELY. IT'S HIGH TIME I FIGURED OUT WHAT THAT SPAWN'S ABOUT. AIN'T NO ONE GOING TO TOUCH MY BUDDY AND NOT PAY FOR IT SOME WAY.*
THANKS, GRANDMA.
* SEE BLOODFEUD MINI-SERIES-- Tom.
C'MON. SERIOUSLY, THE DOC SAYS THERE'S STILL A CHANCE FOR PROBLEMS. SOME SERIOUS. HOW YOU FEELING. REALLY.
I HURT.
HURT LIKE HELL
BUT I NEED YOU TO DO ME A FAVOR. FORGET ABOUT ME. IF CHIEF BANKS IS TIED TO SOME CHILD KILLER, BRING HIM DOWN.
I'M IN PAIN, BUT NOWHERE AS MUCH AS THE PARENTS OF THOSE SLAUGHTERED KIDS.
DO YOU UNDERSTAND?
DADDY! DADDY!
I'LL TAKE CARE OF IT, PARTNER.
MOM'S OUT TALKING TO THE DOCTORS, SHE'LL BE IN SHORTLY.
HOW'R'YA DOING, DAD?
COOL, DAD! YOU LOOK LIKE FRANKENSTEIN!
MOM'S BEEN CRYING LOTS, BUT I'VE BEEN A BIG GIRL.

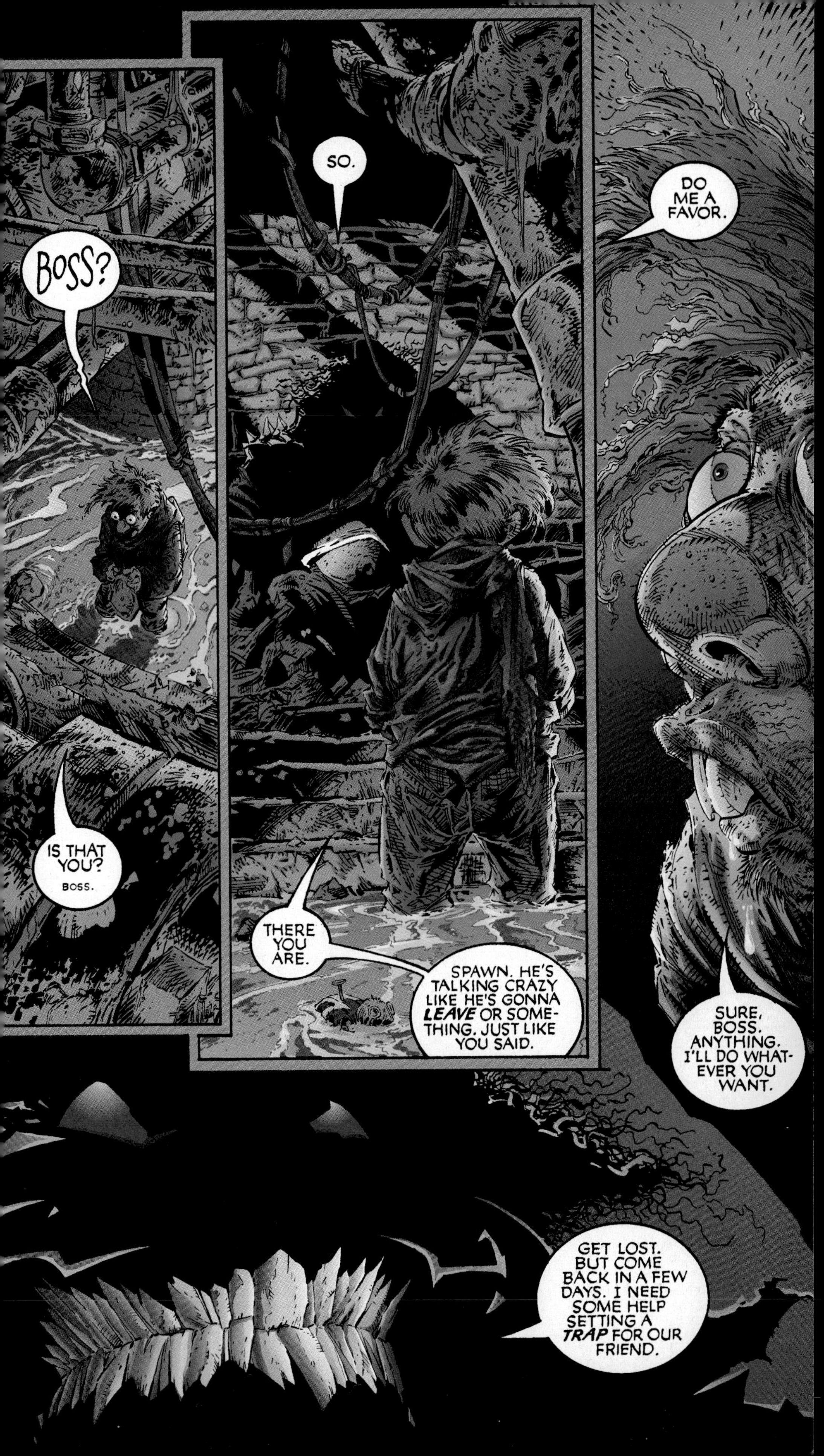
BOSS?
IS THAT YOU? BOSS.
SO.
THERE YOU ARE.
SPAWN. HE'S TALKING CRAZY LIKE HE'S GONNA *LEAVE* OR SOME-THING. JUST LIKE YOU SAID.
DO ME A FAVOR.
SURE, BOSS. ANYTHING. I'LL DO WHAT-EVER YOU WANT.
GET LOST. BUT COME BACK IN A FEW DAYS. I NEED SOME HELP SETTING A *TRAP* FOR OUR FRIEND.

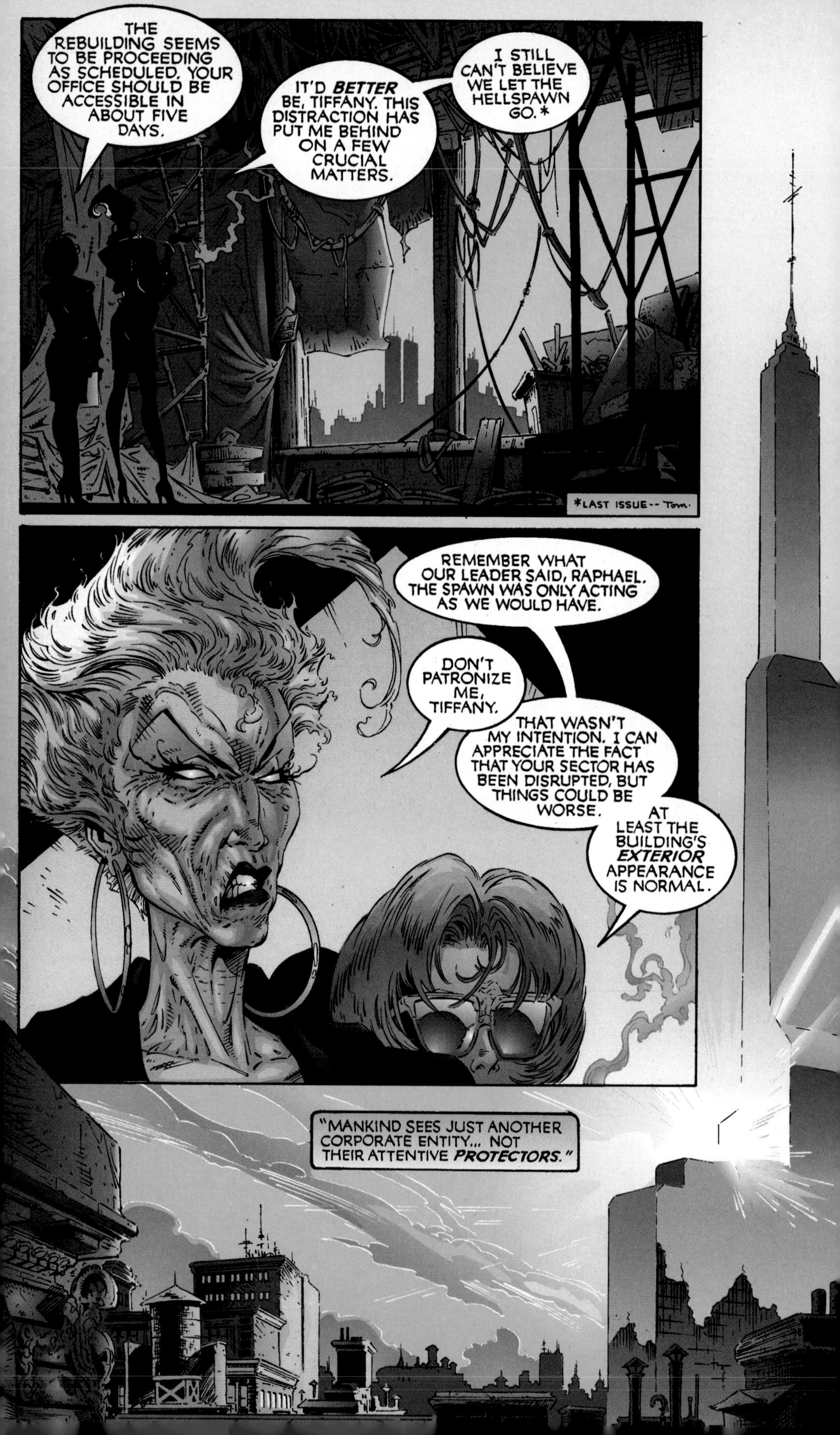
THE REBUILDING SEEMS TO BE PROCEEDING AS SCHEDULED. YOUR OFFICE SHOULD BE ACCESSIBLE IN ABOUT FIVE DAYS.
IT'D *BETTER* BE, TIFFANY. THIS DISTRACTION HAS PUT ME BEHIND ON A FEW CRUCIAL MATTERS.
I STILL CAN'T BELIEVE WE LET THE HELLSPAWN GO.*
*LAST ISSUE-- Tom.
REMEMBER WHAT OUR LEADER SAID, RAPHAEL. THE SPAWN WAS ONLY ACTING AS WE WOULD HAVE.
DON'T PATRONIZE ME, TIFFANY.
THAT WASN'T MY INTENTION. I CAN APPRECIATE THE FACT THAT YOUR SECTOR HAS BEEN DISRUPTED, BUT THINGS COULD BE WORSE.
AT LEAST THE BUILDING'S *EXTERIOR* APPEARANCE IS NORMAL.
"MANKIND SEES JUST ANOTHER CORPORATE ENTITY... NOT THEIR ATTENTIVE *PROTECTORS.*"

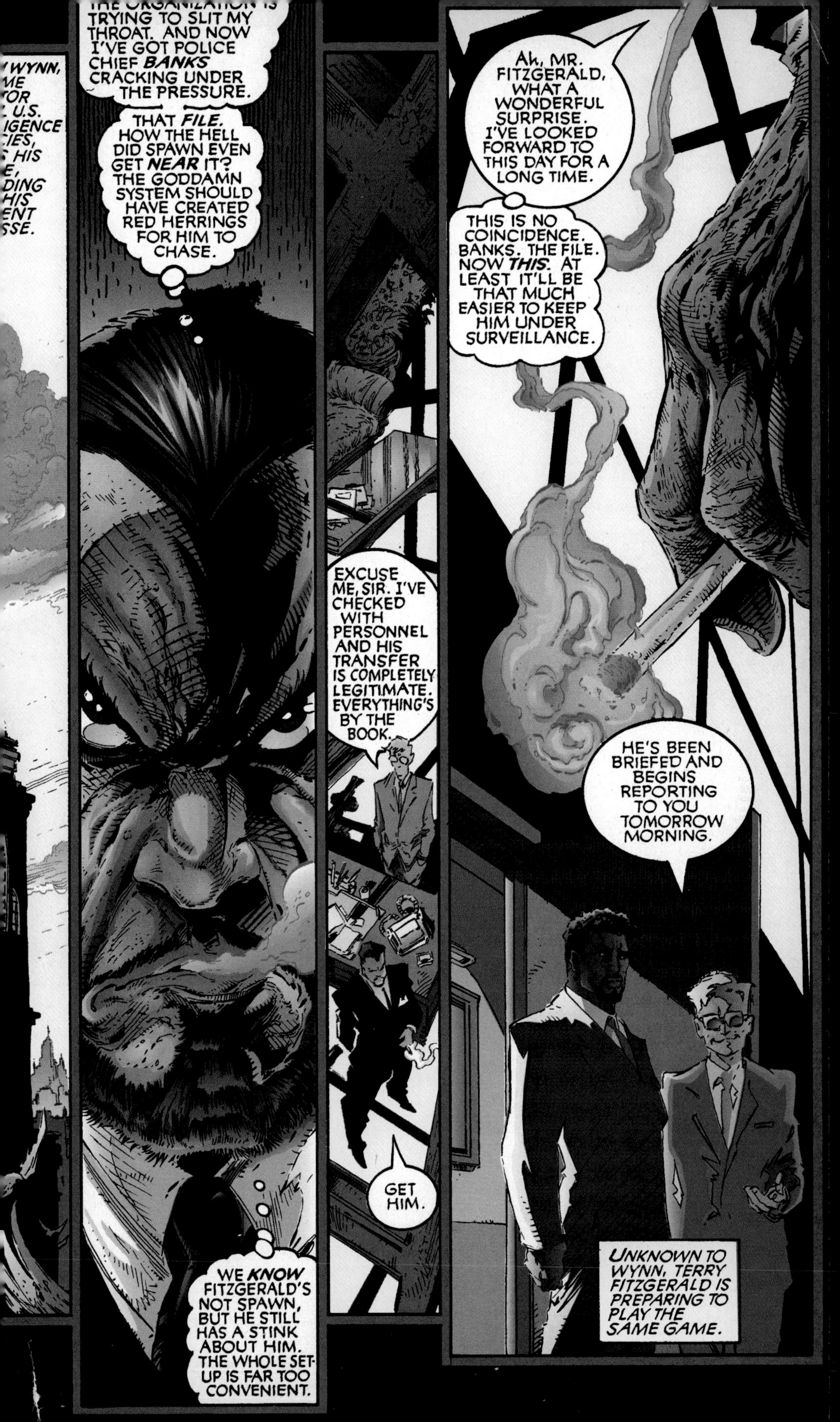
THE ORGANIZATION IS TRYING TO SLIT MY THROAT. AND NOW I'VE GOT POLICE CHIEF BANKS CRACKING UNDER THE PRESSURE.
THAT FILE. HOW THE HELL DID SPAWN EVEN GET NEAR IT? THE GODDAMN SYSTEM SHOULD HAVE CREATED RED HERRINGS FOR HIM TO CHASE.
EXCUSE ME, SIR. I'VE CHECKED WITH PERSONNEL AND HIS TRANSFER IS COMPLETELY LEGITIMATE. EVERYTHING'S BY THE BOOK.
GET HIM.
WE KNOW FITZGERALD'S NOT SPAWN, BUT HE STILL HAS A STINK ABOUT HIM. THE WHOLE SET-UP IS FAR TOO CONVENIENT.
AH, MR. FITZGERALD, WHAT A WONDERFUL SURPRISE. I'VE LOOKED FORWARD TO THIS DAY FOR A LONG TIME.
THIS IS NO COINCIDENCE. BANKS. THE FILE. NOW THIS. AT LEAST IT'LL BE THAT MUCH EASIER TO KEEP HIM UNDER SURVEILLANCE.
HE'S BEEN BRIEFED AND BEGINS REPORTING TO YOU TOMORROW MORNING.
UNKNOWN TO WYNN, TERRY FITZGERALD IS PREPARING TO PLAY THE SAME GAME.

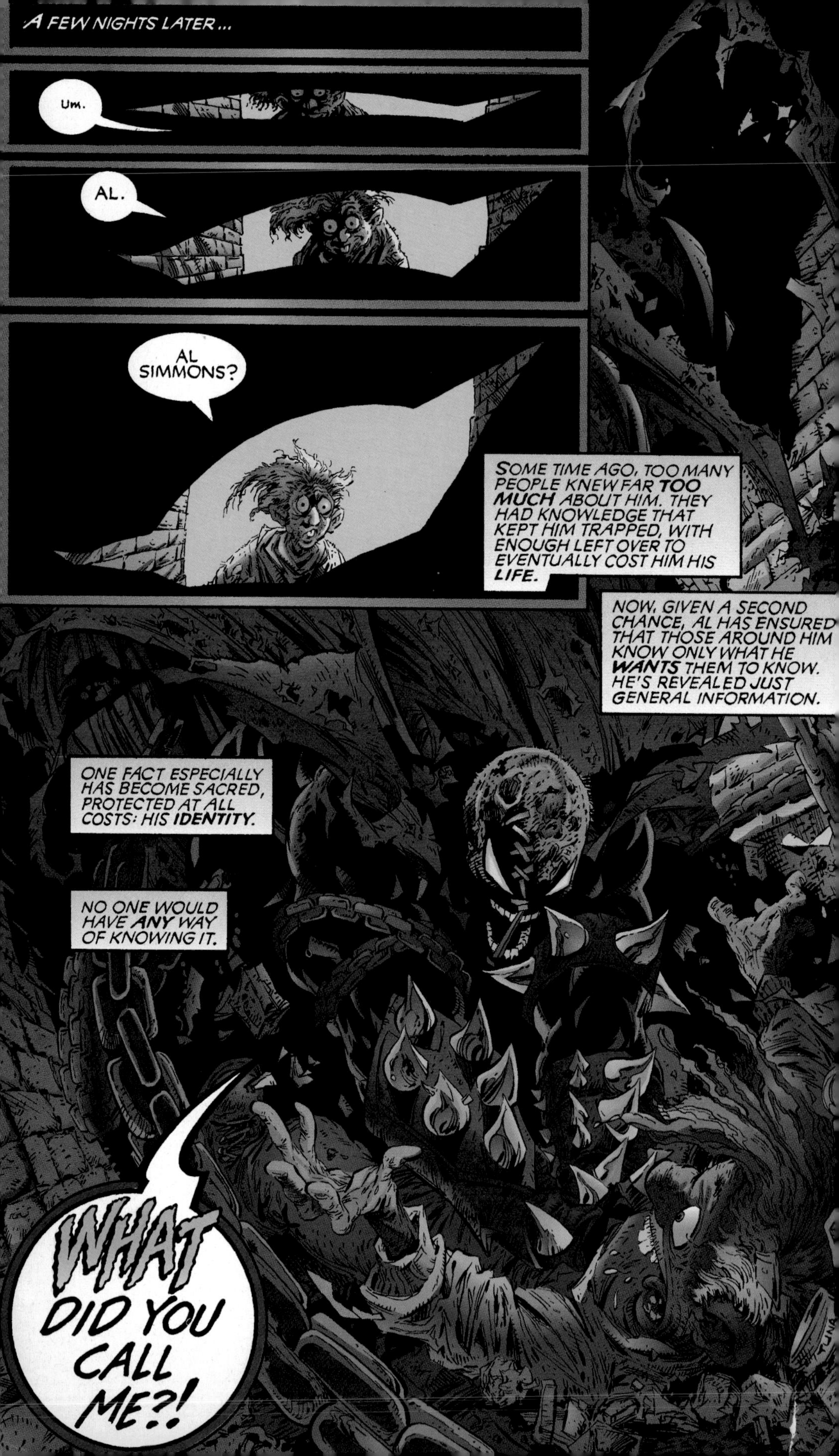
A FEW NIGHTS LATER...
Um.
AL.
AL SIMMONS?
SOME TIME AGO, TOO MANY PEOPLE KNEW FAR TOO MUCH ABOUT HIM. THEY HAD KNOWLEDGE THAT KEPT HIM TRAPPED, WITH ENOUGH LEFT OVER TO EVENTUALLY COST HIM HIS LIFE.
NOW, GIVEN A SECOND CHANCE, AL HAS ENSURED THAT THOSE AROUND HIM KNOW ONLY WHAT HE WANTS THEM TO KNOW. HE'S REVEALED JUST GENERAL INFORMATION.
ONE FACT ESPECIALLY HAS BECOME SACRED, PROTECTED AT ALL COSTS: HIS IDENTITY.
NO ONE WOULD HAVE ANY WAY OF KNOWING IT.
WHAT DID YOU CALL ME?!

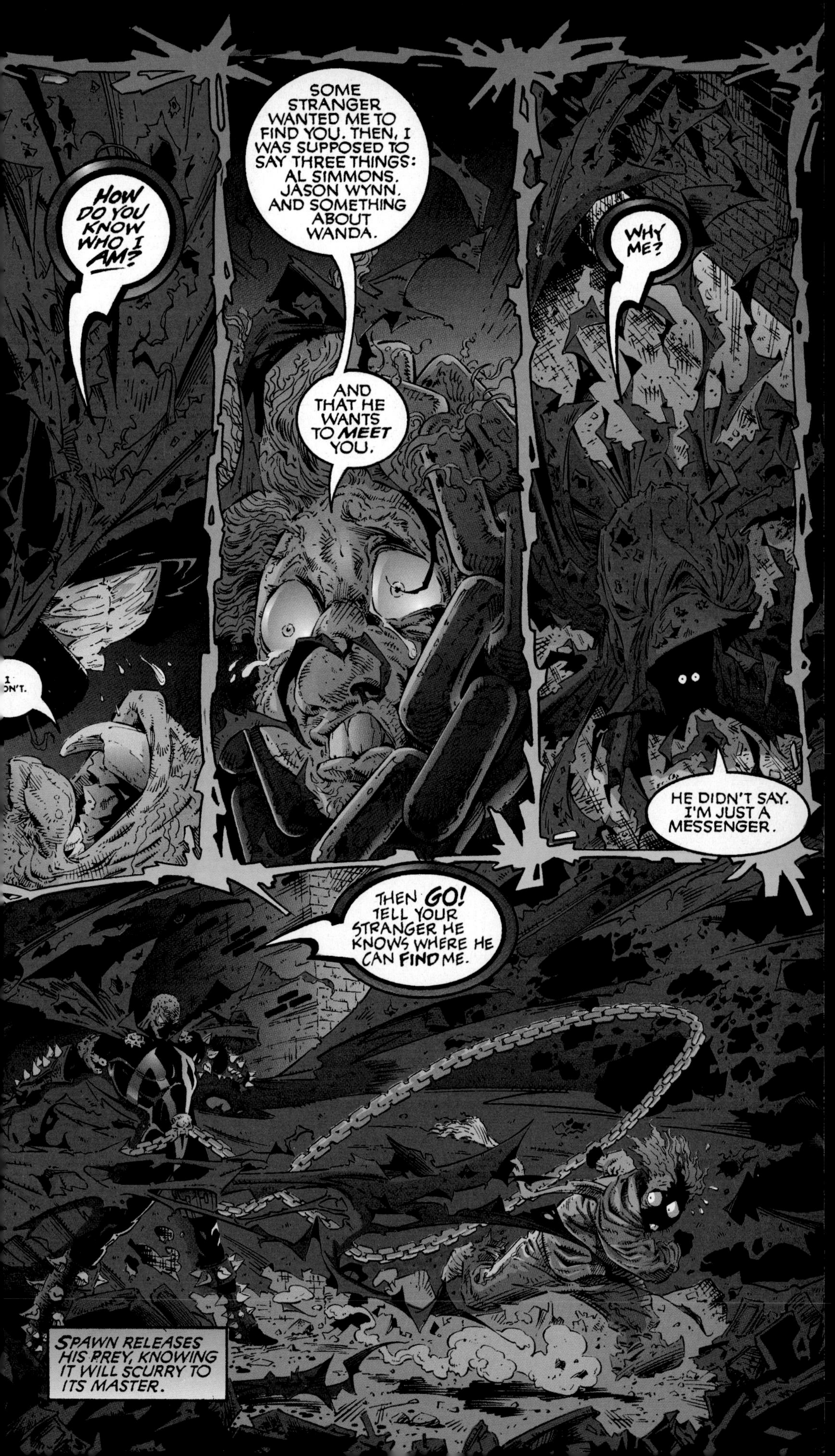
HOW DO YOU KNOW WHO I AM?
SOME STRANGER WANTED ME TO FIND YOU. THEN, I WAS SUPPOSED TO SAY THREE THINGS: AL SIMMONS. JASON WYNN. AND SOMETHING ABOUT WANDA.
AND THAT HE WANTS TO MEET YOU.
WHY ME?
HE DIDN'T SAY. I'M JUST A MESSENGER.
THEN GO! TELL YOUR STRANGER HE KNOWS WHERE HE CAN FIND ME.
SPAWN RELEASES HIS PREY, KNOWING IT WILL SCURRY TO ITS MASTER.

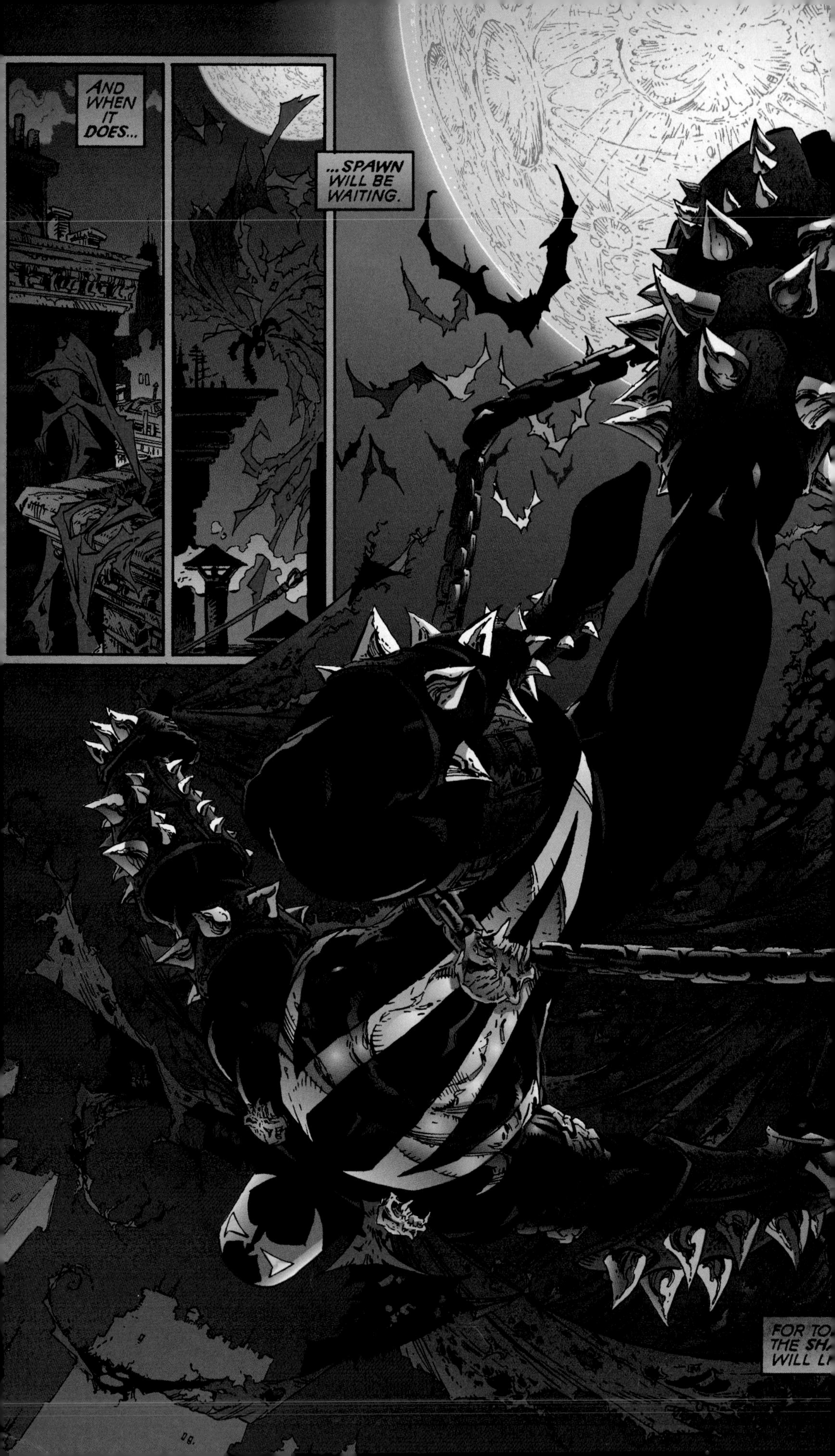
AND WHEN IT DOES...
...SPAWN WILL BE WAITING.
FOR TO THE SH WILL L

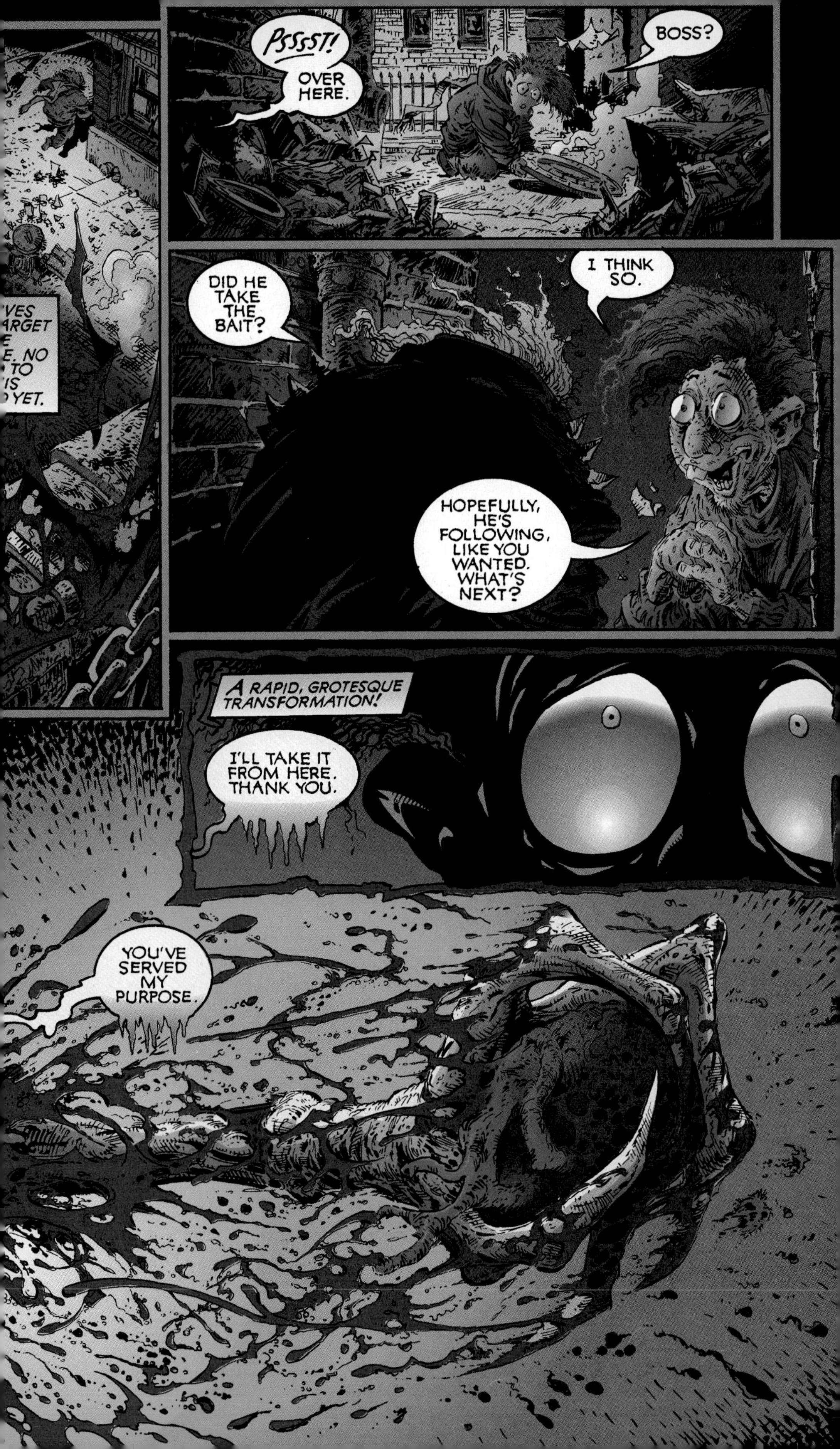
PSSSST!
OVER HERE.
BOSS?
DID HE TAKE THE BAIT?
I THINK SO.
HOPEFULLY, HE'S FOLLOWING, LIKE YOU WANTED. WHAT'S NEXT?
A RAPID, GROTESQUE TRANSFORMATION!
I'LL TAKE IT FROM HERE. THANK YOU.
YOU'VE SERVED MY PURPOSE.

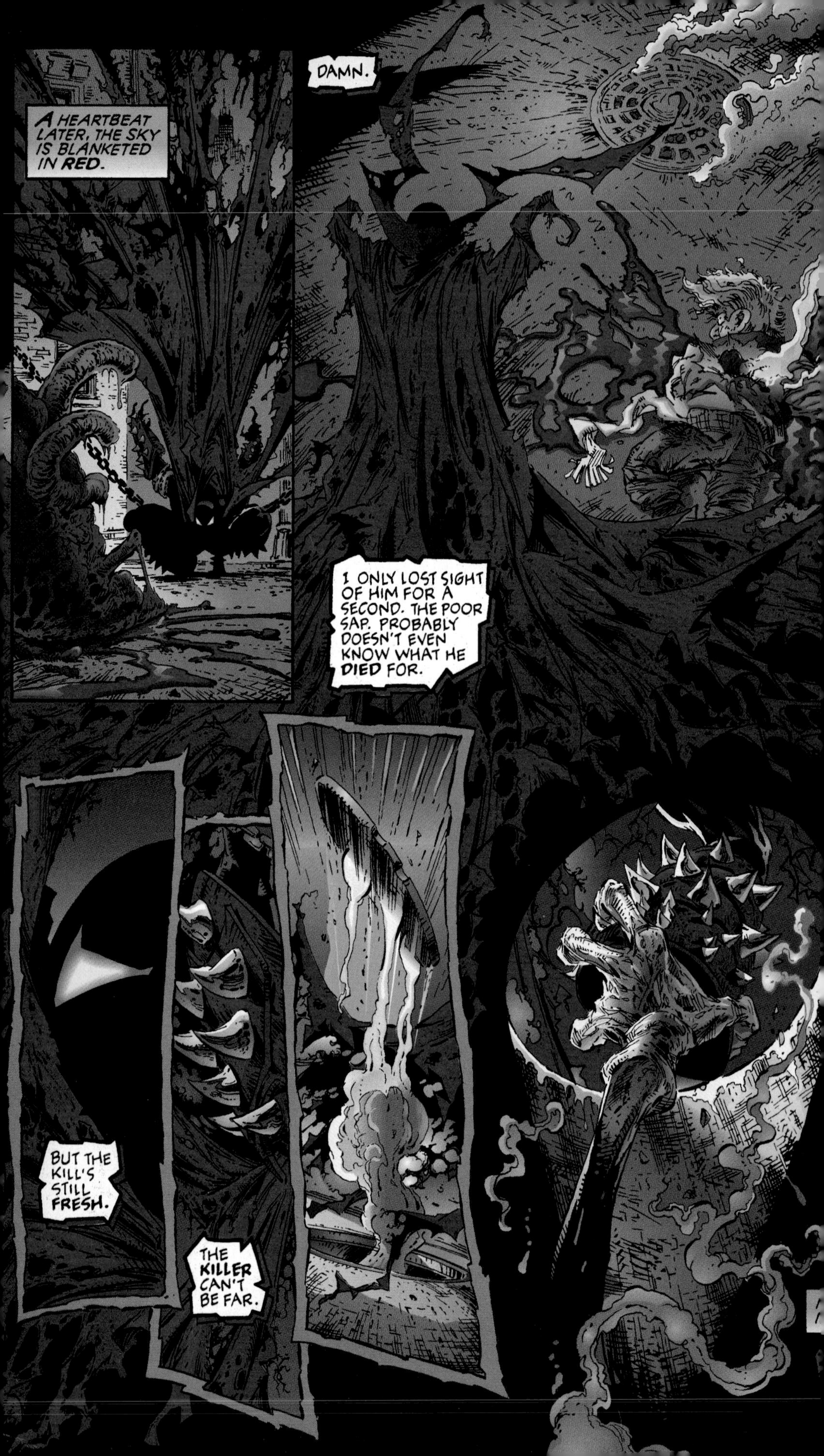
A HEARTBEAT LATER, THE SKY IS BLANKETED IN **RED**.
DAMN.
I ONLY LOST SIGHT OF HIM FOR A SECOND. THE POOR SAP. PROBABLY DOESN'T EVEN KNOW WHAT HE **DIED** FOR.
BUT THE KILL'S STILL **FRESH**.
THE **KILLER** CAN'T BE FAR.

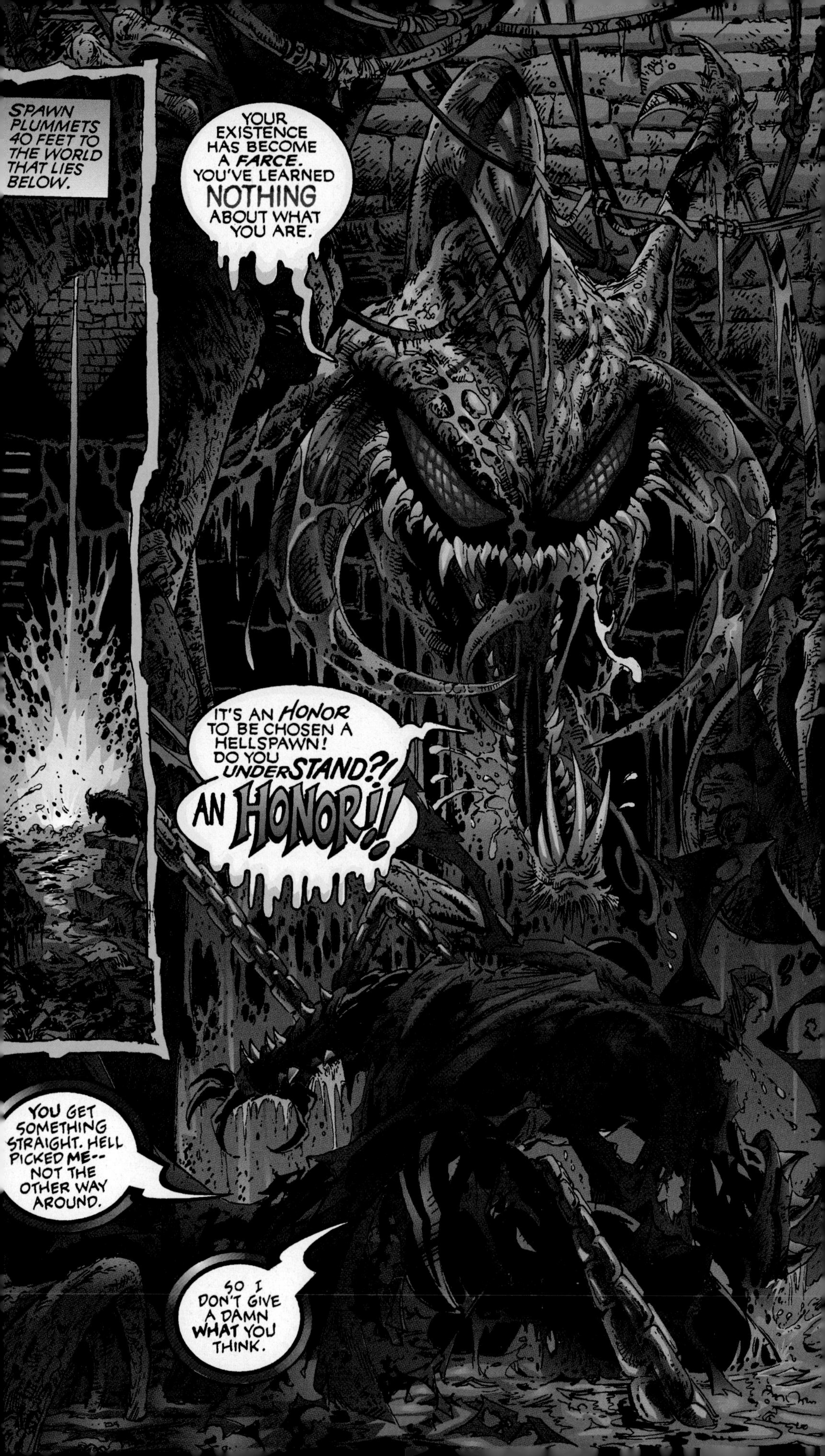

SPAWN PLUMMETS 40 FEET TO THE WORLD THAT LIES BELOW.
YOUR EXISTENCE HAS BECOME A FARCE. YOU'VE LEARNED NOTHING ABOUT WHAT YOU ARE.
IT'S AN HONOR TO BE CHOSEN A HELLSPAWN! DO YOU UNDERSTAND?!
AN HONOR!!
YOU GET SOMETHING STRAIGHT. HELL PICKED ME-- NOT THE OTHER WAY AROUND.
SO I DON'T GIVE A DAMN WHAT YOU THINK.

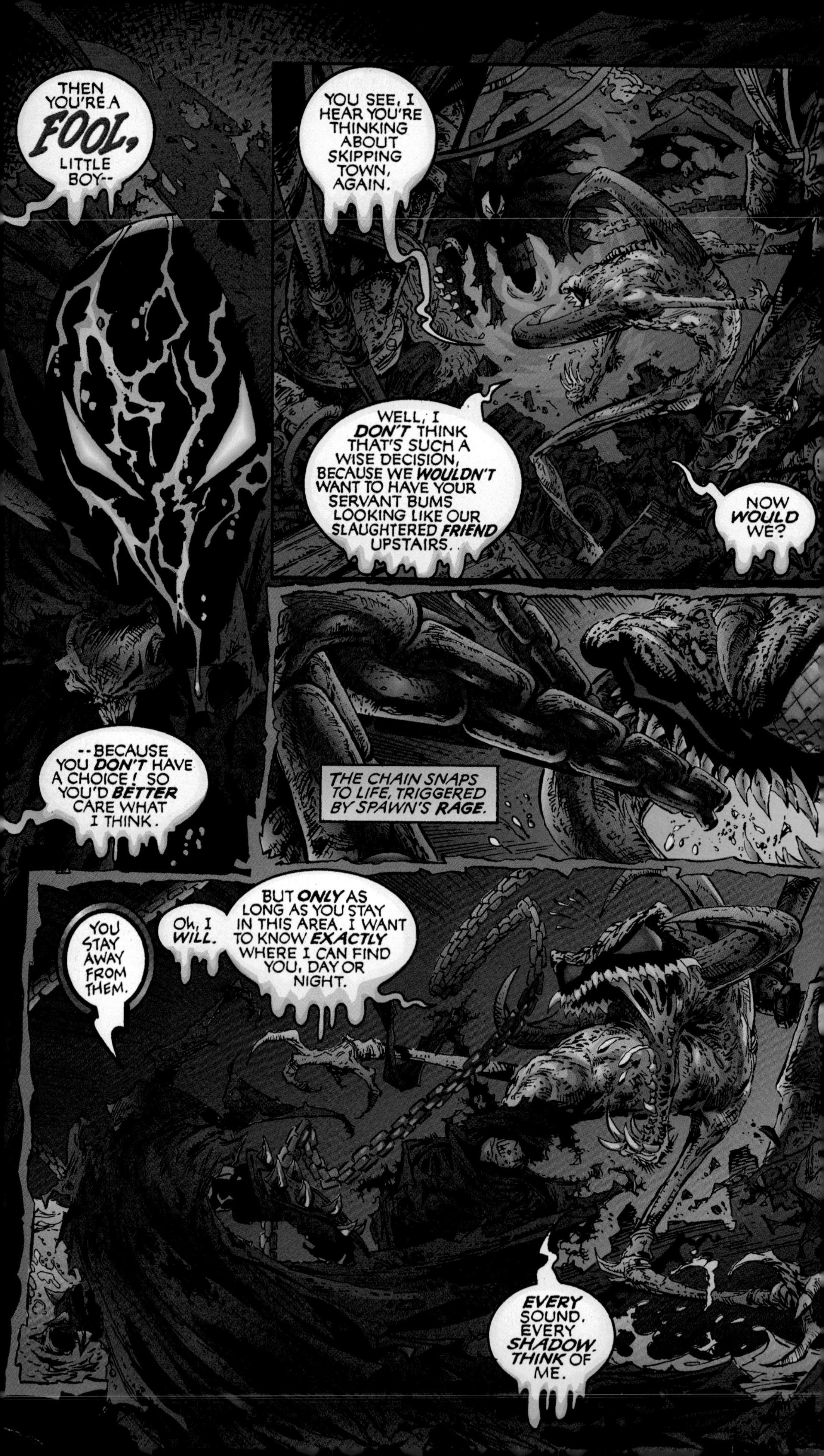
THEN YOU'RE A FOOL, LITTLE BOY--
YOU SEE, I HEAR YOU'RE THINKING ABOUT SKIPPING TOWN, AGAIN.
WELL, I DON'T THINK THAT'S SUCH A WISE DECISION, BECAUSE WE WOULDN'T WANT TO HAVE YOUR SERVANT BUMS LOOKING LIKE OUR SLAUGHTERED FRIEND UPSTAIRS.
NOW WOULD WE?
--BECAUSE YOU DON'T HAVE A CHOICE! SO YOU'D BETTER CARE WHAT I THINK.
THE CHAIN SNAPS TO LIFE, TRIGGERED BY SPAWN'S RAGE.
YOU STAY AWAY FROM THEM.
Oh, I WILL.
BUT ONLY AS LONG AS YOU STAY IN THIS AREA. I WANT TO KNOW EXACTLY WHERE I CAN FIND YOU, DAY OR NIGHT.
EVERY SOUND. EVERY SHADOW. THINK OF ME.

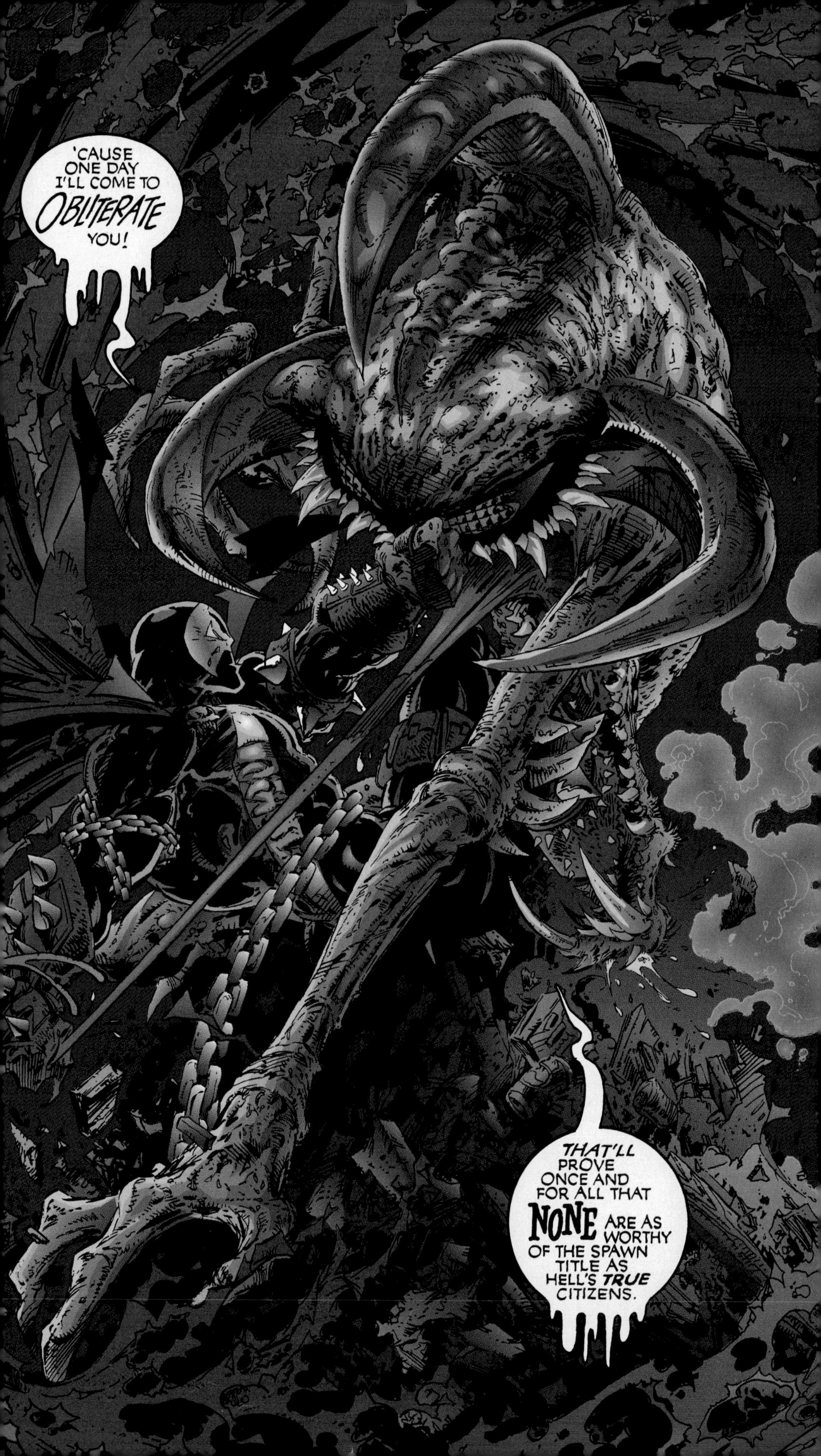
'CAUSE ONE DAY I'LL COME TO OBLITERATE YOU!
THAT'LL PROVE ONCE AND FOR ALL THAT NONE ARE AS WORTHY OF THE SPAWN TITLE AS HELL'S TRUE CITIZENS.

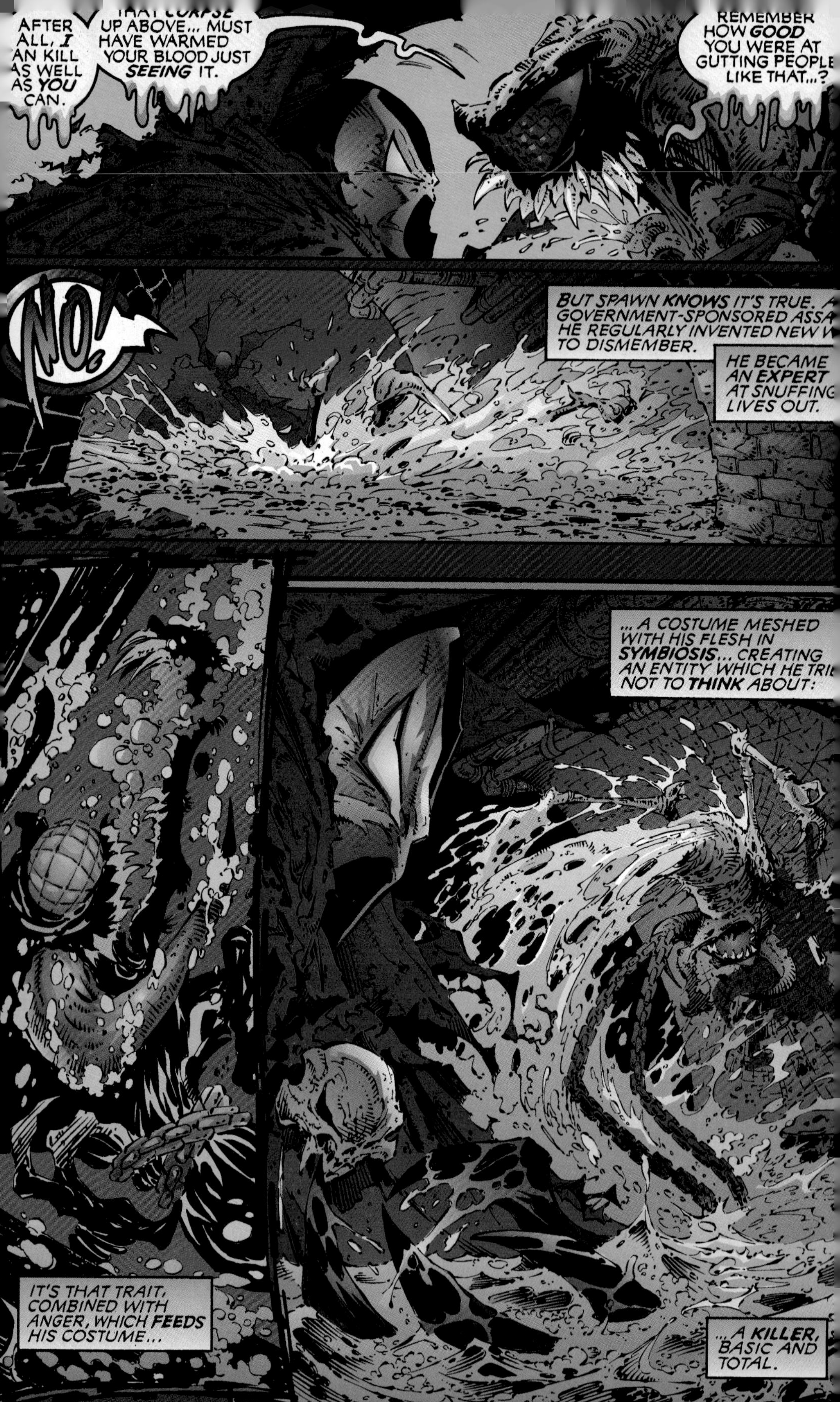
AFTER ALL, I AN KILL AS WELL AS YOU CAN.
THAT CORPSE UP ABOVE... MUST HAVE WARMED YOUR BLOOD JUST SEEING IT.
REMEMBER HOW GOOD YOU WERE AT GUTTING PEOPLE LIKE THAT...?
NO!
BUT SPAWN KNOWS IT'S TRUE. A GOVERNMENT-SPONSORED ASSA HE REGULARLY INVENTED NEW W TO DISMEMBER.
HE BECAME AN EXPERT AT SNUFFING LIVES OUT.
IT'S THAT TRAIT, COMBINED WITH ANGER, WHICH FEEDS HIS COSTUME...
... A COSTUME MESHED WITH HIS FLESH IN SYMBIOSIS... CREATING AN ENTITY WHICH HE TRI NOT TO THINK ABOUT:
...A KILLER, BASIC AND TOTAL.

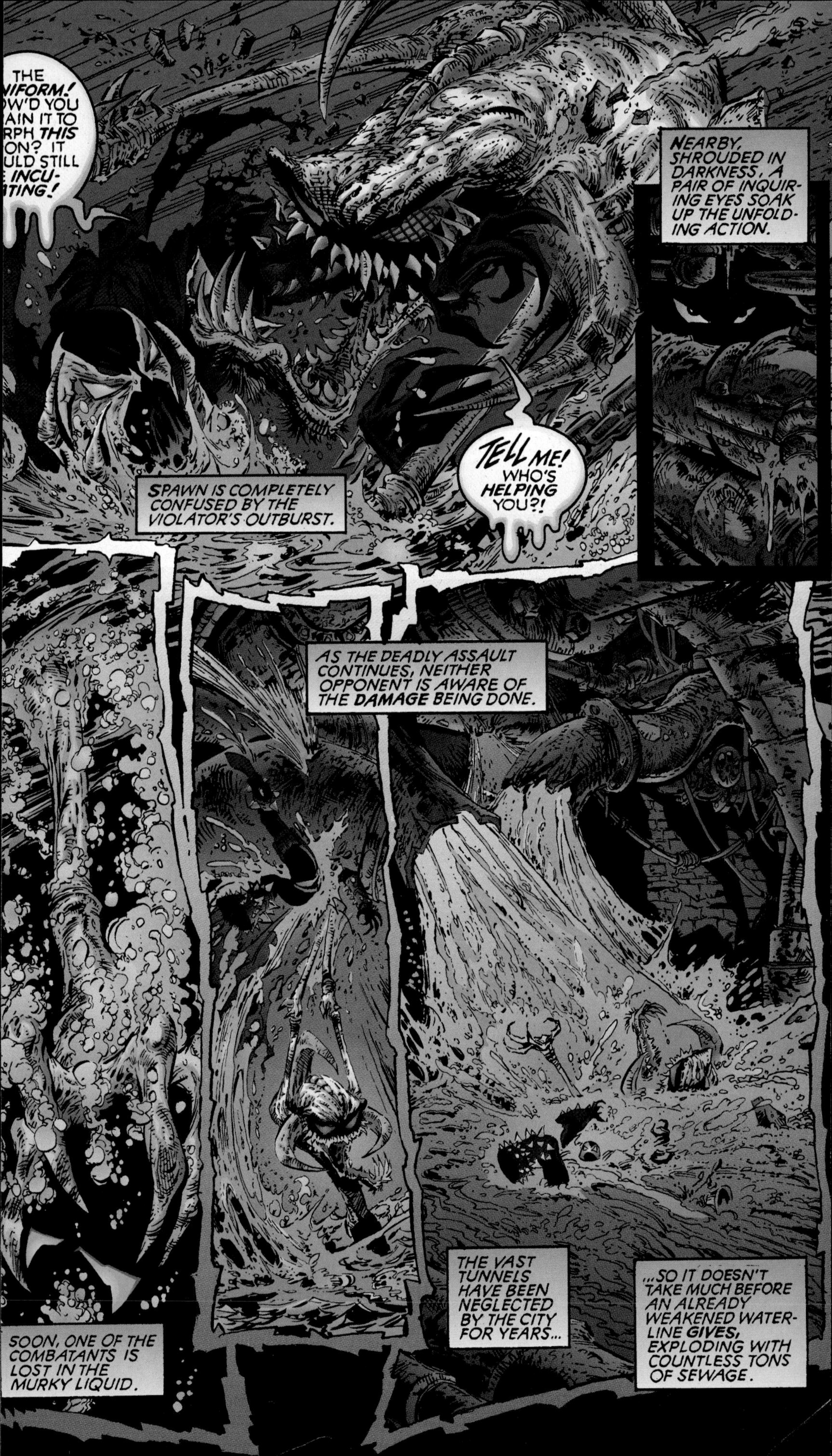
THE
NIFORM!
OW'D YOU
AIN IT TO
RPH THIS
ON? IT
ULD STILL
INCU-
ATING!
NEARBY, SHROUDED IN DARKNESS, A PAIR OF INQUIRING EYES SOAK UP THE UNFOLDING ACTION.
TELL ME! WHO'S HELPING YOU?!
SPAWN IS COMPLETELY CONFUSED BY THE VIOLATOR'S OUTBURST.
AS THE DEADLY ASSAULT CONTINUES, NEITHER OPPONENT IS AWARE OF THE DAMAGE BEING DONE.
SOON, ONE OF THE COMBATANTS IS LOST IN THE MURKY LIQUID.
THE VAST TUNNELS HAVE BEEN NEGLECTED BY THE CITY FOR YEARS...
...SO IT DOESN'T TAKE MUCH BEFORE AN ALREADY WEAKENED WATER-LINE GIVES, EXPLODING WITH COUNTLESS TONS OF SEWAGE.

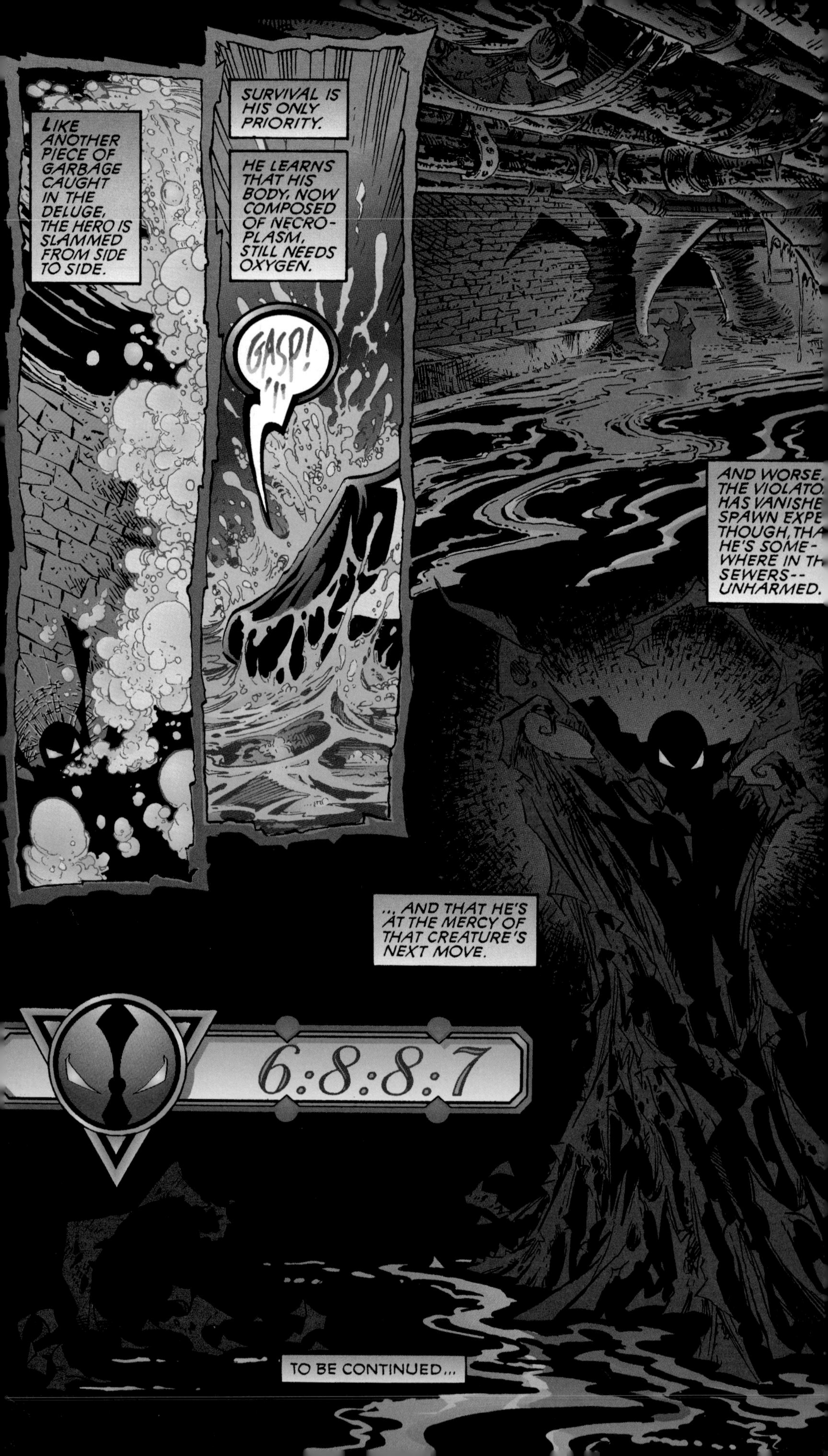

LIKE ANOTHER PIECE OF GARBAGE CAUGHT IN THE DELUGE, THE HERO IS SLAMMED FROM SIDE TO SIDE.
SURVIVAL IS HIS ONLY PRIORITY.
HE LEARNS THAT HIS BODY, NOW COMPOSED OF NECRO-PLASM, STILL NEEDS OXYGEN.
GASP!
AND WORSE. THE VIOLATO HAS VANISHE SPAWN EXPE THOUGH, THA HE'S SOME-WHERE IN TH SEWERS-- UNHARMED.
...AND THAT HE'S AT THE MERCY OF THAT CREATURE'S NEXT MOVE.
6:8:8:7
TO BE CONTINUED...

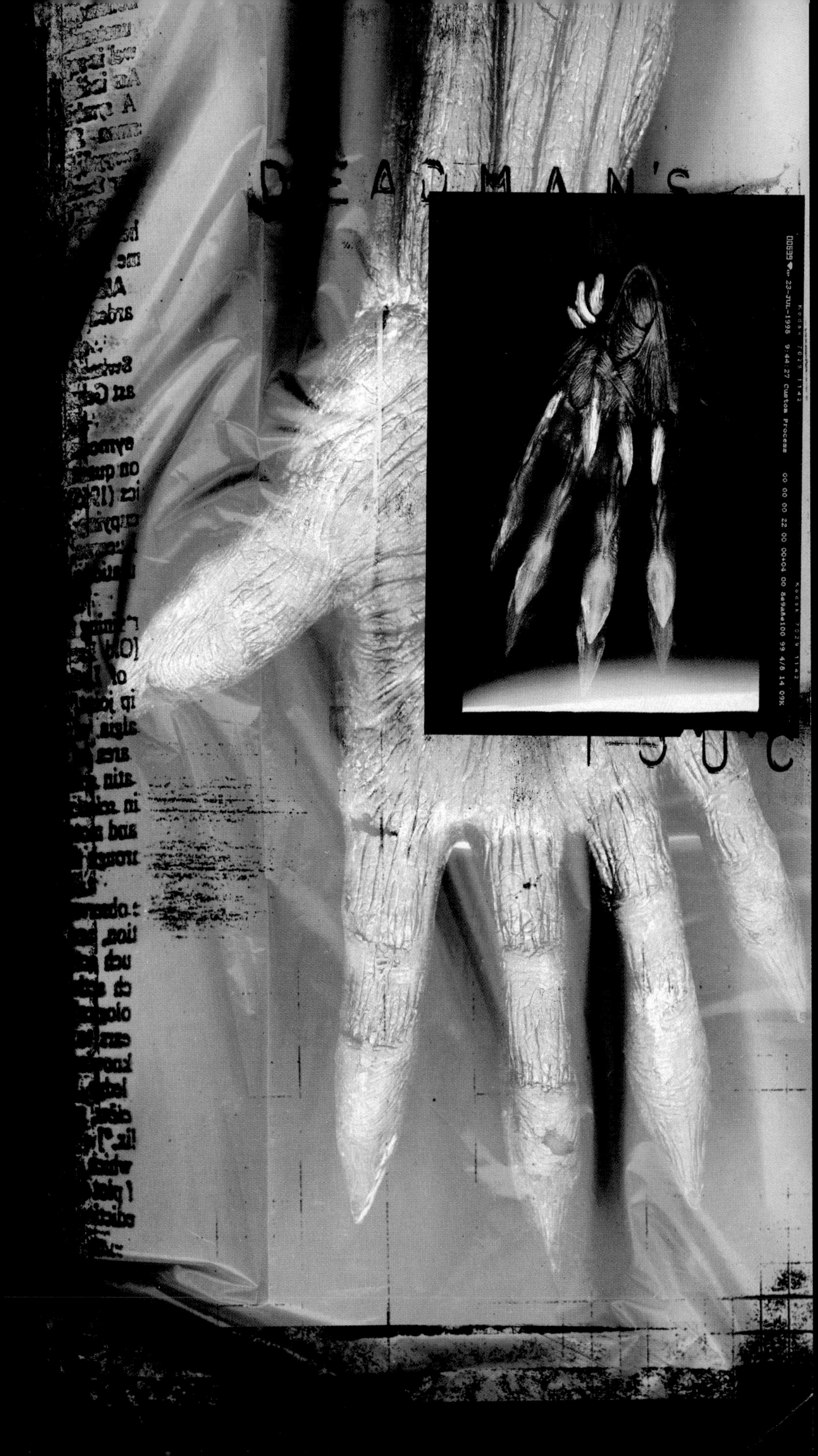
DEADMAN'S

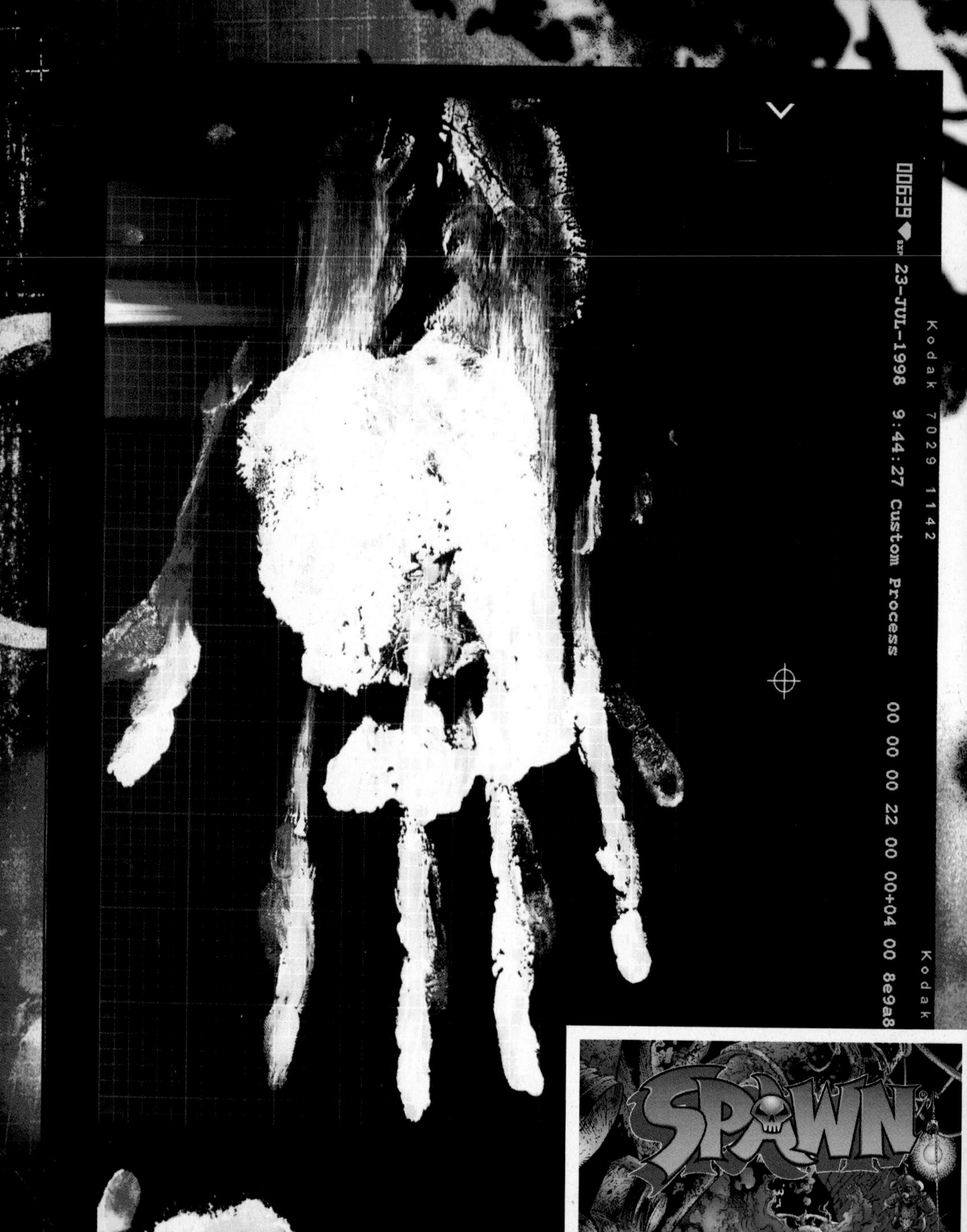
00639 EXP 23-JUL-1998 9:44:27 Custom Process 00 00 00 22 00 00+04 00 8e9a8
Kodak 7029 1142
Kodak

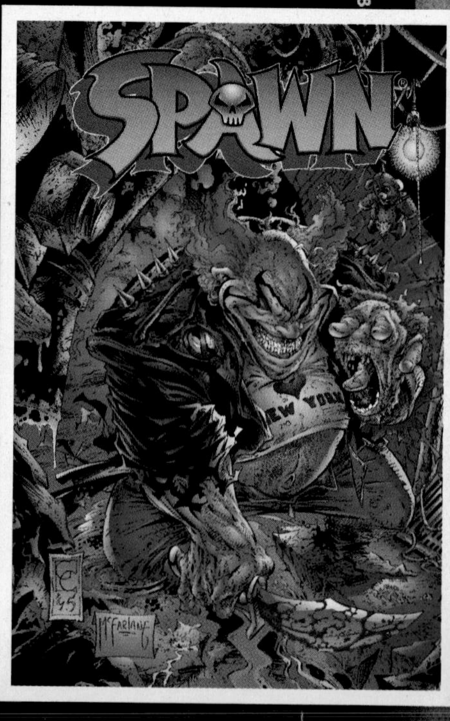
SPAWN

SHADOWS PART II 34

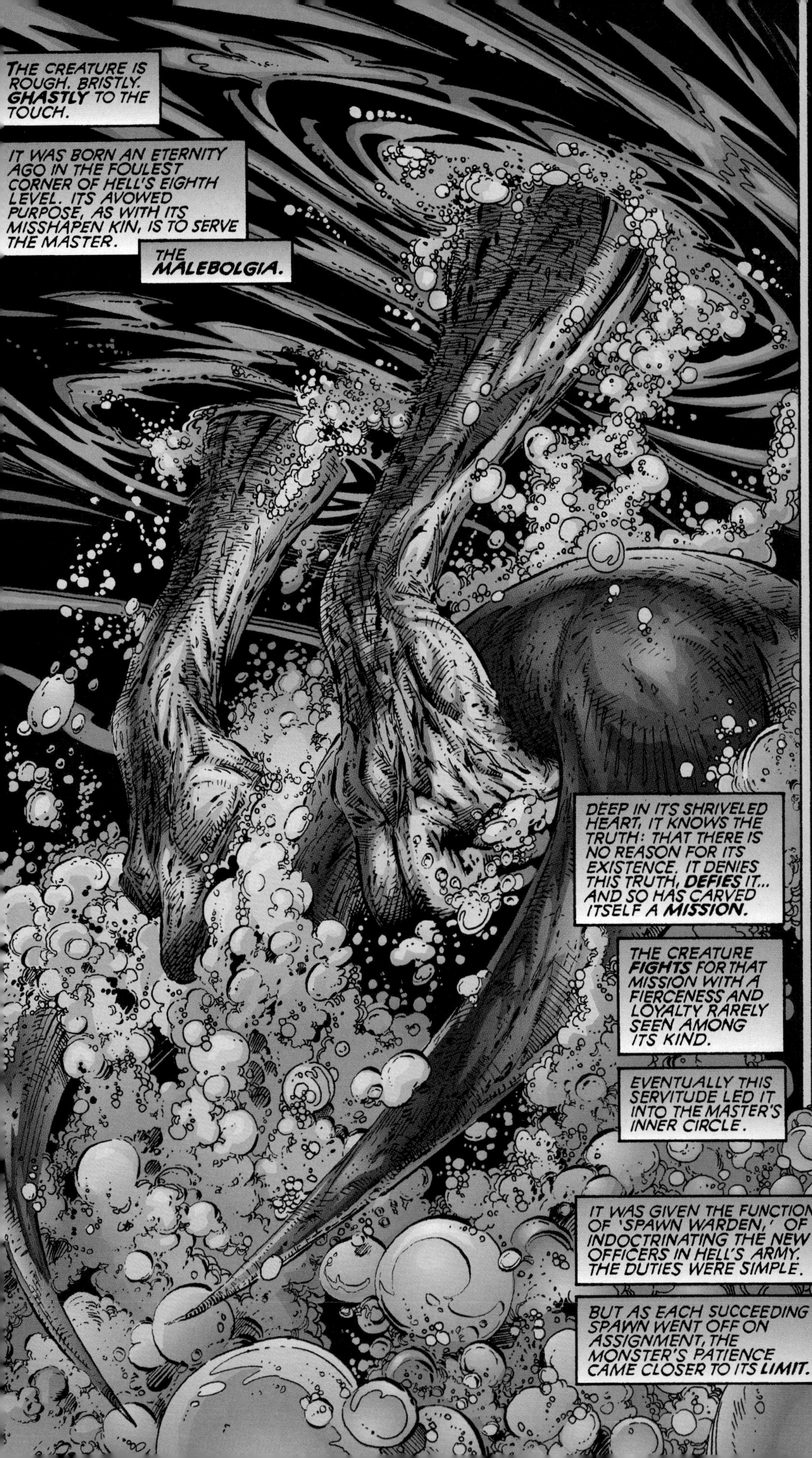
THE CREATURE IS ROUGH. BRISTLY. GHASTLY TO THE TOUCH.
IT WAS BORN AN ETERNITY AGO IN THE FOULEST CORNER OF HELL'S EIGHTH LEVEL. ITS AVOWED PURPOSE, AS WITH ITS MISSHAPEN KIN, IS TO SERVE THE MASTER.
THE MALEBOLGIA.
DEEP IN ITS SHRIVELED HEART, IT KNOWS THE TRUTH: THAT THERE IS NO REASON FOR ITS EXISTENCE. IT DENIES THIS TRUTH, DEFIES IT... AND SO HAS CARVED ITSELF A MISSION.
THE CREATURE FIGHTS FOR THAT MISSION WITH A FIERCENESS AND LOYALTY RARELY SEEN AMONG ITS KIND.
EVENTUALLY THIS SERVITUDE LED IT INTO THE MASTER'S INNER CIRCLE.
IT WAS GIVEN THE FUNCTION OF 'SPAWN WARDEN,' OF INDOCTRINATING THE NEW OFFICERS IN HELL'S ARMY. THE DUTIES WERE SIMPLE.
BUT AS EACH SUCCEEDING SPAWN WENT OFF ON ASSIGNMENT, THE MONSTER'S PATIENCE CAME CLOSER TO ITS LIMIT.

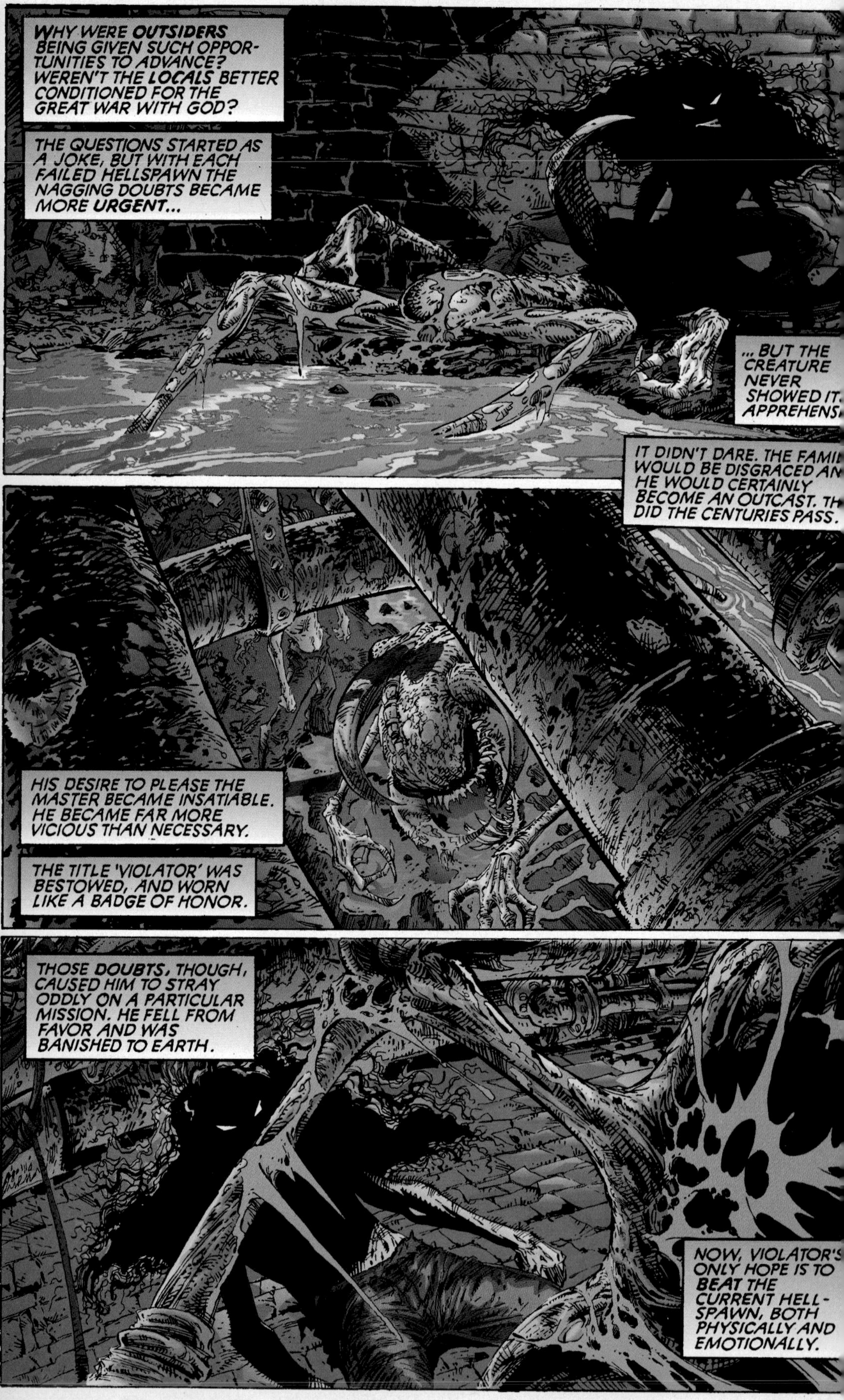

WHY WERE OUTSIDERS BEING GIVEN SUCH OPPORTUNITIES TO ADVANCE? WEREN'T THE LOCALS BETTER CONDITIONED FOR THE GREAT WAR WITH GOD?
THE QUESTIONS STARTED AS A JOKE, BUT WITH EACH FAILED HELLSPAWN THE NAGGING DOUBTS BECAME MORE URGENT...
... BUT THE CREATURE NEVER SHOWED IT. APPREHENS
IT DIDN'T DARE. THE FAMI WOULD BE DISGRACED AN HE WOULD CERTAINLY BECOME AN OUTCAST. TH DID THE CENTURIES PASS.
HIS DESIRE TO PLEASE THE MASTER BECAME INSATIABLE. HE BECAME FAR MORE VICIOUS THAN NECESSARY.
THE TITLE 'VIOLATOR' WAS BESTOWED, AND WORN LIKE A BADGE OF HONOR.
THOSE DOUBTS, THOUGH, CAUSED HIM TO STRAY ODDLY ON A PARTICULAR MISSION. HE FELL FROM FAVOR AND WAS BANISHED TO EARTH.
NOW, VIOLATOR'S ONLY HOPE IS TO BEAT THE CURRENT HELL-SPAWN, BOTH PHYSICALLY AND EMOTIONALLY.

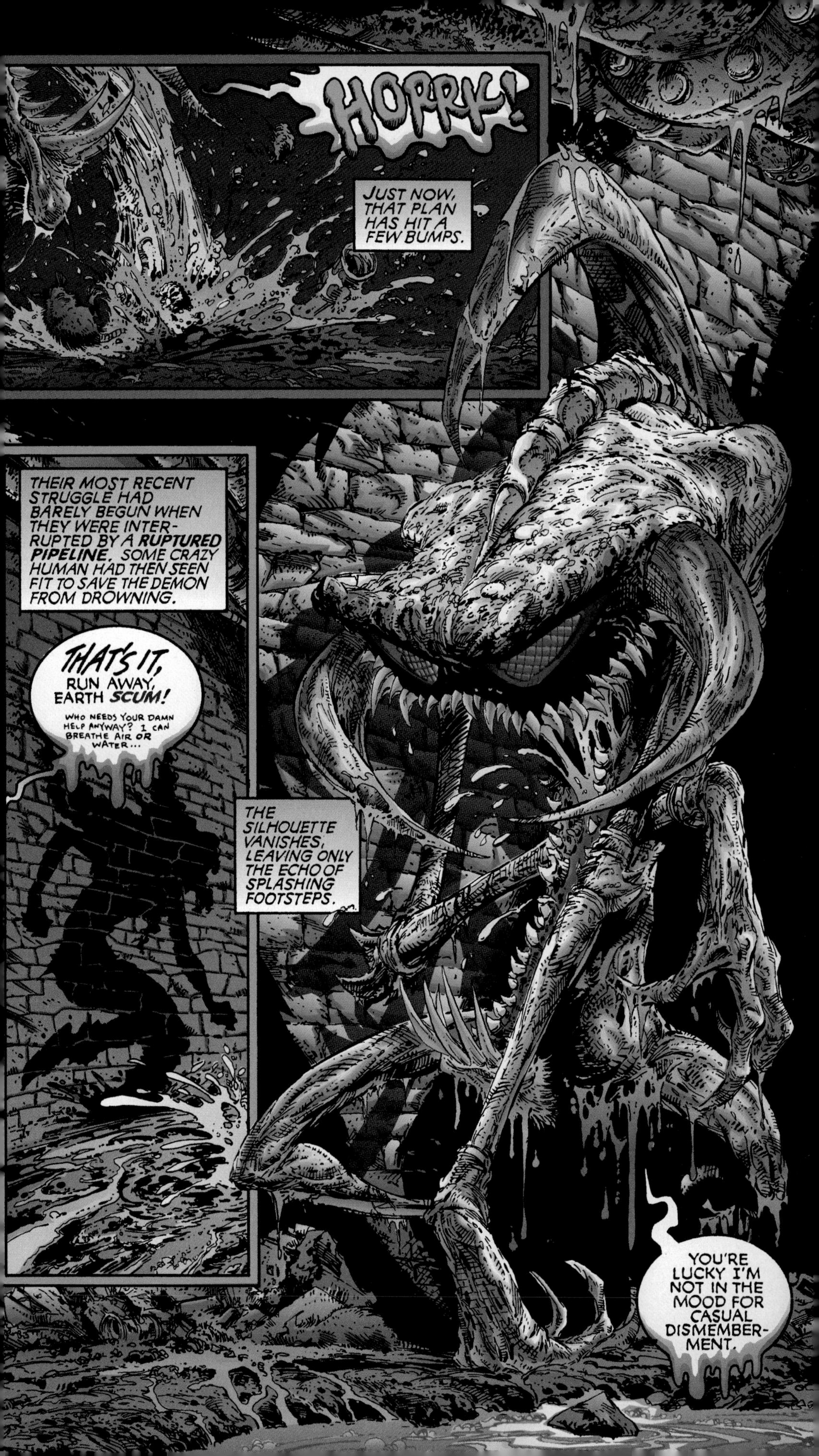
HORRK!
JUST NOW, THAT PLAN HAS HIT A FEW BUMPS.
THEIR MOST RECENT STRUGGLE HAD BARELY BEGUN WHEN THEY WERE INTER-RUPTED BY A RUPTURED PIPELINE. SOME CRAZY HUMAN HAD THEN SEEN FIT TO SAVE THE DEMON FROM DROWNING.
THAT'S IT, RUN AWAY, EARTH SCUM! WHO NEEDS YOUR DAMN HELP ANYWAY? I CAN BREATHE AIR OR WATER...
THE SILHOUETTE VANISHES, LEAVING ONLY THE ECHO OF SPLASHING FOOTSTEPS.
YOU'RE LUCKY I'M NOT IN THE MOOD FOR CASUAL DISMEMBER-MENT.

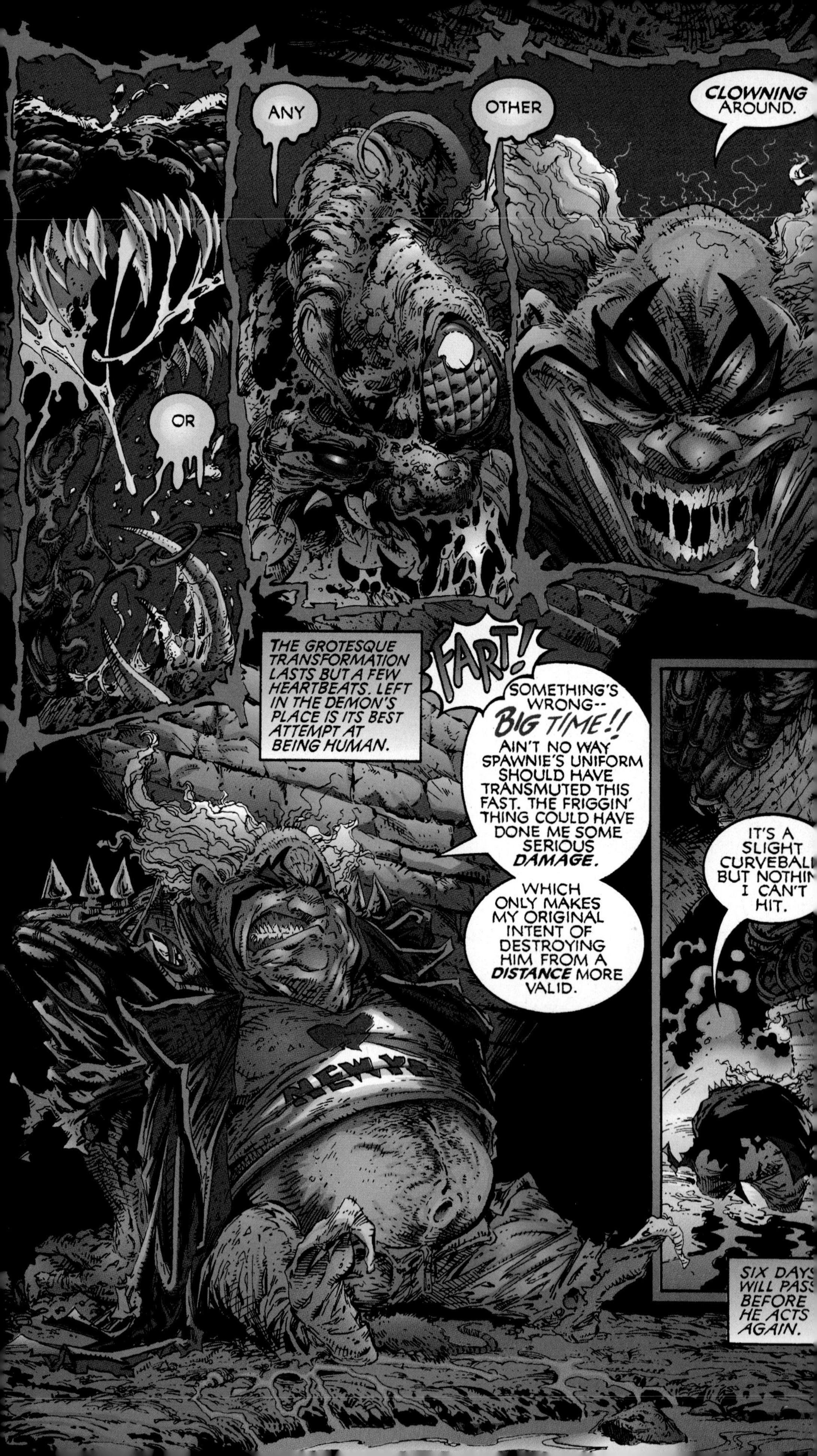

ANY
OR
OTHER
CLOWNING AROUND.
THE GROTESQUE TRANSFORMATION LASTS BUT A FEW HEARTBEATS. LEFT IN THE DEMON'S PLACE IS ITS BEST ATTEMPT AT BEING HUMAN.
FART!
SOMETHING'S WRONG-- BIG TIME!! AIN'T NO WAY SPAWNIE'S UNIFORM SHOULD HAVE TRANSMUTED THIS FAST. THE FRIGGIN' THING COULD HAVE DONE ME SOME SERIOUS DAMAGE.
WHICH ONLY MAKES MY ORIGINAL INTENT OF DESTROYING HIM FROM A DISTANCE MORE VALID.
IT'S A SLIGHT CURVEBALL BUT NOTHIN I CAN'T HIT.
SIX DAYS WILL PASS BEFORE HE ACTS AGAIN.

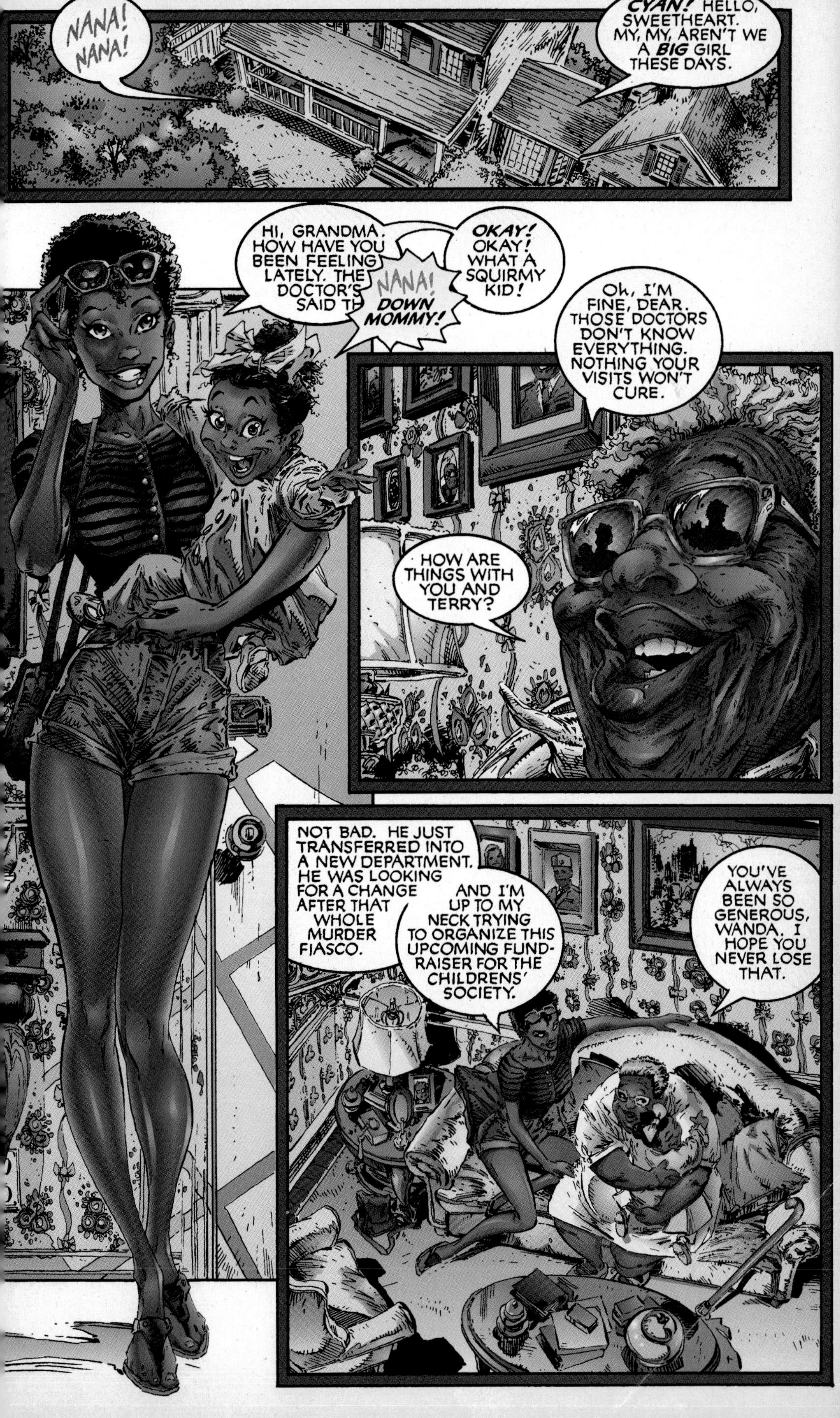

NANA! NANA!
CYAN! HELLO, SWEETHEART. MY, MY, AREN'T WE A BIG GIRL THESE DAYS.
HI, GRANDMA. HOW HAVE YOU BEEN FEELING LATELY. THE DOCTOR'S SAID TH
NANA! DOWN MOMMY!
OKAY! OKAY! WHAT A SQUIRMY KID!
Oh, I'M FINE, DEAR. THOSE DOCTORS DON'T KNOW EVERYTHING. NOTHING YOUR VISITS WON'T CURE.
HOW ARE THINGS WITH YOU AND TERRY?
NOT BAD. HE JUST TRANSFERRED INTO A NEW DEPARTMENT. HE WAS LOOKING FOR A CHANGE AFTER THAT WHOLE MURDER FIASCO.
AND I'M UP TO MY NECK TRYING TO ORGANIZE THIS UPCOMING FUND-RAISER FOR THE CHILDRENS' SOCIETY.
YOU'VE ALWAYS BEEN SO GENEROUS, WANDA. I HOPE YOU NEVER LOSE THAT.

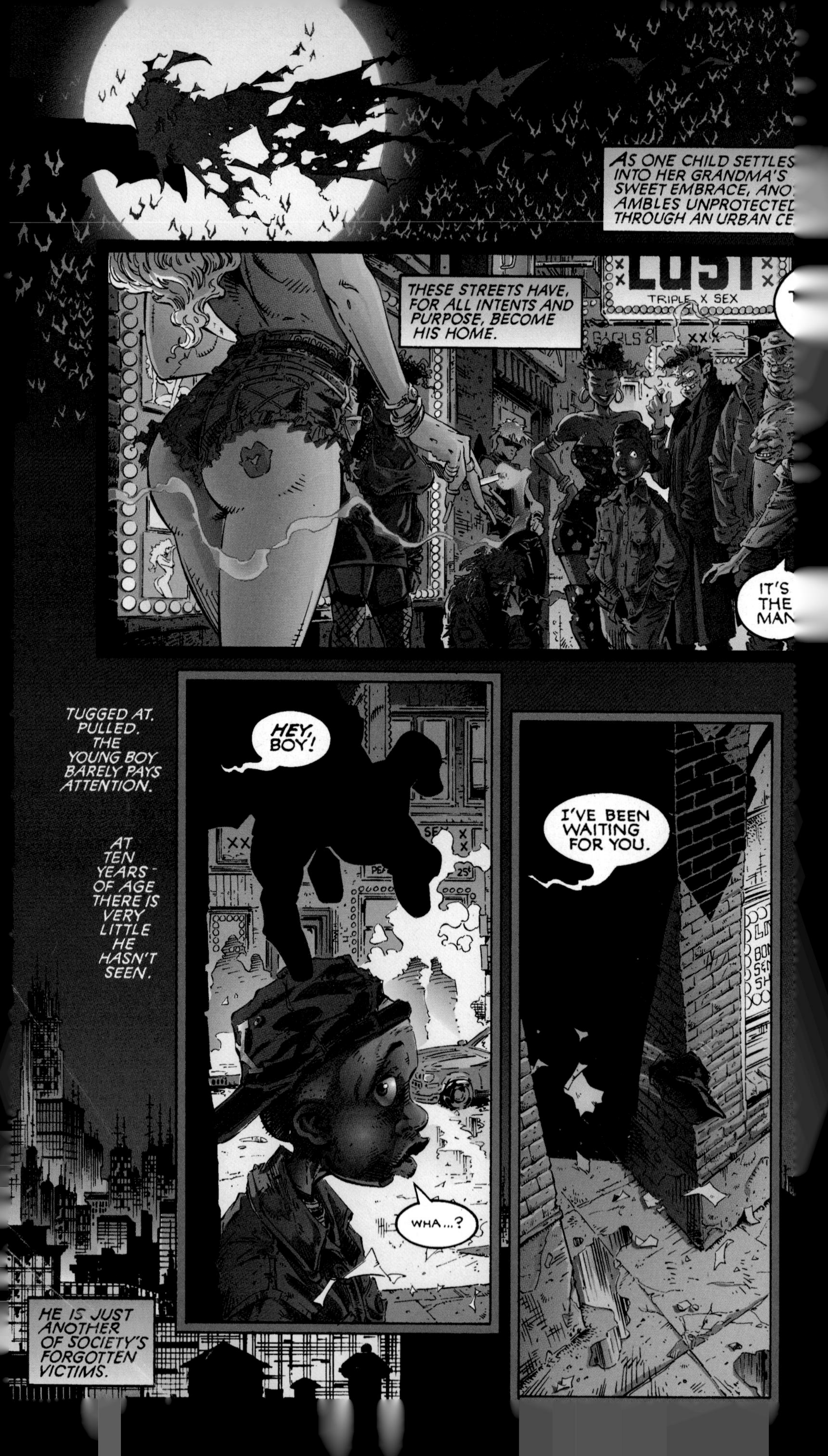

AS ONE CHILD SETTLES INTO HER GRANDMA'S SWEET EMBRACE, ANO AMBLES UNPROTECTED THROUGH AN URBAN CE
THESE STREETS HAVE, FOR ALL INTENTS AND PURPOSE, BECOME HIS HOME.
TRIPLE X SEX
IT'S THE MAN
TUGGED AT. PULLED. THE YOUNG BOY BARELY PAYS ATTENTION.
AT TEN YEARS-OF AGE THERE IS VERY LITTLE HE HASN'T SEEN.
HEY, BOY!
WHA...?
I'VE BEEN WAITING FOR YOU.
HE IS JUST ANOTHER OF SOCIETY'S FORGOTTEN VICTIMS.

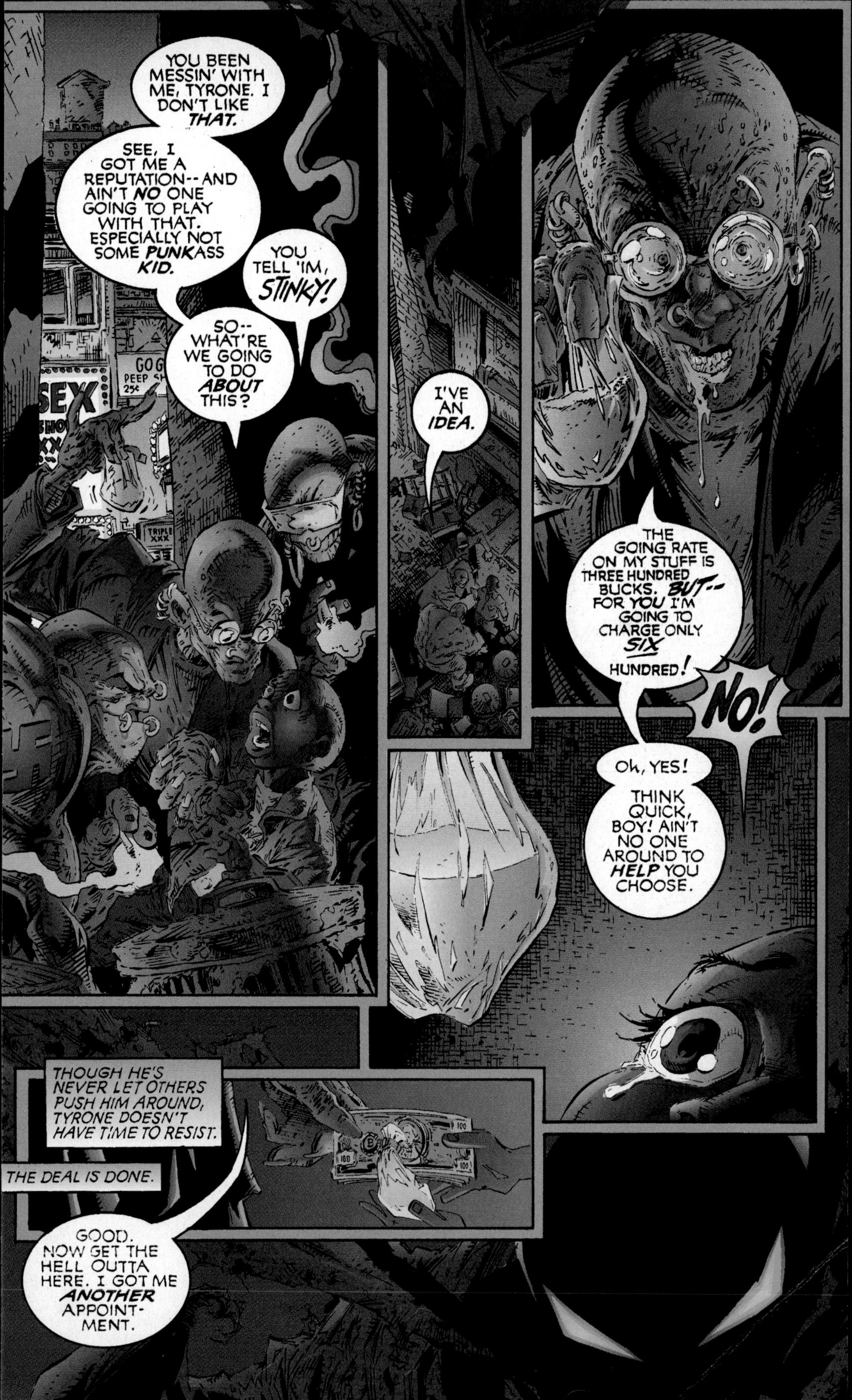
YOU BEEN MESSIN' WITH ME, TYRONE. I DON'T LIKE THAT.
SEE, I GOT ME A REPUTATION--AND AIN'T NO ONE GOING TO PLAY WITH THAT. ESPECIALLY NOT SOME PUNKASS KID.
YOU TELL 'IM, STINKY!
SO--WHAT'RE WE GOING TO DO ABOUT THIS?
SEX
TRIPLE XXX
I'VE AN IDEA.
THE GOING RATE ON MY STUFF IS THREE HUNDRED BUCKS. BUT--FOR YOU I'M GOING TO CHARGE ONLY SIX HUNDRED!
NO!
Oh, YES!
THINK QUICK, BOY! AIN'T NO ONE AROUND TO HELP YOU CHOOSE.
THOUGH HE'S NEVER LET OTHERS PUSH HIM AROUND, TYRONE DOESN'T HAVE TIME TO RESIST.
THE DEAL IS DONE.
GOOD. NOW GET THE HELL OUTTA HERE. I GOT ME ANOTHER APPOINTMENT.

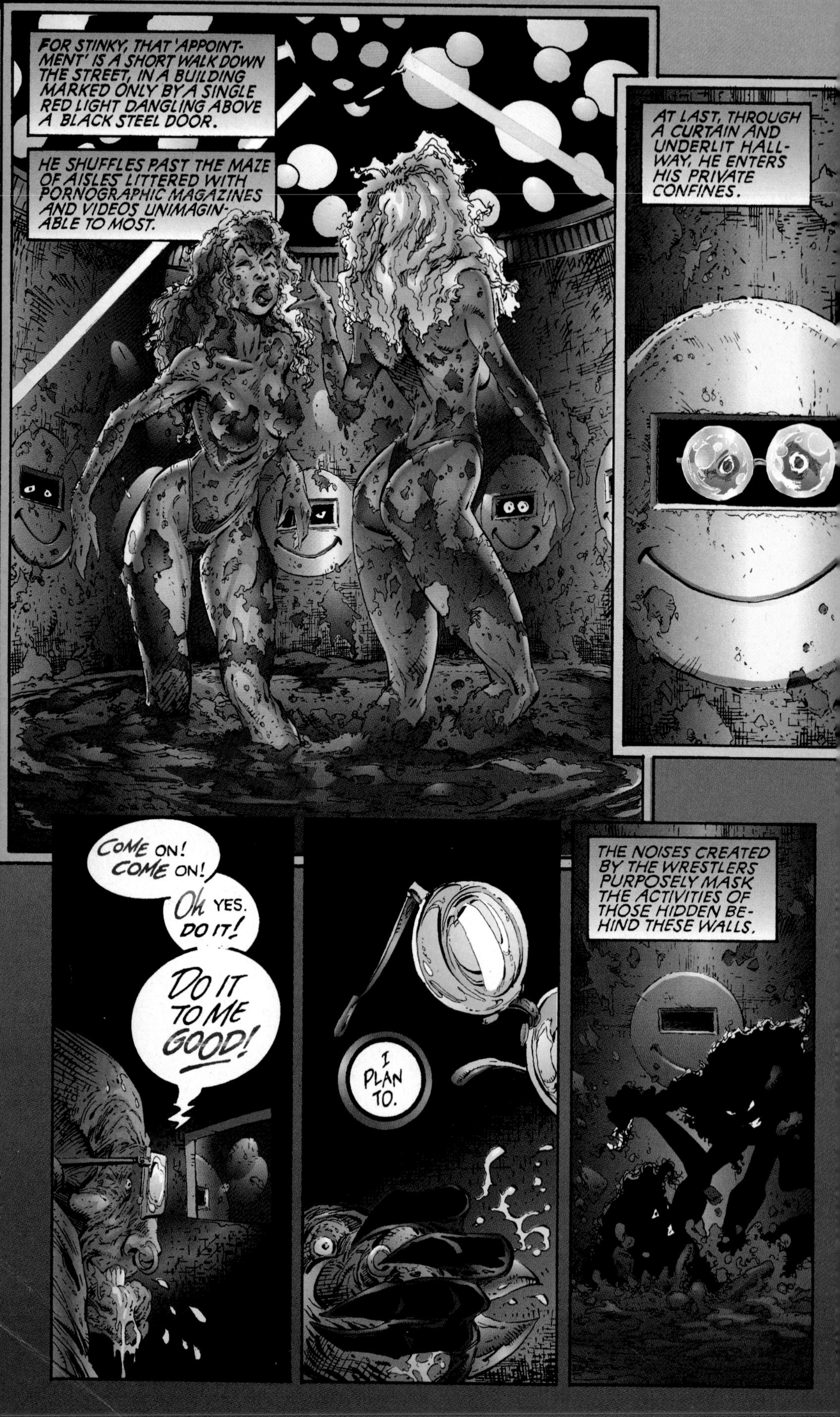
FOR STINKY, THAT 'APPOINTMENT' IS A SHORT WALK DOWN THE STREET, IN A BUILDING MARKED ONLY BY A SINGLE RED LIGHT DANGLING ABOVE A BLACK STEEL DOOR.
HE SHUFFLES PAST THE MAZE OF AISLES LITTERED WITH PORNOGRAPHIC MAGAZINES AND VIDEOS UNIMAGINABLE TO MOST.
AT LAST, THROUGH A CURTAIN AND UNDERLIT HALLWAY, HE ENTERS HIS PRIVATE CONFINES.
COME ON! COME ON!
Oh YES. DO IT!
DO IT TO ME GOOD!
I PLAN TO.
THE NOISES CREATED BY THE WRESTLERS PURPOSELY MASK THE ACTIVITIES OF THOSE HIDDEN BEHIND THESE WALLS.

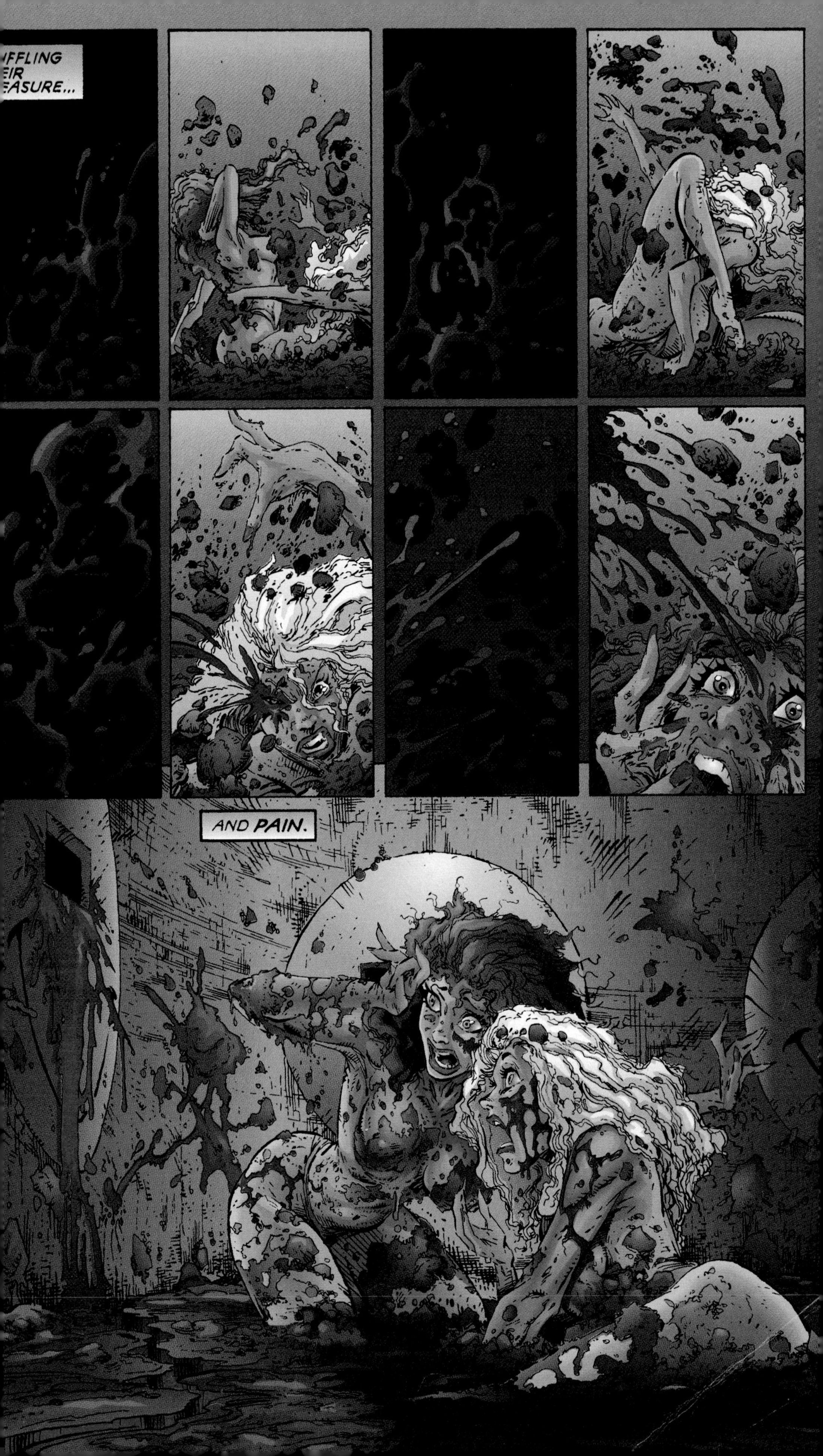

IFFLING
EIR
EASURE...
AND PAIN.

TWISTED IN BETWEEN PURGATORY AND LIMBO IS THE VAST WASTELAND OF HELL'S EIGHTH LEVEL. THE SHADOW OF THIS BLACK VOID CREEPS FAR CLOSER TO THE EARTHLY REALM THAN WE CARE TO THINK ABOUT.

IT'S HERE THAT THE ARMIES OF THE DAMNED ARE ASSEMBLED AND TRAINED, AWAITING THE SIGNAL TO BEGIN THE GLORIOUS WAR AGAINST THE HEAVENS: **ARMAGEDDON.**

THAT EVENTUAL WAR IS THE ONLY PURPOSE FOR THIS CREATURE, *THE MALEBOLGIA,* ONE OF THE HIGH-RANKING DEVILS. HE OVERSEES THE SWELLING SEA OF TROOPS, AND OCCASIONALLY CHOOSES OFFICERS TO LEAD THEM.

HIS LATEST HELLSPAWN-IN-TRAINING IS COMING ALONG AS PLANNED.

Delude yourself all you wish, Simmons, but you cannot run away from yourself.

There is a reason you were chosen from among the tortured millions.

Death. Evil. Blackness. Those seeds were planted in you at birth.

Soon. Very so All sha come t fruitio

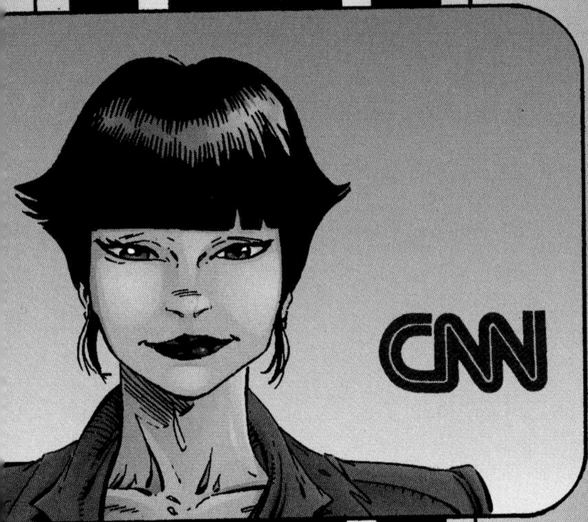
CNN

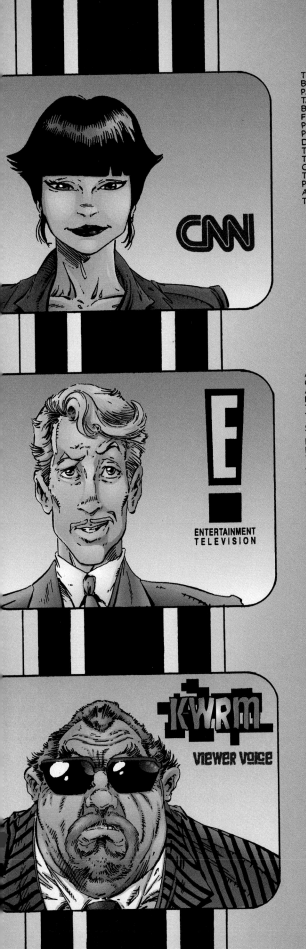

THE SITUATION IN BOSNIA INTENSIFIES AS NEITHER BOSNIAN DIPLOMATS NOR THEIR SERBIAN COUNTERPARTS SEEM WILLING TO RESUME PEACEKEEPING TALKS. THE PRESIDENT'S MUCH-PUBLICIZED VISIT TO BOSNIA WAS CUT UNEXPECTEDLY SHORT, THREE FEWER DAYS THAN PLANNED, AFTER THE BOSNIAN PRESIDENT WALKED OUT DURING OUR PRESIDENT'S PRESENTATION REGARDING THE ONGOING BORDER DISPUTE. CITING FAVORITISM TOWARD THE SERBS, THE BOSNIAN PRESIDENT ADVISED THE COMMITTEE THAT BOSNIAN PARTICIATION WOULD RESUME ONLY IF THE U.S. PRESIDENT WAS REMOVED FROM THE PEACE NEGOTIATIONS. CLOSER TO HOME, POLICE IN NEW YORK CITY ARE STILL INVESTIGATING A GRUESOME MURDER IN THE RED LIGHT DISTRICT. THERE ARE NO REPORTED SUSPECTS AT THIS TIME.

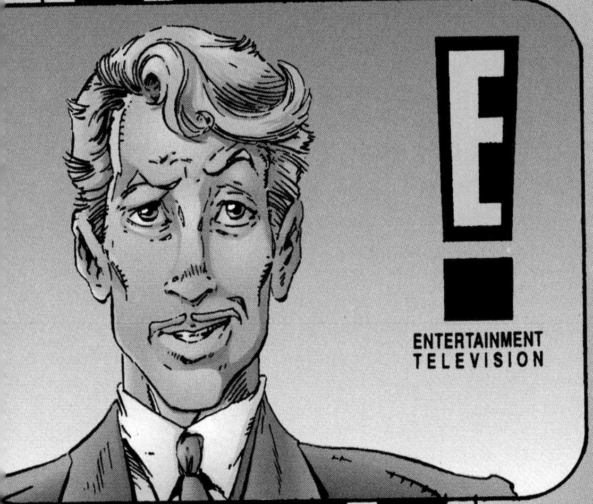
E!
ENTERTAINMENT
TELEVISION

AS THE INTERMINABLE DRUG WAR IN NEW YORK CITY ESCALATES, ANOTHER PAWN FALLS, VICTIM TO A ***GRUESOME*** ATTACK IN A PORN THEATER. POLICE HAD TO RESORT TO DENTAL RECORDS IN AN ATTEMPT TO IDENTIFY THE BODY. SOURCES INDICATE THAT THE VICTIM HAD OVER A ***DOZEN*** BROKEN BONES. A BLOOD SPATTER EXPERT BEGINS HIS INVESTIGATION TODAY IN AN ATTEMPT TO DETERMINE WHAT, IF ***ANY,*** WEAPON WAS USED TO SEVER THE VICTIM'S HEAD. OFFICIALS ARE BAFFLED BY THE EXTENT OF THE MUTILATION, AND CANNOT DETERMINE IF THE ATTACK WAS COMMITTED BY A HUMAN OR SOME WILD ANIMAL. EVEN THOUGH THE RECENT ***VAMPIRE*** CASE HAS BEEN CLOSED, POLICE ARE NOT RULING OUT THE POSSIBILITY OF A CONNECTION. IS THIS JUST ANOTHER MEANINGLESS CRIME, OR A REVENGE HIT FOR A DRUG DEAL GONE BAD? BEFORE A MOTIVE CAN BE SUGGESTED, POLICE SAY THE VICTIM'S IDENTITY MUST FIRST BE DETERIMINED. CREDIT WHERE IT'S DUE. SOUNDS FAIR TO ME.

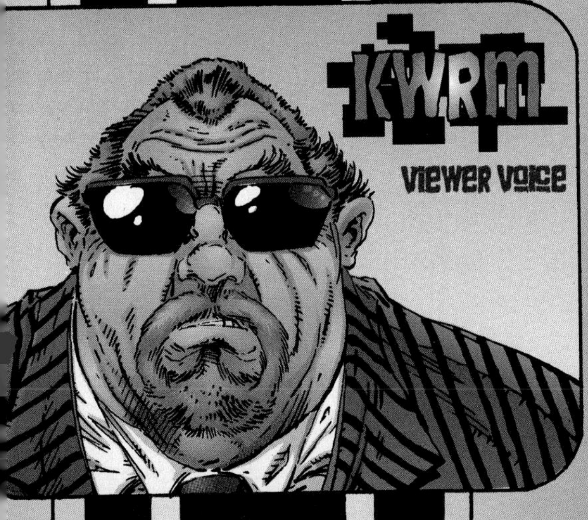
KWRM
VIEWER VOICE

BIG SURPRISE. OUR OVERWHELMINGLY ELECTED PRESIDENT HAS PUT HIS FOOT IN HIS MOUTH ONCE AGAIN, THIS TIME AS HIS PROPOSAL FOR ENDING THE BOSNIAN CONFLICT WENT OVER LIKE A LEAD BALLOON. THE PRESIDENT IS WASTING OUR VALUABLE TIME TRYING TO MAKE HIS MARK IN HISTORY. I GUESS HE'S NOT PLANNING ON RETURNING FOR ANOTHER FOUR YEARS, SO THIS WOULD BE A GOOD OPPORTUNITY. INSTEAD OF GETTING THE JOB DONE, AS ***THIS*** CITIZEN WOULD LIKE TO DO, HE PUSSY-FOOTS AROUND THE ISSUE, ACCOMPLISHING ***NOTHING.*** BACK AT HOME, WE KNOW HOW TO DEAL WITH SIMILAR PROBLEMS. FOR INSTANCE, LAST NIGHT'S GRUESOME MURDER IN NEW YORK. OBVIOUSLY THIS GUY, ANOTHER DRUG-PUSHING PUNK OR MAFIA THUG, GOT WHAT WAS ***COMING*** TO HIM. HE SCREWED SOMEONE OVER AND PAID THE PRICE. SHORT, SWEET, AND TO THE POINT. THE PRESIDENT COULD ***LEARN*** SOMETHING FROM THIS.

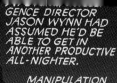

...GENCE DIRECTOR JASON WYNN HAD ASSUMED HE'D BE ABLE TO GET IN ANOTHER PRODUCTIVE ALL-NIGHTER.

MANIPULATION OF NATIONAL SECURITY MISSIONS IS BEST DONE FAR FROM THE LIGHT OF DAY.

WHO DARES!

Awww... DECEPTION AND DECEIT. GIVES ME A WARM, *SQUISHY* FEELING.

DOESN'T MATTER.

WHAT *DOES* IS THAT YOU'LL BE WORKING FOR *ME*, STARTING *TODAY*.

AND I'M HOPING IT'LL BE *PERMANENT*.

YOU SEE, I'VE DONE MY *HOMEWORK* ON YOU, JASON MY BOY. YOU'RE PERFECT FOR *MY* NEEDS AND WHETHER YOU KNOW IT OR *NOT*, WE HAVE A FEW COMMON ENEMIES.

SO, ARE YOU IN OR WHAT? THOUGH, COME TO *THINK* OF IT, YOU DON'T HAVE A *CHOICE*.

I DON'T KNOW HOW YOU GOT PAST SECURITY BUT YOU'VE JUST MADE A *FATAL* MISTAKE!

FORGET ABOUT THE PHONES. THEY'RE DEAD.

BUT THAT'S *YOUR* PROBLEM.

COMBINE THAT WITH TERRY FITZ-GERALD. POLICE CHIEF BANKS. BILLY KINCAID. ET CETERA, ET CETERA, AND I THINK YOU GET MY *DRIFT*.

I'... LISTEN...

SPEAKING OF WHICH, YOU HAVE A THORN IN YOUR SIDE NAMED *SPAWN*.

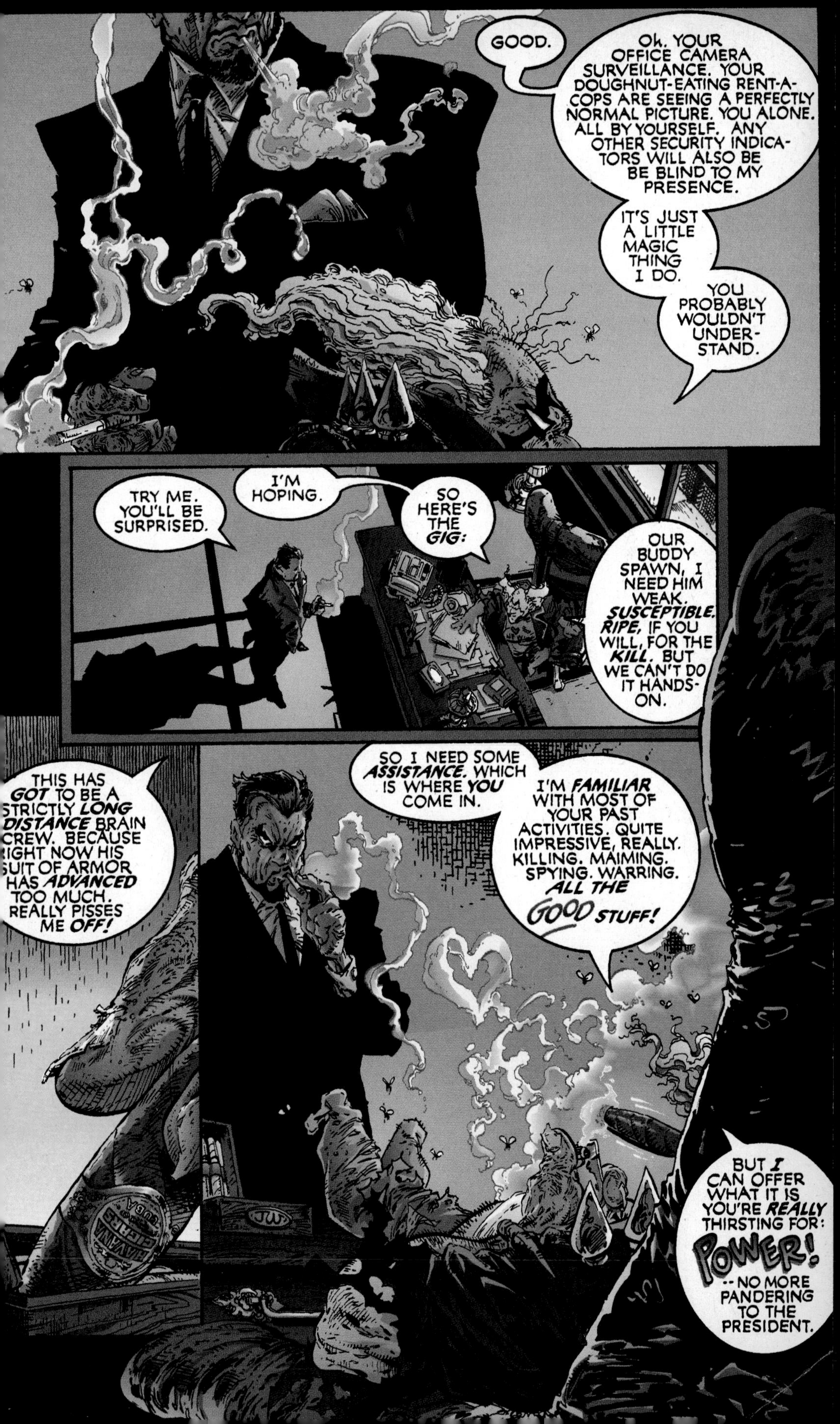
GOOD.
Oh. YOUR OFFICE CAMERA SURVEILLANCE. YOUR DOUGHNUT-EATING RENT-A-COPS ARE SEEING A PERFECTLY NORMAL PICTURE. YOU ALONE. ALL BY YOURSELF. ANY OTHER SECURITY INDICATORS WILL ALSO BE BE BLIND TO MY PRESENCE.
IT'S JUST A LITTLE MAGIC THING I DO.
YOU PROBABLY WOULDN'T UNDERSTAND.
TRY ME. YOU'LL BE SURPRISED.
I'M HOPING.
SO HERE'S THE *GIG:*
OUR BUDDY SPAWN, I NEED HIM WEAK. ***SUSCEPTIBLE. RIPE,*** IF YOU WILL, FOR THE ***KILL***. BUT WE CAN'T DO IT HANDS-ON.
THIS HAS ***GOT*** TO BE A TRICTLY ***LONG DISTANCE*** BRAIN CREW. BECAUSE IGHT NOW HIS UIT OF ARMOR HAS ***ADVANCED*** TOO MUCH. REALLY PISSES ME ***OFF!***
SO I NEED SOME ***ASSISTANCE.*** WHICH IS WHERE ***YOU*** COME IN.
I'M ***FAMILIAR*** WITH MOST OF YOUR PAST ACTIVITIES. QUITE IMPRESSIVE, REALLY. KILLING. MAIMING. SPYING. WARRING. ***ALL THE GOOD*** STUFF!
BUT ***I*** CAN OFFER WHAT IT IS YOU'RE ***REALLY*** THIRSTING FOR: POWER! -- NO MORE PANDERING TO THE PRESIDENT.

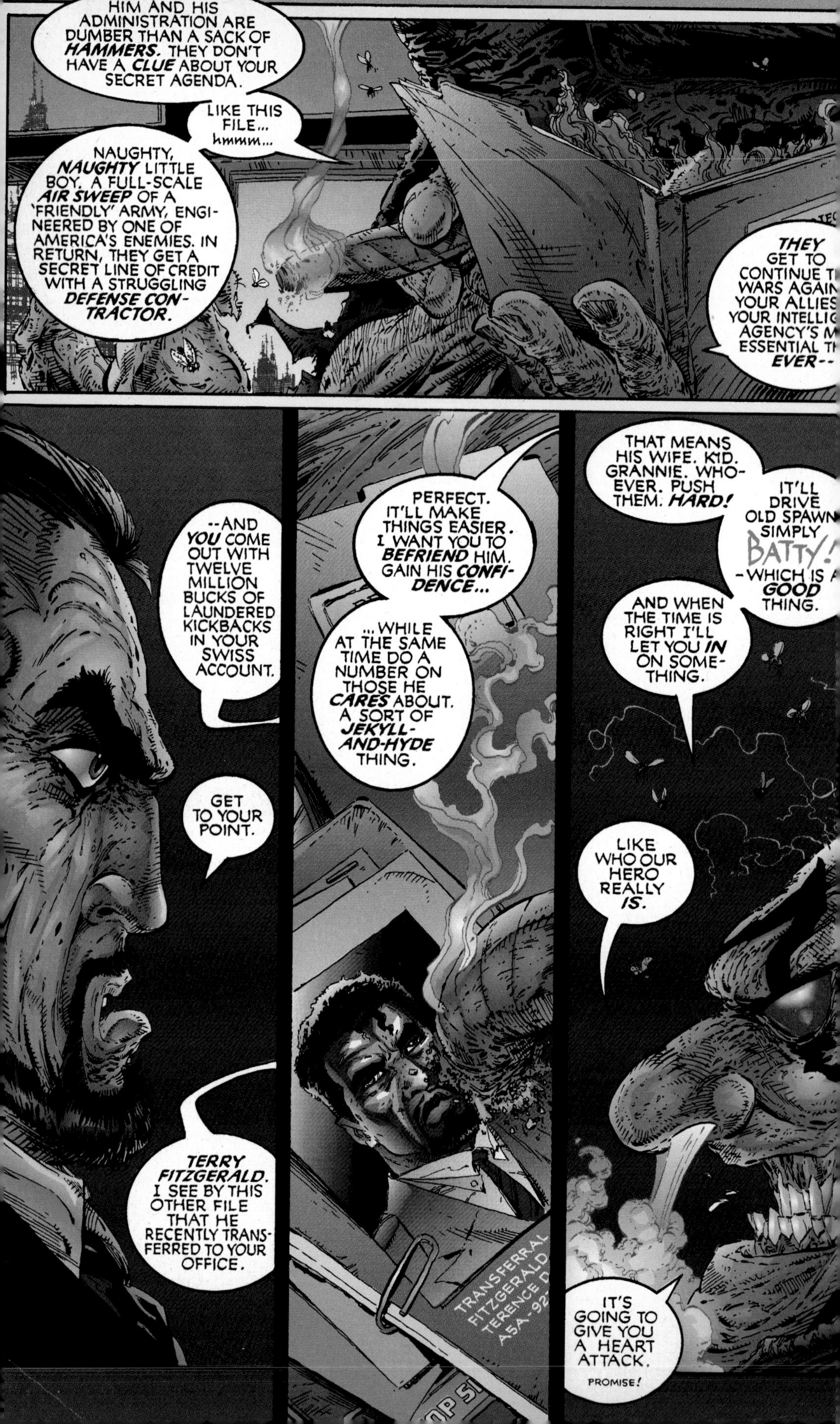
HIM AND HIS ADMINISTRATION ARE DUMBER THAN A SACK OF HAMMERS. THEY DON'T HAVE A CLUE ABOUT YOUR SECRET AGENDA.
LIKE THIS FILE... hmmm...
NAUGHTY, NAUGHTY LITTLE BOY. A FULL-SCALE AIR SWEEP OF A 'FRIENDLY' ARMY, ENGINEERED BY ONE OF AMERICA'S ENEMIES. IN RETURN, THEY GET A SECRET LINE OF CREDIT WITH A STRUGGLING DEFENSE CONTRACTOR.
THEY GET TO CONTINUE WARS AGAIN YOUR ALLIES YOUR INTELLI AGENCY'S ESSENTIAL EVER--
--AND YOU COME OUT WITH TWELVE MILLION BUCKS OF LAUNDERED KICKBACKS IN YOUR SWISS ACCOUNT.
GET TO YOUR POINT.
TERRY FITZGERALD. I SEE BY THIS OTHER FILE THAT HE RECENTLY TRANSFERRED TO YOUR OFFICE.
PERFECT. IT'LL MAKE THINGS EASIER. I WANT YOU TO BEFRIEND HIM. GAIN HIS CONFIDENCE...
...WHILE AT THE SAME TIME DO A NUMBER ON THOSE HE CARES ABOUT. A SORT OF JEKYLL-AND-HYDE THING.
TRANSFERRAL FITZGERALD TERENCE
THAT MEANS HIS WIFE. KID. GRANNIE. WHOEVER. PUSH THEM. HARD!
IT'LL DRIVE OLD SPAWN SIMPLY BATTY! -WHICH IS A GOOD THING.
AND WHEN THE TIME IS RIGHT I'LL LET YOU IN ON SOMETHING.
LIKE WHO OUR HERO REALLY IS.
IT'S GOING TO GIVE YOU A HEART ATTACK.
PROMISE!

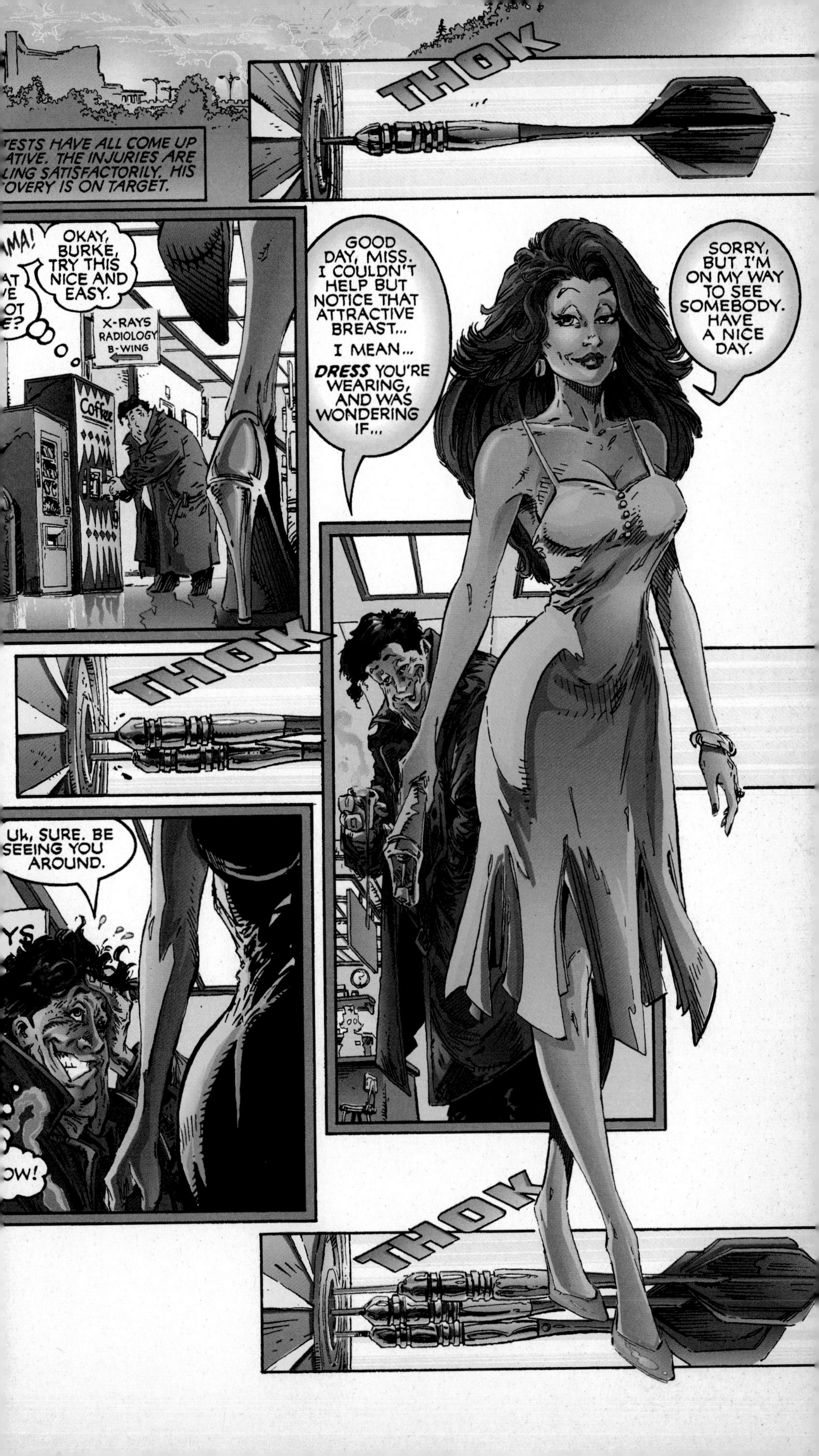
TESTS HAVE ALL COME UP
ATIVE. THE INJURIES ARE
LING SATISFACTORILY. HIS
OVERY IS ON TARGET.
THOK
MA!
OKAY, BURKE, TRY THIS NICE AND EASY.
AT VE OT E?
X-RAYS RADIOLOGY B-WING
Coffee
GOOD DAY, MISS. I COULDN'T HELP BUT NOTICE THAT ATTRACTIVE BREAST... I MEAN... DRESS YOU'RE WEARING, AND WAS WONDERING IF...
SORRY, BUT I'M ON MY WAY TO SEE SOMEBODY. HAVE A NICE DAY.
THOK
UH, SURE. BE SEEING YOU AROUND.
YS
OW!
THOK

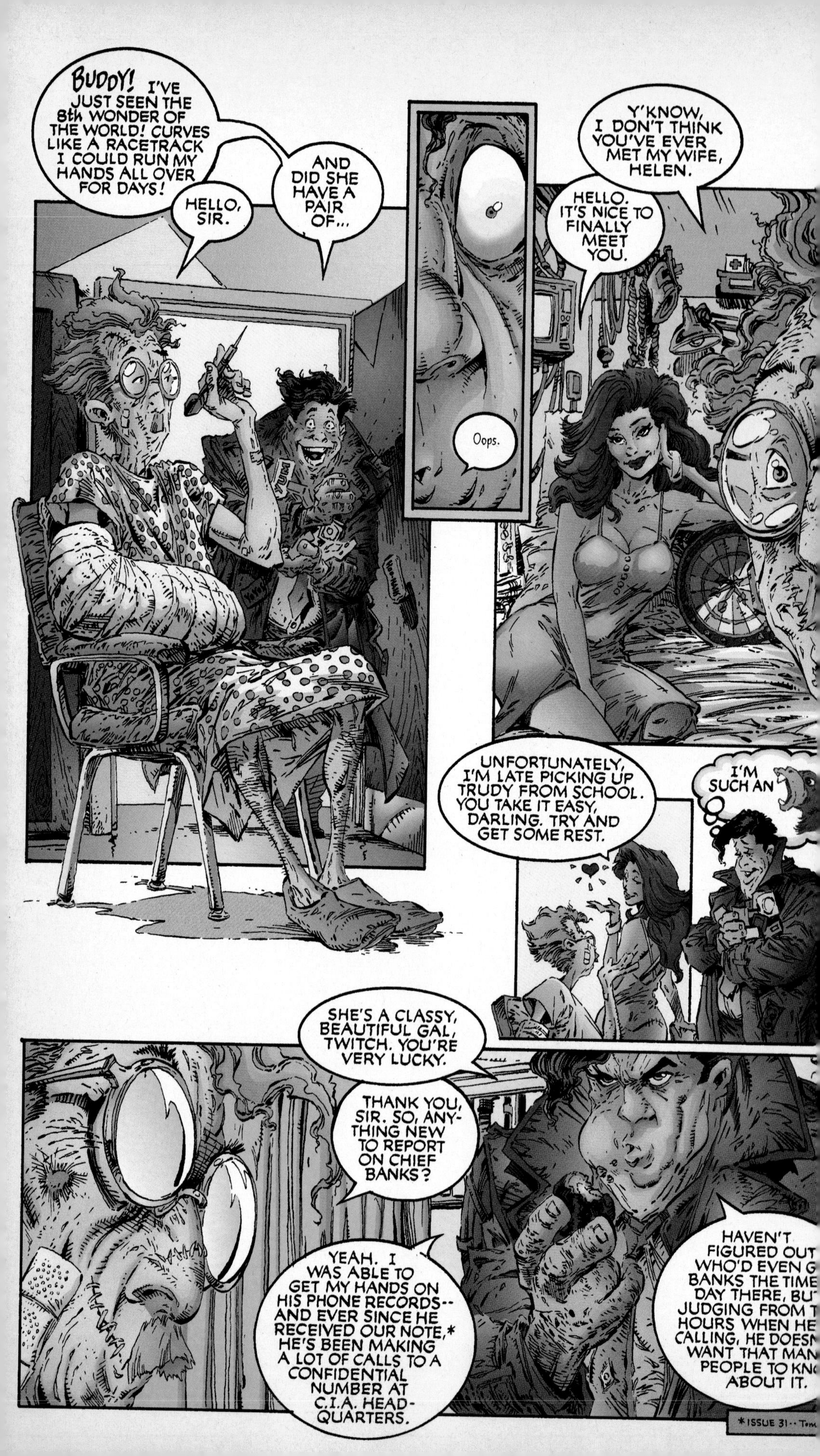

BUDDY! I'VE JUST SEEN THE 8th WONDER OF THE WORLD! CURVES LIKE A RACETRACK I COULD RUN MY HANDS ALL OVER FOR DAYS!
HELLO, SIR.
AND DID SHE HAVE A PAIR OF...
Oops.
Y'KNOW, I DON'T THINK YOU'VE EVER MET MY WIFE, HELEN.
HELLO. IT'S NICE TO FINALLY MEET YOU.
UNFORTUNATELY, I'M LATE PICKING UP TRUDY FROM SCHOOL. YOU TAKE IT EASY, DARLING. TRY AND GET SOME REST.
I'M SUCH AN
SHE'S A CLASSY, BEAUTIFUL GAL, TWITCH. YOU'RE VERY LUCKY.
THANK YOU, SIR. SO, ANYTHING NEW TO REPORT ON CHIEF BANKS?
YEAH. I WAS ABLE TO GET MY HANDS ON HIS PHONE RECORDS-- AND EVER SINCE HE RECEIVED OUR NOTE,* HE'S BEEN MAKING A LOT OF CALLS TO A CONFIDENTIAL NUMBER AT C.I.A. HEADQUARTERS.
HAVEN'T FIGURED OUT
*ISSUE 31--

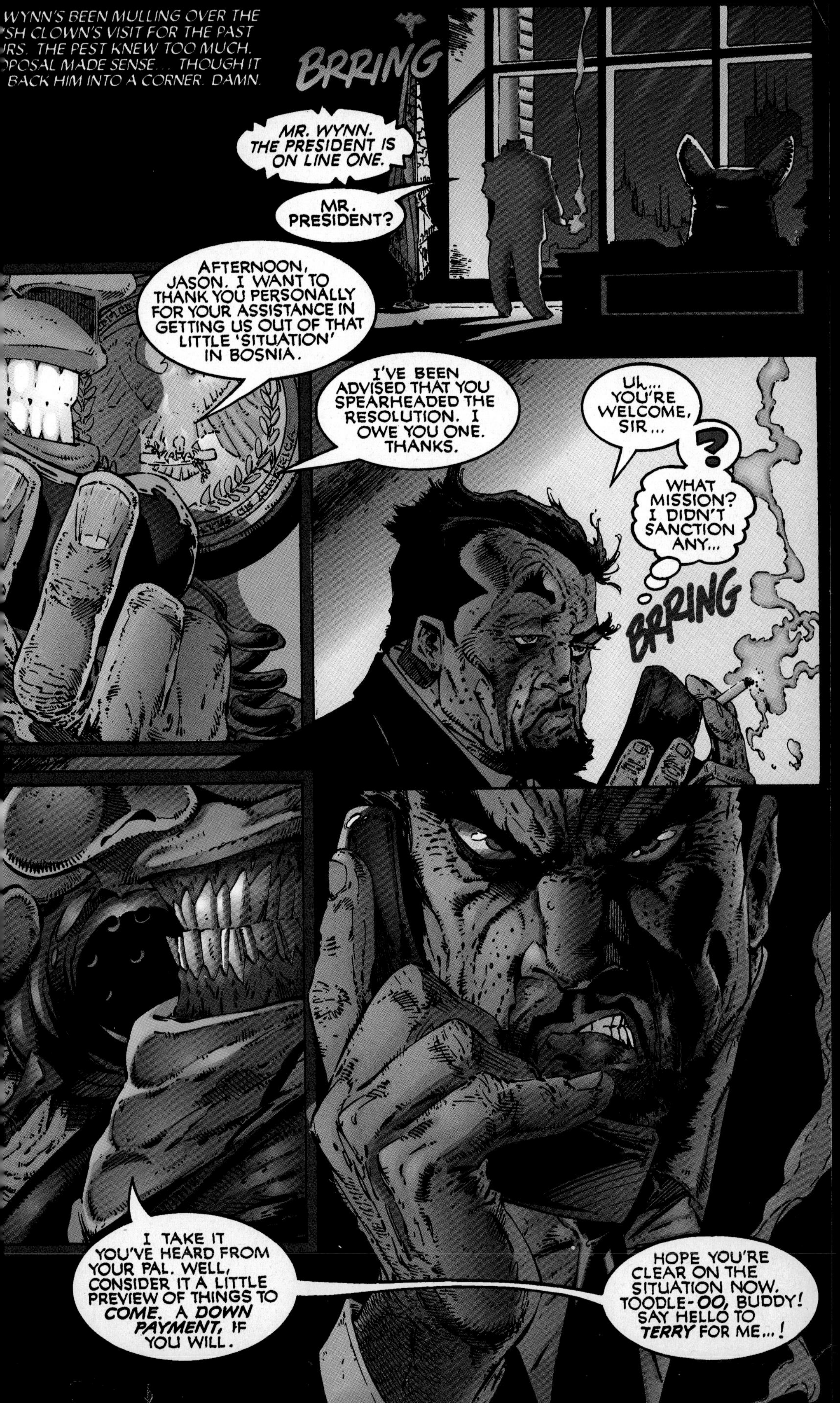
WYNN'S BEEN MULLING OVER THE
'SH CLOWN'S VISIT FOR THE PAST
IRS. THE PEST KNEW TOO MUCH.
OPOSAL MADE SENSE... THOUGH IT
BACK HIM INTO A CORNER. DAMN.
BRRING
MR. WYNN. THE PRESIDENT IS ON LINE ONE.
MR. PRESIDENT?
AFTERNOON, JASON. I WANT TO THANK YOU PERSONALLY FOR YOUR ASSISTANCE IN GETTING US OUT OF THAT LITTLE 'SITUATION' IN BOSNIA.
I'VE BEEN ADVISED THAT YOU SPEARHEADED THE RESOLUTION. I OWE YOU ONE. THANKS.
Uh... YOU'RE WELCOME, SIR...
?
WHAT MISSION? I DIDN'T SANCTION ANY...
BRRING
I TAKE IT YOU'VE HEARD FROM YOUR PAL. WELL, CONSIDER IT A LITTLE PREVIEW OF THINGS TO COME. A DOWN PAYMENT, IF YOU WILL.
HOPE YOU'RE CLEAR ON THE SITUATION NOW. TOODLE-OO, BUDDY! SAY HELLO TO TERRY FOR ME...!

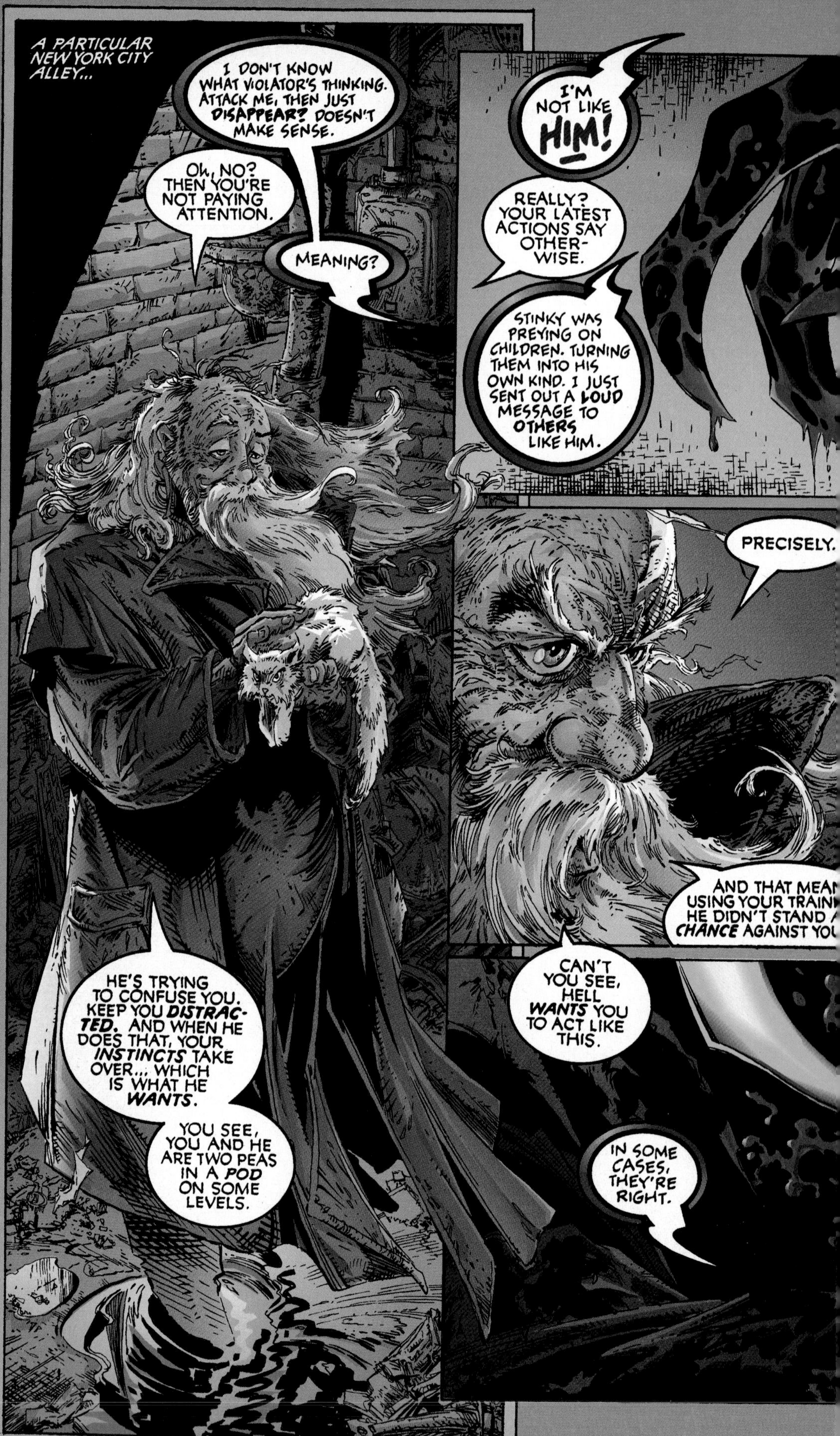
A PARTICULAR NEW YORK CITY ALLEY...
I DON'T KNOW WHAT VIOLATOR'S THINKING. ATTACK ME, THEN JUST DISAPPEAR? DOESN'T MAKE SENSE.
Oh, NO? THEN YOU'RE NOT PAYING ATTENTION.
MEANING?
HE'S TRYING TO CONFUSE YOU. KEEP YOU DISTRACTED. AND WHEN HE DOES THAT, YOUR INSTINCTS TAKE OVER... WHICH IS WHAT HE WANTS.
YOU SEE, YOU AND HE ARE TWO PEAS IN A POD ON SOME LEVELS.
I'M NOT LIKE HIM!
REALLY? YOUR LATEST ACTIONS SAY OTHER-WISE.
STINKY WAS PREYING ON CHILDREN. TURNING THEM INTO HIS OWN KIND. I JUST SENT OUT A LOUD MESSAGE TO OTHERS LIKE HIM.
PRECISELY.
CAN'T YOU SEE, HELL WANTS YOU TO ACT LIKE THIS.
IN SOME CASES, THEY'RE RIGHT.

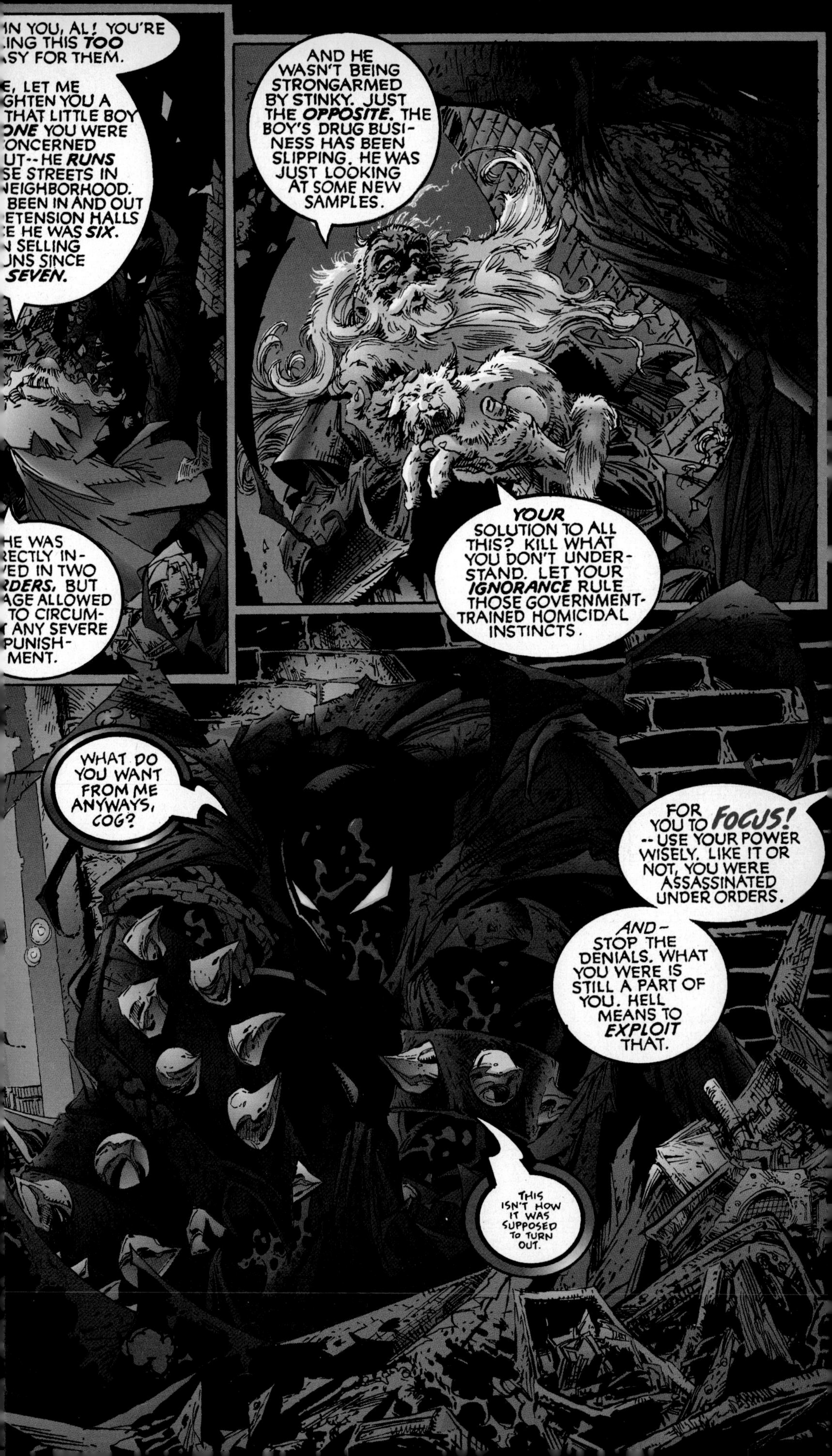

IN YOU, AL! YOU'RE
LING THIS TOO
ASY FOR THEM.
E, LET ME
GHTEN YOU A
THAT LITTLE BOY
ONE YOU WERE
CONCERNED
UT--HE RUNS
SE STREETS IN
NEIGHBORHOOD.
BEEN IN AND OUT
ETENSION HALLS
CE HE WAS SIX.
N SELLING
UNS SINCE
SEVEN.
AND HE WASN'T BEING STRONGARMED BY STINKY. JUST THE OPPOSITE. THE BOY'S DRUG BUSINESS HAS BEEN SLIPPING. HE WAS JUST LOOKING AT SOME NEW SAMPLES.
HE WAS
RECTLY IN-
VED IN TWO
RDERS, BUT
AGE ALLOWED
TO CIRCUM-
T ANY SEVERE
PUNISH-
MENT.
YOUR SOLUTION TO ALL THIS? KILL WHAT YOU DON'T UNDERSTAND. LET YOUR IGNORANCE RULE THOSE GOVERNMENT-TRAINED HOMICIDAL INSTINCTS.
WHAT DO YOU WANT FROM ME ANYWAYS, COG?
FOR YOU TO FOCUS! -- USE YOUR POWER WISELY. LIKE IT OR NOT, YOU WERE ASSASSINATED UNDER ORDERS.
AND--STOP THE DENIALS. WHAT YOU WERE IS STILL A PART OF YOU. HELL MEANS TO EXPLOIT THAT.
THIS ISN'T HOW IT WAS SUPPOSED TO TURN OUT.

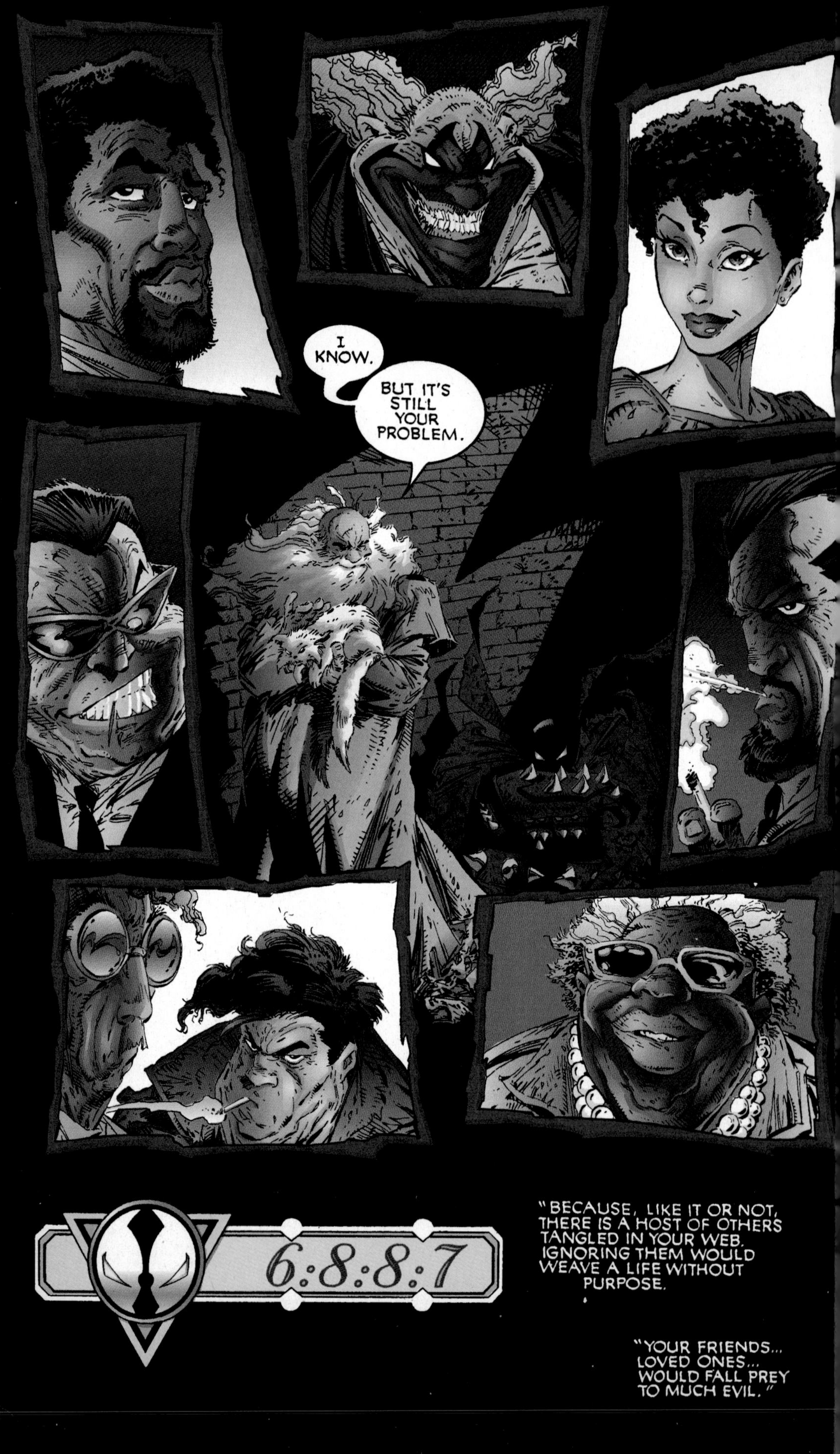
I KNOW.
BUT IT'S STILL YOUR PROBLEM.
6:8:8:7
"BECAUSE, LIKE IT OR NOT, THERE IS A HOST OF OTHERS TANGLED IN YOUR WEB. IGNORING THEM WOULD WEAVE A LIFE WITHOUT PURPOSE.
"YOUR FRIENDS... LOVED ONES... WOULD FALL PREY TO MUCH EVIL."

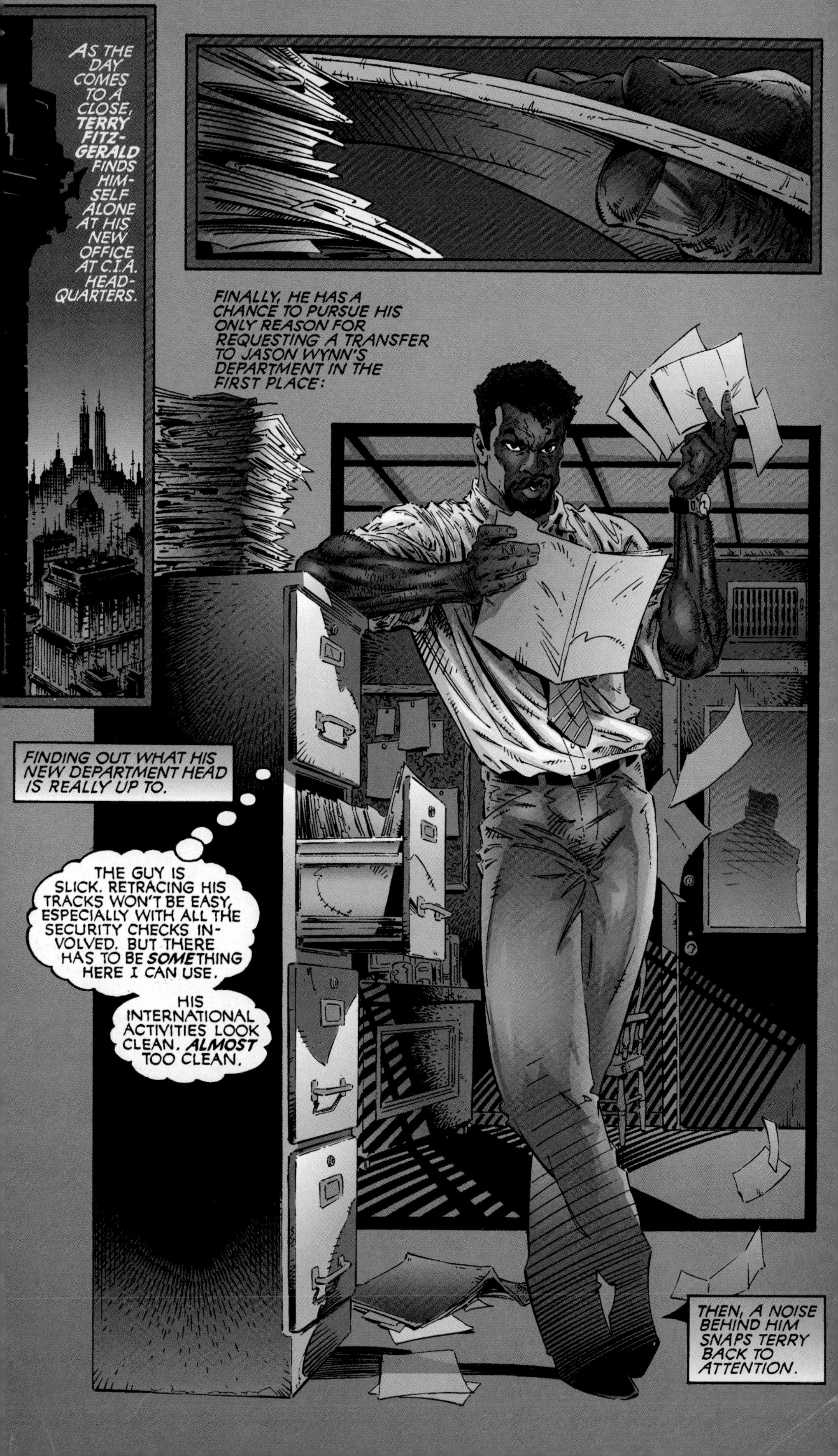
AS THE DAY COMES TO A CLOSE, TERRY FITZ-GERALD FINDS HIM-SELF ALONE AT HIS NEW OFFICE AT C.I.A. HEAD-QUARTERS.
FINALLY, HE HAS A CHANCE TO PURSUE HIS ONLY REASON FOR REQUESTING A TRANSFER TO JASON WYNN'S DEPARTMENT IN THE FIRST PLACE:
FINDING OUT WHAT HIS NEW DEPARTMENT HEAD IS REALLY UP TO.
THE GUY IS SLICK. RETRACING HIS TRACKS WON'T BE EASY, ESPECIALLY WITH ALL THE SECURITY CHECKS IN-VOLVED. BUT THERE HAS TO BE SOMETHING HERE I CAN USE.
HIS INTERNATIONAL ACTIVITIES LOOK CLEAN. ALMOST TOO CLEAN.
THEN, A NOISE BEHIND HIM SNAPS TERRY BACK TO ATTENTION.

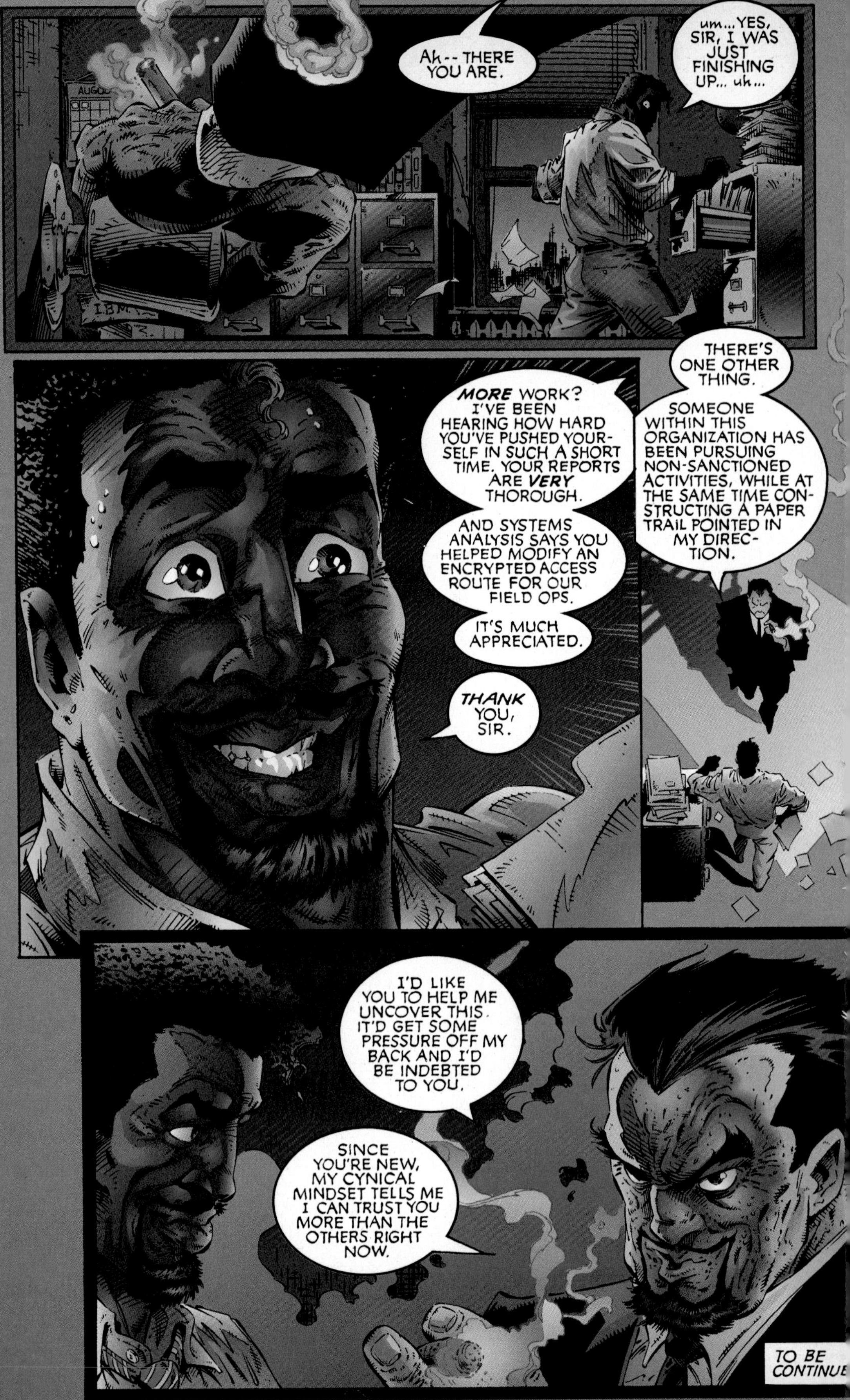
Ah-- THERE YOU ARE.
um... YES, SIR, I WAS JUST FINISHING UP... uh...
MORE WORK? I'VE BEEN HEARING HOW HARD YOU'VE PUSHED YOURSELF IN SUCH A SHORT TIME. YOUR REPORTS ARE VERY THOROUGH.
AND SYSTEMS ANALYSIS SAYS YOU HELPED MODIFY AN ENCRYPTED ACCESS ROUTE FOR OUR FIELD OPS.
IT'S MUCH APPRECIATED.
THANK YOU, SIR.
THERE'S ONE OTHER THING.
SOMEONE WITHIN THIS ORGANIZATION HAS BEEN PURSUING NON-SANCTIONED ACTIVITIES, WHILE AT THE SAME TIME CONSTRUCTING A PAPER TRAIL POINTED IN MY DIRECTION.
I'D LIKE YOU TO HELP ME UNCOVER THIS. IT'D GET SOME PRESSURE OFF MY BACK AND I'D BE INDEBTED TO YOU.
SINCE YOU'RE NEW, MY CYNICAL MINDSET TELLS ME I CAN TRUST YOU MORE THAN THE OTHERS RIGHT NOW.
TO BE CONTINUE